D0342352

MASTERS OF
THE KEYBOARD

Konrad Wolff

MASTERS OF
THE KEYBOARD

Individual Style Elements in the
Piano Music of Bach, Haydn,
Mozart, Beethoven, Schubert,
Chopin, and Brahms

Enlarged Edition

Indiana University Press
Bloomington and Indianapolis

Jacket illustration by Dorothea Schwarzhaupt

First Midland Book Edition 1990

Copyright © 1983, 1990 by Konrad Wolff
All rights reserved

No part of this book may be reproduced or utilized in any form or
by any means, electronic or mechanical, including photocopying and
recording, or by any information storage and retrieval system, without
permission in writing from the publisher. The Association of American
University Presses' Resolution on Permissions constitutes the only
exception to this prohibition.

Manufactured in the United States of America

Library of Congress Cataloging in Publication Data
Wolff, Konrad.
Masters of the keyboard : individual style elements in the piano music
of Bach, Haydn, Mozart, Beethoven, Schubert, Chopin, and Brahms /
Konrad Wolff. — Enl. ed.
      p.   cm.
Includes bibliographical references.
1. Piano music—18th century—History and criticism.
2. Piano music—19th century—History and criticism.
I. Title.
ML705.W64   1990   786.2'09'033—dc20   89-45570
ISBN 0-253-36458-2 cloth
ISBN 0-253-20567-0 paper
1 2 3 4 5 94 93 92 91 90

. . .
and the past stays
amidst the dark infinity of future
like a luminous star
not to be extinguished
ever

Ilse Bing

Contents

Preface to the Enlarged Edition

In accordance with the wishes of the publisher, I have made only the most necessary corrections, without any rewriting, in the text of the first edition. But, at their request, I have added two chapters, about Chopin and Brahms. John Sessions, Laurence Libin, Kathryn Shanks, and Michael Campbell have been most supportive in this endeavor. Diane Jezic, whose recent death has deeply saddened us all, contributed her private research into the connections between Schubert and Chopin. Florence Kirsch has shared her unique wisdom in interpreting Chopin scores with me, from which I feel I benefited a great deal—but will she think so, too, after reading my chapter? I found it a great help to study all the Chopin autographs at the Library of Congress, the Pierpont Morgan Library in New York, the Bibliothèque Nationale, and the British Library (including the Stefan Zweig collection); and I thank the librarians in all these places for having made the autographs available to me.

August 1989

Preface

The individual approach used in this book—dealing with the five composers without comparing each one's music to that of others and without attempting generalizations about style—is intended to fill a gap for today's piano students, wherever they may live and study. The best of them not only have technique and musicality but have learned their history lessons and perfected their theoretical and style-analytical penetrations of a score. All of them know the differences between late Baroque and early classicism and are familiar with the intricacies of sonata form. But I have found, in over thirty years of teaching, that hardly any of them have been able to acquire the quasi-graphological sensitivity for, say, the inner meaning of a melodic pattern that Mozart used in a very different way from Haydn, or for Bach's purposes in reshaping an ordinary Baroque turn of phrase into something new. Nor does the present-day student get a chance to reflect on the general aims—different in each case—that were in the minds of the great masters as they turned to keyboard music. Notwithstanding the assistance I received from certain excellent books, as a whole this field is untrodden ground. However, it helped that I was familiar with the work on Bach and Mozart scores—in the form of improvised cadenzas, finished fragments, and the like—independently undertaken by the American Robert Levin and by the South African Stefans Grové.

The concrete individualization attempted here made it impossible to ask the same questions of each composer or to rely on general guidelines for style analysis. In this respect my book goes one step beyond Charles Rosen's famous treatise, in which stylistic traits of Haydn, Mozart, and Beethoven are lumped together to some extent. In my opinion, universal change-overs occur at certain times through the unconscious collaboration of everybody, from the greatest masters and most profound thinkers to mediocre artists, scholars, audiences, folk singers—even critics. That is why, when I encounter a major composer, I first look at his work as much as possible from his own, subjective viewpoint without trying to classify him according to personal influences, nationality, or historical background. That can come later, if necessary, and always remains secondary.

My basic approach of going through the music composer by composer is totally contrary to the aesthetic credo of my great teacher Artur

Schnabel. He was convinced that what two or more composers have in common is more important than what separates them. I have discarded that approach entirely, because in my performing and teaching experience I have found the smallest individual traits of the greatest value in guiding me. However, I am gratefully aware that some of his other ideas have surely stayed with me subconsciously throughout these more than forty years.

I must also pay tribute to two other men whose contributions to my musical education were most important: Paul Henry Lang, my admired teacher of music history, who first showed me how to research stylistic connections and separations; and Erich Itor Kahn (d. 1956), composer-pianist and my close friend, who made me listen to traditional elements in new music and progressive features in traditional compositions.

Nietzsche says somewhere that a writer ought to read in the same way in which a dancer eats: little yet nourishing. This I have tried to do, and thus have discovered that some earlier writers such as Albert Schweitzer, August Halm, and Donald Tovey still prove to have surprisingly high nutrition value. In the main, however, the study of the piano scores themselves has dominated my work, sometimes perhaps at the expense of exhaustive research. Still, I consider this a scholarly book, and that is why I have refrained from giving concrete playing suggestions, as is fashionable nowadays to do in print. Some of my findings, I trust, will indirectly benefit performances in the presentation of a work as a whole and of its detail.

Friends, colleagues, and students have contributed so much to all aspects of this book—which was first outlined by me as long ago as 1968—that I am able to name only my most important helpmates: Michael Campbell, who read almost the entire manuscript with a special double understanding based on his analytical powers and his performer's intuition; Gail Webb, who, although in the end was dissatisfied with the Bach chapter, by her patient and painstaking editing enabled me to set it down at all; Maynard Solomon, who kindly helped me in the Beethoven research; Florence Kirsch and Bernice Lehmann, both of whom also made valuable suggestions for the Bach chapter; and my assistant, Ella Grzeskowski, whose careful and thoughtful editing is much appreciated. My piano students and the students in my piano literature classes, where I first spoke of the matters explained here, constantly rekindled my incentive to get this book done and, sometimes unconsciously, by their own insights and questions, contributed to it: I owe them very much. Katherine Spielmann's proofreading was a great help; and Michelle Rucket assisted me in preparing the index.

This book is dedicated to Stephan Kuttner. Our close friendship of more than seventy years has never been interrupted or disturbed and continues to make me happy and to stimulate me.

Konrad Wolff

MASTERS OF
THE KEYBOARD

Chapter I

BACH

The piano music of Bach will be approached in the following pages primarily from the old-fashioned premise that he was "the father of music." Though it is now universally recognized that he represented a culmination rather than a beginning and that he was capable, for instance, of writing a Frescobaldi-like toccata on Monday, a cantata based on the tradition of Schütz on Tuesday, a dance suite in the manner of Couperin on Wednesday, a Germanic Baroque chorale prelude for organ on Thursday, and a direct transcription of a Vivaldi concerto on Friday, Bach still remains "the father of music"—for all these styles and traditions became magically fresh and as though newly invented at his hands! The Roman legal term *novation,* meaning the renewal of an agreement by a new reason substituted for the original one (e.g., A loans B a book; then they agree that B is to keep the book as a gift) seems quite fitting to describe the transforming effect his art had on the varied styles Bach utilized. It is, therefore, unprofitable, for the most part, to gather any rules of performance practice for Bach's music from the study of his Baroque predecessors and contemporaries. Bach may have copied another composer's musical style quite carefully, but the musical *spirit* remains exclusively his own.

After an introduction, showing Bach's individualistic approach even to music notation, the first part of this chapter will be devoted to the three basic traits common to all types of his piano music (preludes, fugues, suites, etc.): his attitude toward compositional rules and exceptions; his consistent order of tonalities; and his observance of certain proportions of length, particularly in his binary compositions. The second part will deal with Bach's idioms for different genres of music, and the last with various elements of importance to the performer: melody, grouping, dynamics, and form.

Introduction: Notation

Without entering into the many controversies concerning Baroque notation in general, one can safely say that Bach's notation is at times willfully different.[1] While his contemporaries had a tendency to use abbreviated and simplified notation—such as double-dotting expressed by single dots, or triplet-eighths expressed by sixteenths—Bach wrote exactly what he wanted to hear, wherever possible. As a schoolmaster and conductor, he probably had little confidence in his executants. In case of doubt, the reader should assume that his notation was not in shorthand but precise and complete. When Bach wrote treble and bass in two-part writing without figures, he did not normally invite performers to fill the space in between.* In the "Lament" from his early *Capriccio on the Departure of a Beloved Brother,* the continuo realizations in the right hand stop as soon as the *obbligato* melody starts, strongly deviating from customary practice.**

Bach's attitude on notation once got him into trouble, when his former pupil J. A. Scheibe criticized him for writing out trills and mordents instead of using the traditional embellishment symbols. Scheibe wrote that it "not only takes away from his pieces the beauty of harmony[!] but it also makes the tune unintelligible throughout"![3]

Good examples of mordents written out in full occur in the second part of the C minor Fantasia, BWV 906. In this case, Bach obviously tried to prevent performers from playing incor-

---

*An exception is to be made in some of his chamber music. The figures written out for the Flute Duo in G major, BWV 1039, for example, should perhaps also be realized in the viola da gamba version, BWV 1027, where they are not notated. The opposite view is held by Ulrich Siegele (see Bibliography).

**Indirect proof that this was what Bach meant is given by the *Allegro Siciliano e scherzando* by his son C. P. E. Bach (Fourth Annex Sonata to vol. 1 of his *Essay*). This piece, in F-sharp minor, is written in the same sparse two-part style, with the composer's own fingerings provided—completely ruling out the possibility of adding inner voices.[2]

rect rhythms or wrong auxiliary notes and also from looking at the apparent embellishments as sheer decorations; they are there to punctuate each of Bach's energetic phrases.

It is interesting that Bach—perhaps only he—succeeded in expressing double-dotted rhythms exactly, before 1750, at a time when the symbol of two dots had not yet been invented.* Depending on the situation, he tied a 16th note to a dotted quarter, as in the Allemande of the Second Partita (Ex. 1a), or used a 16th rest, as in the E minor Prelude of the *Well-Tempered Clavier*, Bk. I, (Ex. 1b) and the *French Overture* in B minor (Ex. 1c). It is therefore necessary to conclude that *single* dots notated by Bach must be played as such. Dolmetsch's idea that the subject of the D major Fugue, *WTC*, Bk. I, for example, ought to be played with double dots where single dots appear in the score[5] must be absolutely rejected.**[6]

Ex. 1a Allemande from Partita No. 2, m. 31.

Ex. 1b Prelude in E minor, *WTC*, Bk. I, m. 10.

Ex. 1c *French Overture*, 1st Mvt., m. 8.

A variant of this situation arises when quick upbeat notes are preceded by rests. It was apparently not permissible to affix dots to rest signs; thus, performers got into the habit of prolonging such rests by one half on their own, thereby halving the value of the following upbeat note. Here, too, Bach discovered a precise notation. In the beginning of the left-hand part of the Sarabande

---

*Leopold Mozart claimed to have invented the double dot himself.[4]

**On the recording of this Fugue by Glenn Gould the first dot is played as a double dot, the second as written. While this might seem like a thumbing of the nose at Dolmetsch on Gould's part, there are indeed plausible musical reasons for his discrimination. The first of the dotted eighths is repeated after the dot, while the second opens a descending diatonic progression in which the 16th following the dot—G—forms an essential step.

of the Fifth Partita (Ex. 2a) and in the "St. Anne" Prelude for
organ, BWV 552.1 (Ex. 2b), he combined two successive rest
signs, the second being half as long as the first. The result was
exactly what the notation of a dotted rest would have achieved.

Ex. 2a Sarabande from Partita No. 5, m. 1.   Ex. 2b "St. Anne" Prelude, BWV 552.1, m. 5.

Whether this applies to the opening of the Second Partita
(Grave; Ex. 3a) remains doubtful, however. Bach could have
used two rest signs here, just as in the Fifth Partita, but he used
only a single 16th rest each time. If one takes this literally (which,
let us remember, was mandatory from about 1800 to around
1950, at which point pianists finally learned about the practice of
double-dotting in the French Baroque!), the first of the two upbeats would be twice as long as the second. This does not make
much musical sense. On the other hand, if Bach wanted quick
upbeats—not only following the rests, but also following some
held 8th notes beginning on the first beat of m. 2—why did he
not write them, as he did elsewhere in the same series of Partitas?
(See the examples above.) Perhaps he had in mind a halfway solution in the form of a uniform triplet division in which the var-
iously notated upbeats would be assimilated into the same—or
almost the same—length, more or less equaling the last third of a
triplet. This would lengthen those upbeats notated as 32nds and
shorten those written as 16ths (Ex. 3b). Such a solution would
seem to fit the last measure of the Grave especially (Ex. 3c).
While this seems a stylistically adequate solution, I still prefer to
play the Grave exactly as written—simply because Bach always
expected to be taken literally—and to cope with the resulting

Sinfonia from Partita No. 2
Ex. 3a m. 1 (as written).

Ex. 3b m. 1 (with triplet notation).   Ex. 3c m. 7

unevenness the best I can. Under no circumstances would I rec-
ommend double-dotting the 16th note upbeats completely.

When a simple imprecise notation was *universally* used, however, Bach sometimes accepted it, too. The 16ths in the Courante
of the First Partita (Ex. 4) are certainly meant to be played as
triplet 8ths, and so is the initial upbeat of the head motive of the
Finale of the Fifth *Brandenburg* Concerto. However, as soon as a
polyrhythmic construction appears to have been on Bach's mind,
16ths following dotted 8ths must be played as written to set them
off from any triplets occurring elsewhere in the music. A classic
example is given by the E minor Fugue, *WTC,* Bk. II (Ex. 5).

Ex. 4 Courante from Partita No. 1, mm. 29–30.

Ex. 5 Fugue in E minor, *WTC,* Bk. II, subject.

The quadruple patterns, especially those in dotted rhythm, are
clearly intended to be distinguished from the groups of triplet
8ths with which they alternate and occasionally intersect. The
same principle prevails in the complex *Tempo di Gavotta* of the
Sixth Partita (Exx. 6a, b, c) though its correct application runs
into more problems.[7]

Tempo di Gavotta from Partita No. 6
Ex. 6a   mm. 12–14

Other well-known instances of mixed subdivisions of the beat with occasional polyrhythmic simultaneity occur in the Allemande of the Fifth Partita and the D major Prelude, *WTC*, Bk. II. In my opinion, the separate identity of the two types of subdivisions must be maintained throughout and the kind of assimilation required in the Courante of the First Partita (see above) avoided.

The execution of Bach's ornamentation, a topic most amply treated in the literature,[8] is outside the scope of this book (see p. 61). Still missing in this field is a study of Bach's harmonic laws from which to determine the pitch of auxiliary notes. In the minor mode, the auxiliary notes are built sometimes on the natural scale and sometimes on the ascending melodic scale.* More generally, the auxiliary note is always in the implied tonality and does not necessarily correspond to the key signature. The trill in

---

*The Gigue of the Sixth English Suite, a wild and deliberately dissonant piece, offers a few puzzles. In Ex. 7, I prefer e-natural' as the auxiliary note sounding with the f-sharp' on the second beat. The e-flat in m. 33, following the trill, thus gains more importance, and the whole-tone trill becomes an answer to that in m. 30. The clash with the various e-flats in the bass is not uncommon in this piece; see the downbeat of m. 20 (f–f-sharp''); also e-flat' (top)–e (bottom) in m. 35, last beat, if one plays the auxiliary note correctly in G minor, i.e., as E-flat.

Ex. 7   Gigue from English Suite No. 6, m. 32.

m. 16 of the slow movement of the *Italian Concerto* (Ex. 8), for instance, is to be played with e-flat as an auxiliary, as befits the implied G minor. The coda of this movement, in several places, reveals Bach's complex harmonic thinking, as the turns and mordents are written out here. At the end of m. 42, f-sharp' –g' is easily explained as part of the implied G major chord. The c-sharp'–d' at the end of m. 45 is not quite as obvious, since it is not part of the D major chord; it is, however, explainable in terms of melody, inasmuch as c-natural would have to be re- solved downward. In the beginning of m. 45, on the other hand, Bach wrote the turn using a whole tone below as the lower note (f'); this must be compared to the auxiliary f-sharp on the last beat of m. 10. See also Ex. 9 from the *Chromatic Fantasy,* where many pianists use the lower *whole* tone in the mordent on ac- count of the spelling of this embellishment in sharps (enharmonic change). The notation by itself is not a sufficient reason to do so, since Bach usually did not indicate the auxiliary note precisely, but the whole tone below is perhaps justified by the harmonic direction.

Ex. 8   *Italian Concerto,* 2nd Mvt., m. 16.

Ex. 9   *Chromatic Fantasy,* mm. 55–56.

I. COMMON ELEMENTS IN DIFFERENT MUSICAL GENRES

It was more important to Bach than to other composers to establish a discrete way of writing for each type of composition. His sense of orderliness resisted any mixture of genres, quite the opposite of the Viennese classical composers. Each separate species of Bach's music is put forward with its own musical and instrumental characteristics, depending on purpose and basic idea. In his well-ordered universality, Bach resembles Homer. If we did not know that all his works were created by the same person, we would most certainly conclude that they must have been produced by many masters, so different are their harmonies, textures, forms, and rhythms. (Typically, a good adult pupil of mine, who had successfully learned the entire *Well-Tempered Clavier,* was totally at sea—even technically— when confronted for the first time with one of the French Suites!) Only a few essentials are common to all.

Attitude toward Rules and Exceptions

Bach made his own rules and confirmed their validity by occasionally breaking them. So far, I have not discovered a single rule which he did not break, not even the avoidance of parallel fifths (see Two-Part Invention in F minor; Ex. 10)[9] Bach's treatment of rule and exception is well exemplified by his rule of *avoiding the augmented second* between the 6th and 7th scale tone in

Ex. 10 Two-Part Invention in F minor, m. 25.

the minor mode as a melodic interval.* He consistently thought up varying substitute melodic turns wherever an augmented second would normally be indicated. The first two runs in the *Chromatic Fantasy* provide a spectacular example of the length to which Bach would go in order to avoid augmented seconds. These runs end with g'−a'−b-flat'−e'' (Ex. 11a) and c-sharp''−d''−f'', respectively. Together they form a complete

---

*The only mention of this rule I found in the literature was by Andreas Moser, second violinist of the Joachim Quartet.[10]

harmonic scale that includes the augmented second B-flat–C-sharp. This interval was so loathsome to Bach that he would rather write the startling tritone leap B-flat–E in the first run!* In the motive of the D minor Invention (Ex. 11b), the downbeat of m. 2 logically ought to feature *c-sharp''* and not *c-sharp'*. The subject of the *Art of Fugue,* also in D minor, contains, in addition to the first five tones of the scale, only C-sharp, not B-flat (Ex. 11c); its inversion contains only B-flat, not C-sharp (Ex. 11d). This, perhaps, gives a clue to the nature of the harmonic scale as Bach conceived it: as a five-tone group, tonic to dominant, flanked on either end by semitones, rather than a stepwise scale from tonic to tonic.

Ex. 11a *Chromatic Fantasy,* m. 1.

Ex. 11b Two-Part Invention in D minor, mm. 1–2.

Art of Fugue
Ex. 11c subject

Ex. 11d inversion of subject

Gamut

Gamut

Here, then, is an example of one of Bach's clear, self-defined compositional rules. But an exception was boldly established during the middle section of his Second Duetto in F major from *Clavierübung,* vol. 3. In this haunting canon (Ex. 11e), presumably to be played *piano,* the augmented second is the most audible thematic interval! The section appears in sharpest possible contrast to the consonant melodies in the Italian-style main section, presumably to be played *forte,* which is modeled on the opening of the Violin Concerto in E major. By slurring the two tones of the augmented second every time, Bach draws immediate attention to its importance.**

---

*The augmented seconds that occur later in the *Chromatic Fantasy* are heard as part of a diminished chord and not as melodic progressions.

**Perhaps these slurs indicate a certain way of playing, but I do not know what it might be.

Ex. 11e   Duetto No. 2, mm. 38–42.

On occasion, Bach also broke some of the rules concerning formal devices. As a rule, the *da capo* which forms the last third of long preludes and outer concerto movements is absolutely literal. Yet Bach dramatized the end of the *Italian Concerto*—almost as a nineteenth-century composer would have done—by slightly touching up the texture (Exx. 12a, b).* The modification of the left-hand pattern one measure before the end, in particular, offers the distinct invitation to make a ritard. In the Gigue of the Second English Suite in A minor, following the usual repeat of the second "half," Bach added one more repeat of the entire Gigue—a unique instance, to my knowledge. Perhaps the reason was that he conceived the piece as being faster than other gigues. Another exceptional feature is the addition of a coda to the two sections of the Air in the Sixth Partita (see below, p. 18, footnote).

Italian Concerto, 3rd Mvt.
Ex. 12a   mm. 23–24   Ex. 12b   mm. 209–210

The 48 fugues of both volumes of the *Well-Tempered Clavier* reflect a great many rules of fugue composition that, though based on older music, are essentially of Bach's own making. Yet none of these rules is used consistently throughout the two books! Some are broken just once, while others are breached by exceptions with enough regularity to make them seem partly invalidated by the application of counter-rules. The toccata-like

---

*Beethoven acted similarly at the very end of the Sonata in E major, op. 109, in order to express the subtle changes in mood produced during the course of the variation set prior to the return of the theme.

conclusions of certain fugues belong to the latter category. Typical examples are found in the G major Fugue, *WTC,* Bk. I, and the C-sharp major Fugue, *WTC,* Bk. II. Here the obligatory number of voices is increased during the coda. In accordance with traditional toccata performance, the tempo must broaden at the coda. This practice was expressed as early as 1615, in Frescobaldi's Preface to his Toccatas:[11] "In cadenzas (or cadences) while they are written in smaller note values, one will considerably reduce the speed." To continue to play at the same speed in these Bach examples would be an actual mistake.

When approaching any Bach piece, it is advisable to find out in what way it is exceptional. To give just one example, the construction of the C minor Fugue, *WTC,* Bk. II, is understandable only when one realizes that for the first 18 measures, all four voices of the fugue never appear at the same time. Only shortly before the end (Ex. 13) the bass completes the foursome* and proceeds to render all three forms of the subject (augmented, inverted, and original) in succession. The performer should not, however, underline exceptional passages by octave doubling. Where Bach wanted octave doubling, he wrote it himself (see the end of the *Chromatic Fugue* and the Gigue in the Fifth Partita).

Ex. 13   Fugue in C minor, *WTC,* Bk. 2, m. 19.

NB

Order of Tonalities

In most of Bach's instrumental works the tonal order is clearly planned, and in a majority of instances Bach uses the same order. It applies equally to pieces in the major and the minor mode, pieces in two-part dance form, continuous longer pieces, and more polyphonic or more homophonic music.

---

*Bach does not delay the entrance of the bass as a fourth voice until m. 19, but has one voice drop out as soon as the bass enters.

The order is as follows: After establishing the *tonic key,* frequently over a tonic pedal point, the music progresses to the *dominant* (major dominant, if the tonic key is major; minor dominant, if it is minor). Next there is a modulation to the *relative key*—major or minor, as the case may be. After this, an excursion—usually a very brief one—to the *subdominant* precedes the final return to the *tonic key,* again often over a tonic pedal point.[12] In lengthy movements, each intermediate tonality (except, at times, in the case of the subdominant) is usually completed in a full cadence from which the next segment then departs. Typical of such long pieces are the Preludes of the English Suites, opening movements of the Concertos, and various lengthy opening pieces including some Preludes of the *Well-Tempered Clavier.* In shorter pieces, particularly those in dance form, the delineation between successive keys is more subtle, especially where the texture is polyphonic.[13]

As might be expected, the exceptions to this order are numerous, but they consist mostly of key substitutions and key omissions rather than reversals of the order or repeats of earlier keys, although the latter can happen, too; see D minor Clavier Concerto, 2nd movement, mm. 25–26 and 56–57, both in the subdominant.

The tonal scheme outlined above creates *structure* and *variety,* Bach's two principal goals at all times, for nearly all of the closely related keys are explored or at least systematically visited. The tonal scheme is supplemented by the motivic design, particularly in longer movements, if they are mostly homophonic. For example, to announce each key area in the Preambulum of the Fifth Partita, Bach repeats the head motive (which is four measures long) each time. He does the same in the unusually long Prelude to the A-flat major Fugue, *WTC,* Bk. II. By comparing these two examples it is possible to derive an approximate idea of the relative weight Bach attributed to each of the key areas. Indeed, a comparison of measure numbers shows that corresponding sections are, on the whole, equally long in both works:

	Tonic	Dominant	Relative Minor	Subdominant	End
Preambulum	1–4	17–20	41–44	65–68	95
Prelude	1–4	17–20	34–37	50–51*	77

*first half only

The quick modulation to the dominant and the much longer wait before arriving at the relative minor (or major) are features found in many other Bach scores. The F major Prelude, *WTC*, Bk. II, has four entrances, 16 measures apart, the last in the mediant key, followed by a final entrance in the main key.

Occasionally, in slow movements, an entire bass melody is treated as an ostinato in ground-bass fashion, moving from key to key in an elastic application of the normal tonal scheme. Not every repeat of the ground bass ends in the key in which it started. In the G minor *Adagio* of the D minor Clavier Concerto, for example, the third statement of the ground bass begins in the dominant minor (m. 30) and concludes 12 measures later in the relative major (the next expected key, m. 42).

The substitution of other keys for the expected key happens especially in pieces in the minor mode and may lead to tremendous complexities. The Aria of the *Goldberg Variations* is in G major; the relative key, E minor, is reached in a full cadence in m. 8 of the second part of the Aria (Ex. 14a). Twenty-seven of the 30 variations are in the major mode; the three remaining variations—Nos. 15, 21, and 25—are in G minor. In the first two of these, instead of using the relative major (B-flat major) at the point where the theme cadences in E minor, Bach used the submediant key of E-flat major (Ex. 14b). Since E-flat is only a semitone below E, it is the nearest possible neighbor to the relative minor, and using it enabled Bach to keep both the bass melody and the melodic outline of the treble instead of disrupting them by using B-flat major. For the very slow* and extremely serious Variation 25, however, it seemed necessary to Bach to avoid the major mode altogether, even at this place; so he substituted for the key of E-flat major (itself a substitution for B-flat major), that of E-flat minor (Ex. 14c). This modulation from a

Goldberg Variations

Ex. 14a Aria, m. 24.   Ex. 14b Var. 21, m. 11.

---

*Bach marked this variation *adagio* in his personal copy.[14]

Ex. 14c Var. 25, m. 23.

minor key to its submediant minor—though it became dear to
Schubert a century later—has, to my knowledge, no parallel
elsewhere in Bach.

In dance forms, Bach's observance of the same order of tonalities results in a second half that is more complex than the
first. While there is only one key change (tonic to dominant) in
the first half of a dance, the second half has at least two (dominant to relative key; relative key to tonic) and often three, if the
subdominant is included after the relative key. From there the
next step is to make the second half longer than the first—the
result is the nucleus of the proportions of a sonata movement![15]

Bach always thought ahead. As soon as he cadenced in one
key, he was on his way to the next cadence in a new key. This is
where the observance of the tonality order becomes of practical
importance for the performer. Most people are unaware of the
existence of tonal directions prior to the final cadence.* Bach's
harmonies must be explained not only in terms of what precedes
them but also in view of their relationship with what follows. If,
in a C major piece, for example, Bach concludes a phrase in A
minor and proceeds to F major (i.e., from the relative minor to
the subdominant), all the chords of the connecting phrase must
also be heard as part of the next key. (Any D minor chord, for
instance, must be understood immediately not just as the fourth
degree of A minor, but as the sixth degree of F major.) Bach
expected his listeners to be familiar enough with his normal order
of tonalities to recognize and enjoy such a double relationship.

In the Prelude to the Sixth English Suite in D minor, the section composed in the dominant minor ends with a Picardy third
in m. 113 (Ex. 15a), and 14 measures later, a cadence in B-flat
major (relative major of the subdominant) substitutes for the ex-

---

*The pianist-composer Erich Itor Kahn once complained about this defect.[16]

pected cadence in F major. Within that passage, mm. 113–15 contain a number of D minor chords; these chords ought to be heard as the mediant of the upcoming B-flat major as well as the subdominant of A minor or as the tonic key of the piece. A little later in the same section, the harmonic progressions include several triads not belonging to B-flat major proper, but momentarily annexed to it. This harmonic event illustrates an additional important feature of Bach's treatment of tonality, namely, that he always included the *dominants and subdominants of each degree triad,* notwithstanding their deviating sharps and flats. In m. 118 (Ex. 15b), on the last 8th note, we find the dominant seventh of E-flat (the subdominant)—including A-flat, which is not in the B-flat major scale! Furthermore, a D major chord opens m. 120 (Ex. 15c), its major third justified as part of the dominant chord of G minor.

Prelude from English Suite No. 6
Ex. 15a   m. 113

Ex. 15b   m. 118

Ex. 15c   mm. 119–20

What follows is even more daring: the supertonic, C major, appears in the music, preceded by *its* dominant seventh. No modulation is induced or implied by any of this; the goal of a cadence in B-flat major not only remains undeflected but is strengthened in that the D major and C major chords mentioned above aid the top voice in its chromatic descent to the major third of B-flat major.

The habitual use of seemingly remote chords within a given key stems from Bach's concept of *enlarged tonality,*[17] in which the chord inventory of each key comprises not only the triads (and their seventh chords) on each of the seven degrees, but all secondary dominant and subdominant chords of these triads as well. In their totality, these chords form a large "family," so to speak, in which the in-laws of each member—though not related by birth—are included as equals. The key of C major can thus regularly feature any number of D major chords, E major chords, A major chords, etc., in their role as secondary dominants, all being part of the enlarged tonality.

One particular instance must be mentioned here. When writing in the minor mode, Bach frequently harmonizes the raised sixth of the melodic scale with the help of the dominant of the natural seventh, or its relative minor. In the C minor Prelude, *WTC*, Bk. I (Ex. 16a), Bach uses the dominant seventh of B-flat as harmony for the A-natural in the middle voice, which is on its way to B-natural and C (Ex. 16b); see also the E minor Prelude, *WTC*, Bk. I, m. 10.

Prelude in C minor, *WTC*, Bk. I
Ex. 16a   mm. 15–18

Ex. 16b   Condensed harmony

If we are bewildered by the occurrence of sharps and flats contrary to the key signature, such as described here, it is our own fault for not having studied Bach's harmonic vocabulary sufficiently. Bach did not aim at creating surprise effects; to maintain order was always his foremost concern. He often established signposts for the listener and performer, indicating the direction he intended to follow. Upon reaching a dominant, for instance, he frequently would insert a diminished chord—to be played *diminuendo*—to indicate a motion toward the relative minor. See the F major Invention; G major French Suite, Allemande and Courante; and Ex. 4 above. In this Courante, the diminished chord precedes the cadence in E minor by fully 16 measures; without it the tonal direction might remain unclear to the listener.

Sharp dissonances are found mainly where the music is firmly established in a single tonality and not threatened by immediate modulation. In the great majority of cases, they are part of the minor mode,* and in nearly every instance they are caused by clashes between two different forms of the minor scale occurring simultaneously. In the slow movement of the *Italian Concerto* the third of the subdominant chord happens to be sounded in the left hand just as the ascending melodic scale reaches b-natural' in the right hand (Ex. 17). If Bach's dynamic marking of *piano* is carefully observed in the left hand, the result is most convincing, giving the effect of muted timpani.

Ex. 17 *Italian Concerto*, 2nd Mvt., mm. 10–11.

Proportions of Length

Most obviously in the dances, but also in nearly all of Bach's other works, the different sections stand in a pre-planned mathematical relationship to each other. A certain concern for *proportions of length* was part of the composer's task.[18] But while all others "composed" a large piece by fitting small segments together symmetrically, Bach mentally looked at the musical space occupied by the whole work and then subdivided it into regular, or nearly regular, sections.

---

*One of the basic differences between Bach and Mozart (who loved to create dissonance also in a straightforward major): cf. the slow movement of the E-flat major Quartet, K. 428, and the Finale of the *Jupiter* Symphony.

For a long time afterward, the great composers did not look at compositional forms as spaces filled in an orderly distribution of measures—not even Mozart, mathematically gifted as he was, and certainly not Beethoven and the Romantics. Not until the twentieth century—when Stravinsky was commissioned to write modern ballets; Honegger wrote sound tracks for films; and Bartok developed a new, abstract approach to form[19]—was there a resumption of Bach's concept, and was the significance of his spatial planning finally recognized for what it was.

In Bach's binary compositions the two parts are, as a rule, of equal length;[20] see, for example, the Allemande and Courante of the Second Partita. However, this rule is quite frequently changed to make room for a longer second part (see p. 14). In this case, the various proportions are usually based on simple mathematical ratios, such as twice as long (Giga of the First Partita; Passepied of the Fifth Partita; Sarabande of the First French Suite). Ratios of 2:3 (that is, 16:24 measures) occur in the Burleska of the Third Partita; 3:4 (12:16 measures) in the Sarabande of the First Partita; 3:5 (12:20 measures) in the Scherzo of the Third Partita. Certain tendencies prevail in certain Suites. Thus it happens that in the Second Partita the second part tends to be long everywhere, while in the First Partita equality between the sections prevails. Perhaps this was one of the ways in which Bach realized the relative gravity of the Second Partita compared to the graceful symmetry of the First.

More complex ratios sometimes exist on the surface, but most of the time they can be reduced to simpler ones by analysis. In the Aria of the Fourth Partita, for example, the second section has 36 measures, while the first has only 16. A form analysis shows that the second section is twice as long as the first; that is, 32 measures, with the addition of a four-measure coda.* The second section of the E major Invention begins with an episode in the mediant minor** and consequently becomes twice as long as the first, not counting the last two measures forming the coda.

---

*In all such cases, the second repeat ought to be omitted, since it is unlikely that Bach wanted the coda to be played twice. This suggestion is strengthened by evidence in the Air of the Sixth Partita, where the coda follows separately, just once, after the repeat of the second section. (See above, p. 10).

**A similar episode in the same key occurs in the corresponding place in the final Rondo of the Violin Concerto in E major.

Bach probably had a mixture of two-part form and rondo form in mind (as in the Rondeau of the Second Partita).

Any study of Bach's music, especially of a binary piece, ought to begin with counting the measures of each section in order to find out how the musical material is distributed. Quite frequently, wherever the organization is symmetrical, the external symmetry serves to compensate for internal asymmetries. In the Allemande of the Second English Suite, for instance, in which the two sections are of equal length, only the very opening and the very closing measures correspond; in the rest the identical material is quite differently distributed, so that the recapitulations happen earlier or later.

If, as in French overture style, the second section is faster than the first, it obviously has to consist of a greater number of measures, if it is to be of the same duration. Here complications may arise. The two sections of the Aria of the *Goldberg Variations,* as well as of nearly all the variations, contain 16 measures each. Variation 16, entitled "Ouverture," consists of a slow first section in 2/2, the regular 16 measures, and a fast second section in 3/8, which is 32 measures long; if performed so that two 3/8 measures equal one 2/2 measure ($\downarrow. = \downarrow$), the two sections should be equal in length. Unfortunately, this does not work out. The second section is obviously much faster than that; in fact, it is probably meant to be four times as fast as the first.*[21] As a result, the first section lasts twice as long as the second; this is unsatisfactory but seems unavoidable. A similar problem arises in the C-sharp major Prelude, *WTC,* Bk. II, which is an overture in form if not in style.

In longer pieces, especially in ternary Preludes, of which Bach wrote a great number, measure-counting is not of the same importance, but even here it is sometimes surprising how many exact equals and multiples they contain. The first section of the Prelude of the Second English Suite in A minor constitutes exactly one-third (55 measures) of the piece, the middle section also consisting of 55 measures. It may seem strange that the entire piece is 164 and not 165 measures long, but this is because m. 55 is both the end of the first section and the beginning of the

---

*Bach ends the second section with a nominal *da capo* by way of a single G major chord written in 2/2—minimal lip service (on paper) to traditional overture form!

second.* In the *Art of Fugue,* Contrapunctus VIII, the main subject enters in the 94th of 188 measures. In the D-sharp minor Fugue of *WTC,* Bk. I, the inversion is presented in a canon after 43½ measures, exactly at the midpoint (as Diran Alexanian, the great cellist and scholar, once pointed out to me).

One can continue *ad infinitum,* but it is not necessary. Must performers be aware of Bach's planning of space? I say emphatically "Yes," for, next to the order of tonalities, nothing helps as directly in organizing the interpretation.

II. BACH'S IDIOMS

Bach's stylistic differentiation among the various species of music is most noticeable in the different aspects of *harmony.* The Preludes of the *WTC,* for example, were just that, pieces intended to "prelude," i.e., to establish the key awareness the listener needs prior to hearing an unaccompanied fugue subject. For the most part, they lack melodic motives, replacing them by a tapestry of motivic patterns which draw attention to the harmonic events. Their harmonies are more straightforward than in Bach's other works and thus can become the focus of attention. Normally, the Preludes open and close with extended pedal points on the tonic. The bass is the last to leave and the first to return home.

The Fugues, on the contrary, feature *melody* as they embody Bach's complex *polyphony,* with the side effect of creating frequent dissonances. Moreover, Bach liked to use major sevenths and tritones as melodic intervals in many themes (see Fugues in G major, *WTC,* Bk. I; E minor, *WTC,* Bk. I; B-flat minor, *WTC,* Bk. II, and especially B minor, *WTC,* Bk. I), intervals which inevitably influence the harmonic character. (His most dissonant writing, however, is found in the canons of the *Musical Offering* and *Art of Fugue;* here the melodic contours are wholly sovereign.)

In Bach's dances and pieces in dance style, it is essentially the *rhythm* that establishes the idiom of each particular dance form and the harmonic rhythm; the harmonic changes are usually

---

* "Takterstickung," in Marpurg's terminology.[22]

confined to the crossing of barlines and sometimes mid-measure divisions. This implies the existence of subspecies (Allemandes, Courantes, etc.) whose rhythmic patterns remain approximately the same whether they occur in an English Suite, a French Suite, or a Partita. Such is the case despite the slight difference in genre between these series of movements: the French Suites are essentially two-part writing, concise, and without introductory pieces; the English Suites are longer, more dissonant, and more rhythmically complex; and the Partitas are brilliant (see below) and, in French style, ornately decorated. The rhythmic identity of each dance form cuts across these differences.

As to the particular rhythmic type of dance motion, Bach, while leaning on Froberger and other predecessors, went his own way in sharpening the precision with which each type is identifiable. These types are not always correctly defined in the various studies of Bach's music. Here are a few of the most important: *Allemande:* The meter is in fast eighth notes rather than slow quarter notes. This enables the performer to establish a relaxed yet lively pulse and to evoke the "walking" character, which is followed by the "running" of the ensuing *Courante.* The passage beginning in m. 71 of the first movement of the Fifth *Brandenburg* Concerto establishes an Allemande rhythm through the accompaniment in even eighth notes. *Sarabande:* Bach's Sarabandes are the only dances which are rigorously cast in four-measure periods. In each period, except for the third measure, the note or chord occurring on the second beat is held through the end of the measure. Typical is the Sarabande of the C minor Partita, in which there are held notes on, and only on, these beats, indicating, as well as establishing, the Sarabande dance rhythm ♩♩|♩♩| ♪♪♪|♩♩| . Ratner's example[23] of the slow movement of the *Jupiter* Symphony is wrong, since the second beat of m. 2 is short. *Bourrée:* The dance consists of units of four measures each, in which the first measure is preceded by a short upbeat and the fourth is subdivided in vigorous quarter notes (half beats) in its first half ♪|♩♩|♩♩|♩♩|♪♪♪| . *Passepied:* The "foot" is "passed" at the end of the first full measure in a slide (*Schleifer*) whose rhythmic function must be projected in performance. (See the Fifth Partita and the *French Overture.*) In the English Suite in E minor, the slide stands at the beginning of the measure. *Gigue:* As a round dance in whirling motion, its exact rhythms were changeable, and Bach realized them in many different ways.

To sum up, somewhat oversimplifying the differences among genres, one might say that in preludes the harmonic element is dominant, while fugues are ruled by the melodic and dances by the rhythmic element. To give one particular example, Bach's use of *enharmonic changes* illustrates how his harmonic language depends on genre. Not a single enharmonic change is found in the *Well-Tempered Clavier!* Someone not familiar with any other compositions by Bach would come to the conclusion that he avoided enharmonic changes altogether, and it would be impossible to guess that their absence is caused simply by the specific character of this particular collection of preludes and fugues. Bach clearly intended the *Well-Tempered Clavier* to be an embodiment of the spirit of moderation, as befits educational music. The affects expressed in it, strong as they sometimes are, are held within strict boundaries of length and intensity. This is easy to see in a comparison with his preludes and fugues for organ or his *Chromatic Fantasy and Fugue.* Except for the toccata-like endings of some fugues (see above, p. 11), the rhythms are also more strictly measured than in the majority of Bach's works; it is this almost complete absence of unmeasured rhythms in particular which accounts for Bach's omission of enharmonic changes.

The situation is quite different wherever Bach reverted to expressive declamation. In recitative style the ear indeed has no difficulty absorbing the startling reversal of tonal regions engendered by enharmonic changes. To quote just two passages, enharmonic changes dominate the beginning of the recitative in the *Chromatic Fantasy* (especially mm. 49 ff.; Ex. 18a) and the second half of the Sarabande of the Third English Suite in G minor (Ex. 18b).*

The *Clavierübung,* consisting of four volumes, comprises the Partitas (vol. 1), the *Italian Concerto* and the *French Overture* (vol.

---

*The extreme affects which Bach obviously associated with this harmonic process may be studied in No. 60, "Erbarm Es Gott," of the *St. Matthew Passion,* which is a desperate appeal to stop the whipping of Jesus.

Ex. 18a *Chromatic Fantasy,* m. 49.   Ex. 18b Sarabande from English Suite No. 3, mm. 17–18.

2), the Duets (vol. 3*), and the *Goldberg Variations* (vol. 4). But as
the title of the collection indicates, these various types of pieces
combine into a new, independent genre, one in which the focal
point is the brilliance of the keyboard writing. When Schumann
listed the entire *Clavierübung* among existing collections of piano
etudes,[24] he was one of the very few people—then or now—to
realize this emphasis. In the *Clavierübung,* Bach deliberately explored the virtuosities of both composing and performing. Vol-
ume 2 is a showcase for the composer. The Italianisms of the
Italian Concerto were meant to contrast with the Gallicisms of the
French Overture, as can be deduced from the way in which Bach
juxtaposed the two pieces, calling one "in the Italian taste" and
the other "in the French manner." Bach's Italian style was
influenced by Vivaldi, his favorite composer. The music is distinguished by its textural simplicity: minimal embellishments and
polyphony, and the top voice leading, especially in the episodes;
see the markings of *forte* for the right hand and *piano* for the left.
Like the D minor Clavier Concerto, the *Italian Concerto* was
modeled after a (real or imagined) *violin* concerto. This becomes
apparent in the texture of the slow movement (one line plus continuo), the figurations in the top voice of the Finale (for example,
mm. 9ff.), and other details inexplicable in a keyboard concerto
but normal in a violin concerto.

The French style of the Overture (also of some Partitas and
most of the *Goldberg Variations*) seems to originate with a totally
different kind of composer. Here we discover playful ornaments,
piquant polyphonic rhythmic games—especially in the Fifth
Partita, and in the Passepied and Gigue of the *Overture***—and

---

*Part of vol. 3 is for organ.
**Dance rhythms sometimes illuminate the character of other Bach pieces. This Gigue,
for example, explains *Goldberg* Variation No. 7; the Burleska of the Third Partita (Ex. 19a)
makes clear the solid, almost vulgar, rhythm of the D minor Fugue, *WTC,* Bk. I (Ex.
19b).

Ex. 19a Burleska from Partita No. 3, m. 5.   Ex. 19b Fugue in D minor, *WTC*, Bk. I, m. 2.

total equality between the lower voices and the treble. The performer who is aware of these stylistic contrasts will observe and enjoy these sophisticated nuances in the *French Overture* while giving prime attention in the *Italian Concerto* to architectural designs, tonal beauty, and direct expression of strong feelings.

Virtuosity of the performer is emphasized by Bach's keyboard style especially in the third and fourth volumes. The Duets, in particular, which have often been described as another set of two-part inventions, are, on the contrary, virtuoso pieces meant not just to be studied but to be performed. Virtuosity is carried even further in the *Goldberg Variations,* where it becomes part of the overall design. In each group of three variations, the first is a character piece of some sort and the last is a canon. The middle piece is always devoted to various new techniques, which increase in difficulty with each successive group. Some of these techniques were not to be used again until the late Beethoven works and some compositions by Liszt, and they were utterly unheard-of in Bach's time.

III. MUSICAL ELEMENTS OF IMPORTANCE TO THE PERFORMER

Melody

Despite careful attention to other aspects of Bach's music, scholars neglected his melodic principles until the turn of the twentieth century, when Heinrich Schenker and August Halm[25] became aware of them, and composers like Reger, Busoni, Schoenberg, and Stravinsky began to emulate them, each in his own way. Melodic analysis, a relatively new branch of music theory, cannot be confined here to a single method. On the following pages, various analytical approaches will be applied to Bach's fugue subjects and other motives. Not all of them are of value to the music of other composers.

1. While the three basic types of melodic patterns—*diatonic,*

chromatic, and *triadic*—are usually combined in most eighteenth-century music, Bach's melodies are often devoted exclusively or principally to one of these at a time. In the *Chromatic Fugue,* for example, half-steps dominate the subject initially, followed by parts of the D minor scale, and finally by the three tones of the dominant triad (Ex. 20).* This diversity is compensated for by the steady rhythmic device of three even quarter notes in alternate measures.

Ex. 20 *Chromatic Fugue,* subject.

In the subject of the D minor Fugue, *WTC,* Bk. II (Ex. 21), the same patterns are more closely interrelated. The opening diatonic ascent to the dominant is a decoration of the D minor triad; it returns at the end in a simple inversion of the same triad, but this inversion is not employed anywhere else in the Fugue. Between the diatonic and triadic elements of the motive is a de-

Ex. 21   Fugue in D minor, *WTC,* Bk. II, subject.

scending chromatic scale from the upper tonic down to the lower dominant.** Where the three melodic interval types are combined, they ought to be distinguished by their different articulation. Thus, it is often appropriate to associate *legato* with diatonic progressions, super-*legato* (meaning a very slight overlap) with chromaticism, and non-*legato* with triadic passages. These guidelines work well in the subject of the *Chromatic Fugue,* for example, if the triad in m. 7 is played with just enough separation to be heard melodically as well as harmonically—without a

---

*Note that in the harmonization of the Fugue Bach does not necessarily follow the harmonic implications of the unaccompanied melody.

**Contrary to customary practice, the chromatic descent does not function as a chaconne motive here, but remains part of the larger thematic material.

noticeable interruption of sound*—while the two preceding
measures are completely *legato* (yet not overlapping as in the
chromatic beginning).

In the subject of the D minor Fugue, *WTC,* Bk. II, the
chromatic descent must be treated differently because it needs
more emphasis than super-*legato* can provide. On a modern
piano, it is best played with a separate emphasis on each note,
resulting in a sort of non-*legato,* since in slow playing the articulation of each new tone has an interrupting effect simply by its
relative loudness, considering the obsolescence of sound on the
instrument. The concluding triad can be played non-*legato* without accents, as in the preceding example. The diatonic figures of
the first measure may be played as a series of written-out slides
(Ex. 22), similar to the filled-in broken thirds which Bach later
inserted in the First Invention in the so-called Yale manuscript;
this requires the same type of *legato* as in mm. 5 and 6 of the
Chromatic Fugue.

Ex. 22 Two-Part Invention in C major, m. 1, Yale manuscript.

2. Sometimes the identity of a thematic unit is revealed
through a study of its *melodic directions.* There is no better illustration than the B-flat minor Fugue, *WTC,* Bk. II (Ex. 23). Its
rhythmic contrasts, sharp interruptions, and staccato articulations
mask a series of flowing, ascending scale fragments. (This is not
the only instance of such procedure in Bach's works: the directly
descending scales in 16th notes at the end of the Rondeau of the
Second Partita are hidden from immediate perception with the
same ingenuity.) The performer's most important task is to prevent the open interruptions in the theme from interfering with its
hidden flow. The second and third tones of m. 2, for instance,
being leading tone and tonic, can easily bring the phrasing of the
fugue subject to a premature cadence unless the performer begins

---

*Generally speaking, since any fugue subject is basically just the raw material from
which Bach fashions the fugue itself (a table of contents, so to speak), he would wish that
it be performed as objectively as possible—avoiding rubato, sound interruptions unless
marked, and unilateral phrasing—while at the same time establishing the basic character
of the piece.

Ex. 23   Fugue in B-flat minor, *WTC*, Bk. II: subject, outline, and corresponding tritones.

tritone   third   third   third   third   *tritone*

a new phrase on a′, but avoids any rhythmic distortion or modification of note values, and carries it over the ensuing rest (see
para. 3 below). Additional important directional features occur in
m. 3, where, from the second note on, the first four notes of the
fugue subject are repeated in a continuous rhythm; in mm. 2 and
4 open tritones (e-flat′–a′ and g-flat′–c′) correspond to each
other, though situated at opposite ends of the measure.

It is the clarity of these melodic directions that prompted Bach
to use such abrupt rhythmic patterns. Both features combined
make possible the complex polyphonic detail of this model
fugue, which can be regarded as a precursor of the *Art of Fugue*.[26]
Its "pitch vocabulary," consisting of the first five tones of the
B-flat minor scale flanked by semitones at either end, is also the
same as in the *Art of Fugue* (original and inversion taken together;
see above, p. 9).

3. While most composers used *rests* indiscriminately throughout their melodies, with a more or less interrupting effect, Bach
apparently followed his own strict principles in the very few rest
marks that one can find *within* his themes. Mostly these marks do
not indicate a breath between successive phrases; on the contrary,
they hold the two ends of a single phrase together by separating
them. In the subject of the G minor Fugue, *WTC*, Bk. II (Ex.
24), the motivic germ extends from the second beat of each
measure to, and including, the downbeat of the next; that is, over
the rest mark. To phrase, as some people do, from the last note

Ex. 24   Fugue in G minor, *WTC*, Bk. II, subject.

in each measure through to the second beat of the following one would obstruct Bach's melodic interval plan. Musical logic suggests highlighting the rising fourths over each barline by ending each subphrase with the downbeat. There is evidence that this is what Bach wanted, since the Fugue begins on a second, not on a third beat—always a clear indication of Bach's phrase structure. In the E-flat major Fugue, *WTC,* Bk. II, a structural rest mark follows the second tone (B-flat), which is the first tone of a scale descent to G. The interruption of sound at this place has a curious double effect. Not only does one perceive the scale descent more clearly through its interruption, but also all rising intervals become more perceptible. (If one were to hold the B-flat in m. 2 for three quarters instead of two, ignoring the rest, the decrease in clarity would be evident at once.) Bach's habit of inserting rests *into* a phrase or motive, rather than using them to *separate* phrases, goes so far that, occasionally when writing in French style, he even separates a trill from its afterbeat (*Nachschlag*) by a rest (see the *French Overture* in B minor, m. 8; E minor Prelude, *WTC,* Bk. I, m. 10; also Exx. 1b, c).

This is not to say that Bach never used rests to separate two phrases. But when he did, his procedures were also somewhat unusual. The beginning of the slow movement of the *Italian Concerto* includes two such rests in mm. 12 and 14 (Ex. 25). Their purpose is obviously to attract attention to the modulation in the lower voices (in which there are no rest marks), for they are missing in the corresponding place in the second half of the movement, where no such modulation occurs. Or consider the long rest which follows the initial note in the subject of the A major Fugue, *WTC,* Bk. I (Ex. 26). Bach treats this note as a

Ex. 25 *Italian Concerto,* 2nd Mvt., mm. 12–14.

Ex. 26 Fugue in A major, *WTC,* Bk. I, subject.

imitation

phrase in itself so that it may counterbalance the pattern of five two-note groups which follow immediately. The rest after this a' enables the listener to keep the 9/8 meter in mind while enjoying various polyrhythms in what follows.

In a polyphonic composition, when one voice pauses at the end of a more or less lengthy statement, the final note must not necessarily be held for its full notated value, or else numerous places in the fugues would be unplayable.* This rule applies, in my opinion, to the quarter notes (beats 2 and 4) in the tenor of the F minor Fugue, *WTC*, Bk. I, m. 5 (Ex. 27). By *not* holding them for their full length, the performer can more effectively highlight the long note on beat 2 of the following measure (c'). Of course, such notes are not meant to be played *staccato*, but with a *legato* touch, as if the performer meant to hold the note all the way through.

Ex. 27 Fugue in F minor, *WTC*, Bk. I, m. 5. Ex. 28 Fugue in B-flat minor, *WTC*, Bk. II, m. 13.

The situation is different when notes marked *staccato* are also surrounded by rests, as in the B-flat minor Fugue, *WTC*, Bk. II (Ex. 28) They ought to be "plucked" in the manner of a string *pizzicato*. The same approach applies to the curious retrograde appearance of the name B A C H (H C A B) in the bass of m. 51 of the B-flat major Prelude, *WTC*, Bk. II. Thus, all four notes bearing the letters of the name ought to be "plucked"; the rests here act as quotation marks.

4. In many cases it is helpful to investigate Bach's themes for their *dissonant melodic intervals*. They play an important role in the melodic construction. Descending sevenths—major, minor, and diminished—in particular, are used strategically, often in the lowest voice, to activate the crossing of barlines or the transition from the first half of a measure to the second. The Fugue of the Toccata in E minor, Sixth Partita, offers a striking example (Ex.

---

*After all, Bach, too, genius though he was, had no more than five fingers on each hand!

29). A descending minor seventh bridges mm. 2 and 3 of the
subject; then, as a second voice enters with the theme, the first
voice continues with three additional melodic sevenths (diminished, major, and minor) in rhythmic diminution. The second half of the Sarabande of the C minor Partita (Ex. 30) is built

Ex. 29   Toccata from Partita No. 6, mm. 28–31.

Ex. 30   Sarabande from Partita No. 2, mm. 17–19.

on descending sevenths in the bass. In the Gigue of the Fifth
French Suite in G major, the ascending octaves in the treble in m.
2 (Ex. 31a) become descending sevenths in the free inversions of
the second half (Ex. 31b). In the A minor Fugue, BWV 894 (Ex.

Gigue from French Suite No. 5
Ex. 31a   mm. 2–3

Ex. 31b   mm. 26–27

32a), Bach wrote an entire series of ascending six-tone scales.
Each scale starts one tone lower than the preceding one, so that a
descending seventh separates successive scales; it is this interval
that holds the melodic line together. This analysis is confirmed
by an orchestral introduction to the same fugue subject, written
15 years later, when Bach rewrote this fugue to become the
Finale of the *Triple Concerto* in A minor, BWV 1044. In this introduction, Bach traced the outline of the motive in overlapping
descending sevenths (Ex. 32b).[27] The pianist is probably not taking too much liberty in also applying the faintest hint of such an
overlap to the subject of the Fugue itself, with the highest tone of

Ex. 32a Fugue in A minor, BWV 894 and 1044, subject.

Ex. 32b *Triple Concerto*, BWV 1044, orchestral introduction to Finale, mm. 1–3.

each scale being held just long enough to be heard with its lower seventh for a fraction of a second.

5. *Beat Melody*. Bach's bass lines in contrapuntal writing differ in one important respect from those of later composers—Haydn, Beethoven, Brahms, and others—in that Bach kept the principal strong beats in the bass free of nonharmonic notes so that they would provide a harmonic foundation. This concern may have been due to his training in the harmonization of Lutheran hymns, in which logical progressions from chord to chord are essential. (One may therefore assume that Bach would not have approved of the subject of Beethoven's *Hammerclavier* Fugue, with appoggiaturas appearing on a great number of beats following the first few measures.)

But Bach went even further. It is apparent from his variations and melodic decorations in chorales, canons, etc., that, true to the ideas of the late Baroque, he conceived of melody, as of all art, simultaneously on a grand scale and in the minutest detail. This enabled him to produce *organic* works of art in which, according to Kant's definition,* the detail is unthinkable without the whole and vice versa. As an example, almost a symbol, of this double concern for smaller and larger melodic units, the bass notes on strong beats have a curious double function; in addition to being part of the total bass line they form an independent, slower-moving melody which is gained by leaving out all the notes in between. The performer who is aware of this "beat melody," as I call it, will be greatly helped in his understanding of the melodic essence. This beat melody is as important as the

---

*See chapter 2, Haydn, p. 64.

Urlinie of Schenker, but obviously totally different, since it is gained not by looking at all the tones but only at those falling on the principal beats of a measure.

When the beat melodies appear in the bass, they carry the harmonic rhythm; occasionally they are supplemented by strong upbeats on notes in between, but mostly they do so by themselves. Notwithstanding their *obbligato* character, they thus become (to use Claude Frank's expression) a "built-in continuo" part, not necessarily identical to the more familiar device of a thematic outline within a variation (as in Schubert's *Wanderer* Fantasy, second movement, mm. 39ff.). In the secondary theme of the Finale of the *Italian Concerto* (Ex. 33a), for instance, the thematic outline consists of ever-expanding ascending lines: F to C, F to D, F to E (beginning on the last quarter note of m. 26), and F to the higher F and back (Ex. 33b). The beat melody, however, presents a different and harmonically accurate picture, inasmuch as the third ascending line begins on G (downbeat of m. 27), not on F (Ex. 33c).*

Italian Concerto, 3rd Mvt.
Ex. 33a mm. 25–28

Ex. 33b Outline

Ex. 33c Beat melody

The reason why a beat melody can be entirely different from a melodic outline is found in the metric emphasis through which the beat melody, by definition, is generated. In the F-sharp major Fugue, *WTC*, Bk. I, only 7 of the 16 notes of the subject are beat notes (Exx. 34a, b). The beat melody reveals (1) a start on the tonic, ignoring the initial upbeat (which would surely be part of an ordinary melodic outline); (2) a direct descent, d–

---

*The accuracy of this thematic construction is further enhanced by a comparison of this theme with the subject of the B major Fugue, *WTC*, Bk. II, which greatly resembles it.

Fugue in F-sharp major, *WTC*, Bk. I
Ex. 34a Subject

Ex. 34b Beat melody

sharp–b–g-sharp; and (3) a final rise from g-sharp to a-sharp, contradicting the falling triad of the theme and its melodic outline. A comparison of the beat tones of the two fugue themes in A-flat major and G sharp minor, *WTC,* Bk. II, shows the first to be descending and the second to be ascending; this is not noticeable in ordinary listening and analysis.[28]

Occasionally, beat melodies in the bass can help determine the best tempo. A nonharmonic tone in the bass on the third eighth in 3/8 time (for example, in the D minor Invention (Exx. 35a, b), usually indicates that this tone should not be heard as a beat—in other words, that the tempo is quite fast. Compare this with the D major Invention, also in 3/8, which has harmonic tones on each beat in the bass, while the treble includes frequent passing tones and appoggiaturas. In this case, the tempo is slower so that each measure is felt as having three beats, not one, as in the D minor Invention.

Two-Part Invention in D minor
Ex. 35a m. 4   Ex. 35b Beat melody, mm. 3–4.

As always, there are exceptions, especially where the character of the piece is in some way extreme. The harshness of the clashes between the two voices of the E minor Fugue, *WTC,* Bk. I ("the ill-tempered Fugue of the *Well-tempered Clavier*") violates Bach's laws of beat melody in a fast tempo. The tragic character of the slow B minor Fugue in the same book, which bears one of Bach's rare tempo markings to avoid any misunderstanding, is brought out precisely by the deliberate, accented appoggiaturas on the beat in the middle of the fugue subject (Ex. 36a), creating dissonances of extraordinary harshness when they appear in the bass.* The tempo marking may actually have been inserted to indicate the absence of any meaningful beat melody here, at the end of the entire book, in the key in which Bach was later to write his great Mass.

Ex. 36a   Fugue in B minor, *WTC*, Bk. I, subject.

Ex. 36b   Fugue in B minor, *WTC*, Bk. II, subject.

Grouping

Bach's series of continuous short, equidistant notes with no obvious clues as to phrasing and dynamics are often puzzling to performers. They are found in both melody and accompanying voices, and they frequently appear in reversible counterpoint to slower-moving melodies. Their articulation is not confined to the narrow limits in which the harpsichord of Bach's time was forced to operate. Except in the *Clavierübung,* Bach had other keyboard instruments in mind as well as the harpsichord when he wrote for clavier. Furthermore, as a performer of genius, he was almost certainly able to overcome some of the usual instrumental handicaps, especially in achieving a good *legato* and an unusual variety of dynamic nuances. However, it should also be remembered that he could leave a lot to the imagination of the public, since his listeners were quite used to hearing similar music performed by voices or by string instruments.** Without such appeal to the imagination, a masterwork like the *Italian Concerto* would be unthinkable. Yet to anyone with experience in listening to Baroque concerto literature, the alternations between *tutti* and *solo* passages

---

*The first three notes of the B minor Fugue, *WTC,* Bk. II, are identical with those in Bk. I; I have no doubt that they should be equally slow (Ex. 36b).

**The situation can be compared to the playing of classical symphonies as piano duets: if one knows the symphony one will automatically supply the missing orchestration in the imagination.

in the piece's outer movements are as clearly perceptible as if they were being played by different people.

Therefore, one can be sure that Bach, in his infrequent mordents and trills, was not trying to make up for the missing opportunity to accent a single tone on a harpsichord; their main function was melodic decoration. If this is true, then the mordents in small print added by some otherwise excellent editors, such as Bischoff and Landshoff, on the basis of contemporary copies made by Bach's pupils, are unnecessary and, in most cases, to modern ears misleading in that they are likely to overemphasize downbeats. (It is a strange psychological phenomenon that a downbeat note or one that anticipates a downbeat by syncopation will sound longer and louder without even the slightest accent or prolongation.)

Usually, a grouping of small note values (whether there are four or six under one beam) begins on the second note under the beam and extends to the first note under the next beam. In other words, all the notes under the beam, except the first, are part of a long upbeat to the next beat. On the piano, this can be realized in performance by marking the second tone under each beam very slightly and so precisely that the accent does not spill over to the next tone. It is unnecessary and therefore wrong to add any rhythmic punctuation by way of a short hesitation after each beat tone.* Such punctuation may have been the rule in the eighteenth century, but today a listener's tolerance of extra time taken between phrases in fast-moving music has become minimal, thanks to all the dynamic gradations available on the modern piano. Therefore, even if historically unjustified, perfect evenness of rhythm, except at a slow tempo, must be strongly recommended.

Evenness of *rhythm,* however, does not necessarily imply evenness of *connection* or *separation.* Indiscriminate *legato* and indiscriminate *non-legato* are equally wrong. Certain nuances of duration will easily go together with the minimal dynamic stress of the second note under each beam. This combination creates an eloquent speechlike pattern corresponding to the melodic ups and

---

*I once heard Andrés Segovia try this in a guitar arrangement. To my ears, these interruptions of the beat sounded totally artificial.

downs within the metric frame. Thus, the last note in a measure will usually be abbreviated slightly in order to separate it from the ensuing downbeat. This unobtrusive *non-legato* across the barline is too small to be consciously noticed by the listener. The desperate connection that Czerny and other nineteenth-century editors maintained through their fingerings and phrase marks over the barline in order to provide an uninterrupted *legato* was as much a misunderstanding of Bach's music as is, conversely, the brittle avoidance of any melody-sustaining *legato* at all found on some current Bach recordings.*

In triple meter—3/4 or 3/8—a quick passage of even 8ths and 16ths, respectively, can sometimes be successfully divided into two equal halves, with the first three notes played *legato,* the second three *non-legato.*[30] Bach occasionally marked string passages in this manner. Such phrasing has the advantage that the *non-legato* notes are naturally perceived as a long upbeat to the following measure ("and 3 and|1 and 2"). It works extremely well in the fast section of the *French Overture* (Ex. 37); in the Courante from the Fifth Partita (alternate measures; Ex. 38); in the Fantasia of the Third Partita (Ex. 39); and in the D minor Invention, mm. 11ff. In *Goldberg* Variation 19 this phrasing helps establish the jubilant, *Gloria*-like character, which is often missed in performance.

Ex. 37 *French Overture,* 1st Mvt., mm. 22–23.

Ex. 38 Courante from Partita No. 5, mm. 1–3.

Ex. 39 Fantasia from Partita No. 3, mm. 24–26.

---

*The *non-legato* across the barline is of tremendous value in finding useful fingerings. It enables the pianist, even when sightreading, to reset the hand position or confirm the preceding hand position as a new measure begins. A few examples of this fingering are found in Bach's own fingerings for the early version of the C major Prelude and Fugue, *WTC,* Bk. II.[29]

The two types of grouping may alternate. In the A major Fugue, *WTC,* Bk. I, the second type of phrasing—three *legato* notes followed by three *non-legato* notes—works best for the top voice (Ex. 40a).* Thirteen measures later (Ex. 40b), however, it is preferable to revert in the bass to the system described earlier, in which each group extends from the second note of the beam to the first note of the following beam. A similar combination of the types of phrasing solves the problems of the G major Fugue, *WTC,* Bk. II.

Fugue in A major, *WTC,* Bk. I
Ex. 40a   m. 23

Ex. 40b   m. 36

Both systems of phrasing are iambic rather than trochaic; they lead *to* the downbeat, not away from it. This corresponds to the practice of Bach's time. In some Bach pieces, such as the Prelude in D-sharp minor, *WTC,* Bk. II, it is possible, as a practice device, to play the entire piece in a loose, jazzlike kind of dotting—*notes inégales,* so to speak, though there is hardly a historic connection—without damaging the melodic line (Exx. 41a, b). The opposite, trochaic rhythm (as in Scottish folk songs), is, of course, impossible even to attempt (Ex. 41c)!

Obviously, these rules are nothing more than a general outline and tentative approach to phrasing. As always in Bach, nothing

Prelude in D-sharp minor, *WTC,* Bk. II
Ex. 41a   m. 1   Ex. 41b   Iambic rhythm (yes).

Ex. 41c   Trochaic rhythm (no).

*The articulation marks in Exx. 37–40 are mine.

is ruled out. For thematic or other reasons, completely different groupings of even 16ths frequently become necessary or desirable. Ralph Kirkpatrick has explained the necessity of studying the individual traits of each single phrase.[31] When the pattern of the counterpoint in the *Chromatic Fugue,* consisting of an 8th preceded by two 16th notes (Ex. 42a), is transformed during the course of the Fugue into a pattern of even 16ths in the left hand (Ex. 42b), the identity of the new pattern with the old must be established in the phrasing. The four-note groups must clearly begin on the third note under each beam. This same pattern of two 16ths followed by one 8th—which usually, if not precisely, is called "anacrusis"—not only permeates the entire series of *Brandenburg* Concertos but was used by Bach whenever he needed a continuous rhythmic pattern to sustain a long piece at moderate speed, as, for example, the F minor Fugue, *WTC,* Bk. I (Ex. 43).

Chromatic Fugue
Ex. 42a m. 8   Ex. 42b m. 85

Ex. 43   Fugue in F minor, *WTC*, Bk. I, m. 7.

In many other cases, as is often pointed out, it is very helpful to imagine how a string player would phrase a certain pattern. If three out of four melody notes proceed stepwise while the fourth is a jump away, the accepted solution on a string instrument would be to play the three adjacent notes *legato* and the fourth note separately. (Most of the time this fourth tone is the last under the beam, but it can also be the first.) Bach himself indicated this phrasing in mm. 9–10 of the Finale of the *Italian Concerto.* Similar patterns appear at the end of the fugue subject in the C minor Toccata (Ex. 44; slurs marked by Bach), in the motive of the C minor Invention, and many other places.[32]

Ex. 44   Toccata in C minor, fugue subject.

However, some modes of articulation may differ from those customarily employed by string players, for instance, the articulation of slow, written-out mordents occurring on weak beats. Here the first of three notes may be played by itself, the next two in a strong two-note *legato* with emphasis on the first note of the pair. To adopt this phrasing in the E major Prelude, *WTC*, Bk. I (Ex. 45), for the three notes played on the second beat (not those on the third!) provides balance for the entire theme. The same applics to the second (not the first) beat of the subject in the C-sharp minor Fugue, *WTC*, Bk. II (Ex. 46), and to the weak beats of the treble melody in m. 9 of the B-flat major Prelude, *WTC*, Bk. II (Ex. 47). The anticipations in the lower voice, being imitations by nature, and despite their belonging to strong beats, will have to be phrased identically.

Ex. 45   Prelude in E major, *WTC*, Bk. I, m. 1.

Ex. 46   Fugue in C-sharp minor, *WTC*, Bk. II, subject.

Ex. 47   Prelude in B-flat major, *WTC*, Bk. II, m. 9.

Another standard pattern, possibly of operatic origin, which Bach became fond of in his later years, consists of expressive "feminine" endings at the beginning of a measure, preceded by a single upbeat note. This grouping dominates the F minor Prelude, *WTC*, Bk. II, and the opening movement of the Flute Sonata in B minor, but it is also present in the G-sharp minor Prelude, *WTC*, Bk. II, and the middle section (Ex. 48) and coda of the three-part Ricercar of the *Musical Offering;* see also the first movement of the *Italian Concerto,* where the upbeat note is split into two 16ths (Ex. 49). In these instances, the two-note phrase is

Ex. 48   Ricercar a 3 voci from *Musical Offering*, m. 108.

Ex. 49   *Italian Concerto*, 1st Mvt., m. 3.

to be played *legato* and *diminuendo,* the upbeat detached but not *staccato*.

Occasionally, as in the Gavotte of the *French Overture* (Ex. 50), Bach puts a scale motive of four continuous notes under the same slur to indicate that it should be not subdivided in violin tradition, but rather played as the scale fragment it is. The same principle must be observed with even greater consistency in longer scale motives, such as those in the opening of the Fifth Partita; or the F major scales that become part of the motivic design of both the first and last movements of the *Italian Concerto* (Exx. 51a, b; see especially the Finale, mm. 150 ff., Ex. 51c). The analogy with

Ex. 50   Gavotte from *French Overture*, mm. 1–2.

Italian Concerto
Ex. 51a   1st Mvt., mm. 25–26.

Ex. 51b   3rd Mvt., mm. 1–4.

Ex. 51c 3rd Mvt., mm. 150–52.

string articulation stops here. In the first engraving of the Fourth
Partita, which was presumably made by Bach himself aided by
his older sons, the Courante shows its groupings clearly as the
beams of the 8th-note scales extend across the barlines. Whenever
scale passages of this kind are juxtaposed with other types of
melodic figuration, they must be differentiated in performance,
as in the later sections of the Prelude of the Sixth English Suite in
D minor. The principal theme begins with five fast, unphrased,
ascending scale notes. These are followed at first by slower, then
by faster phrases, cast in the usual string-like manner of phrasing
(Exx. 52a, b, c, d).

In Bach's contrapuntal textures the bass emerges just by virtue
of clear articulation.*

Prelude from English Suite No. 6 (phrase marks mine).
Ex. 52a m. 38   Ex. 52b m. 42

Ex. 52c m. 44   Ex. 52d mm. 52–53

---

*One of the more common errors made by young pianists is to play fugue subjects too
loudly when they appear in the bass. This deprives the music of its harmonic rhythm,
because the harmonic tones within the subject cannot be heard as such when their loudness is out of proportion. On the other hand, as long as the themes in the bass are
meticulously phrased and articulated within the normal tone proportions between the
registers — proportions which are different for the modern piano and for the
harpsichord — the resulting harmonic clarity will benefit the polyphonic clarity as well.
This principle applies even in the exceptional case when the left hand is marked *forte* and
the right is *piano* (for example, the Finale of the *Italian Concerto*, mm. 25–28; see Ex. 33a);
even here the *forte* has to remain within the general sound proportions. The softly played
counterpoint above is then heard as a harmonic-rhythmic companion to the tune, not as
an independently viable countermotive. The music world owes much to Edwin Fischer,
the first, and probably the only, pianist of the post-Busoni generation to establish beautiful relationships between the sonorities of the right and the left hand in Bach's piano
music.

Polyphonic Writing

According to Forkel, Bach's first biographer, Bach "considered his parts as if they were persons who conversed together like a select company. If there were three, each could sometimes be silent and listen to the others till it again had something to the purpose to say."[33]

This excellent image, used by Bach himself, clarifies why he worked for a *combination* of voices rather than for their *opposition*. A few examples will illustrate this. In m. 111 of the *Chromatic Fugue* (Ex. 53), the bass snatches the last three notes of the theme from the middle voice, so that the theme ends in a different voice from the one in which it began. In the opening statement of the subject of the (double) Fugue in G-sharp minor, *WTC*, Bk. II

Ex. 53 *Chromatic Fugue*, m. 111.

(Ex. 54), the step up from G-sharp to A-sharp between mm. 99 and 100 is fully understandable only in retrospect, when seen in the light of a corresponding step up in the countersubject just half a measure earlier. Through this device of two steps completing each other, Bach creates a combination in which two equally important themes are ideally coordinated. A similar combination exists in the Gigue of the Fifth Partita: The descending fifth at the opening of m. 2 is completed by the ascending fourth following the second tone of the countersubject in the second half of the

Ex. 54   Fugue in G-sharp minor, *WTC*, Bk. II, mm. 97–101.

piece (Ex. 55). This connection between the two themes becomes obvious as soon as they are played together (for example, at m. 60). Both skips are forceful interjections of the same melodic

Ex. 55 Gigue from Partita No. 5, mm. 55–56 (staccato marks mine).

Ex. 56a *St. Matthew Passion,* 1st Chorus, m. 59.

character as the "Wohin?" in the first Chorus of the *St. Matthew Passion* (Ex. 56a).*

According to the custom of his time, Bach notated his music in strict part writing, with separate stems for each voice whenever more than one tone was played or held in the same hand. But that does not necessarily mean that Bach mentally separated these tones into different voices; in many cases it was just a part of the notation conventions of the time. This may lead to misunderstandings in the present. The music written for the right hand at the opening of the Allemande of the Second English Suite, for example, gives the impression of two-part writing (Ex. 57a); the g-sharp' of the lower part, on the fourth beat, appears as a counterpoint to the melody, as it would be if it were played softer. In reality, this g-sharp' is as much a part of the melody as the f'' that follows. This becomes apparent in m. 13 (Ex. 57b), where the inversion of the theme is presented by a single voice. The

---

*Other examples of such interjections are in the E minor Prelude, *WTC,* Bk. II (Ex. 56b); the Fantasia from the A minor Partita (possibly based on the Prelude; Ex. 56c); the Allegro from the *French Overture,* m. 38f.; the three-part Ricercar from the *Musical Offering,* m. 18. Many of these are marked *staccato* by Bach. Most of these exclamations are not thematically developed.

Ex. 56b Prelude in E minor, *WTC*, Bk. II, mm. 1–4.   Ex. 56c Fantasia from Partita No. 3,
                                                              mm. 9–11.

[Wo-hin?] [Wo-hin?] |"Wo-hin?" "Wo-hin?"|

Allemande from English Suite No. 2
Ex. 57a m. 1   Ex. 57b m. 13

NB   NB

same practice appears in the Finale of the *Italian Concerto*. Compare mm. 17–18 (Ex. 58a) with the upper part of the left hand in mm. 145–46 (Ex. 58b) and with the top voice of mm. 77–90.

Italian Concerto, 3rd Mvt.
Ex. 58a mm. 17–18   Ex. 58b mm. 145–46

In a contrapuntal score it is up to the performer to discriminate between truly contrapuntal lines and simple *continuo* basses. The Sinfonia in D major (Ex. 59) begins in the treble alone; what looks like a counterpoint in the bass is in reality only an introductory accompaniment in *continuo* fashion, comparable to the opening of many movements in the violin sonatas (where the bass is actually provided with figures). Wherever these introductory *continuo* basses exist they are recognizable by their lack of further thematic development. Yet caution must be applied in distinguishing them from thematic lines. For example, the repeated 8th notes, isolated by rests, which appear so innocuously in the bass

Ex. 59 Sinfonia in D major, mm. 1–2.

of the C minor Fugue, *WTC,* Bk. II (Ex. 60), are thematic assertions of the tonic note and must therefore be played distinctly, as
though on an organ pedal.

Accents are an important part of playing polyphonic music because they help distinguish the voice leading—but only as long
as they remain within the confines of sheer declamatory emphasis, as with syllables in speech. For example, in the sturdy second
theme of the Finale of the *Italian Concerto* (Ex. 33a), marked *forte*
regardless of which hand it is to be played with, some discreet
rhythmic accents will enhance clarity and energy.

Ex. 60   Fugue in C minor, *WTC,* Bk. II, mm. 23–26.

Only in rare instances are syncopated accents acceptable.
Albert Schweitzer requested them with regularity. A prominent
example in his book[34] prescribes accents on the long notes in
mm. 31–33 of the first movement of the *Italian Concerto* (Ex. 61).
Only the first of these is justified, not because it falls on a syncopation of the next downbeat, but because it fortifies the end of a
written-out mordent, establishing its connection with f″, the next
tone.* In the following measure the long note is also the top note,
so there is no need to reinforce it. Besides, to give the same accent
in two successive measures of a melody would be far too monotonous for Bach.

In addition to the accented interjections discussed above, there
are occasional trochaic phrase endings calling for the same kind
of exclamatory emphasis. In the F major Duetto (*Clavierübung,*
vol. 3), the first two notes, an ascending major third, are repeated in diminution at the higher octave in m. 4; they should be

Ex. 61   *Italian Concerto,* 1st Mvt., mm. 31–32.

(no accent)

---

*A final accent seems desirable for all of Bach's mordents, since it broadens the emphasis
of the beat on which the mordent begins. See the right-hand opening of the slow movement. Some performers use overlapping *legato,* which helps establish a broad, gentle
accentuation.

played detached and individually emphasized. This becomes abundantly clear in m. 116 (Ex. 62), where they appear inverted in the lower voice directly before the recapitulation. It could be that Bach wanted similar articulation in the left hand at the ends of mm. 2 and 3 of the *Italian Concerto.*

Ex. 62   Duetto No. 2, mm. 113–16.

Dynamics

It is mainly because of the lack of gradual increases and decreases of sound on a harpsichord that Schweitzer,[35] quoting Vianna da Motta, introduced to a larger public the idea of "terraces" of loud and soft dynamics in Bach's music. These unattenuated contrasts between sections doubtlessly fulfill an architectural function, in that they clarify the piece's structure, especially at first hearing. However, in the more than 70 years since Schweitzer's book first appeared, it has become clear that modest degrees of *crescendo* and *decrescendo* were by no means unattainable on keyboard instruments, even on the harpsichord.

Thus, regardless of historical arguments, the question at the present time is whether, as Schweitzer advocates, to restrict the interpretation of Bach's works by refraining from gradual changes of dynamics. To do so, one would have to assume that the idea of a transition was alien—even repugnant—to Bach. There is nothing in his music that would justify this assumption; on the contrary, every so often one finds a gradual increase toward the end in the Preludes of the *Well-Tempered Clavier,* gradually prepared reentries of fugue themes, and other mediating techniques by which the various parts are connected rather than confronted with each other.

Da Motta and Schweitzer were overreacting against the performance practices of the late nineteenth century, with the continuous *mezzoforte* level which swarmed with small, yet constant, deviations toward a little louder and a little softer, allegedly to provide "variety."* Sometimes the only long line to be observed in fugue playing was a continuous *crescendo* from a very soft beginning right through to a thundering conclusion. I heard Eugen d'Albert perform the *Chromatic Fugue* in 1922; his playing, impressive as it was, could have been depicting the spread of an epidemic from the outbreak of an isolated case to a general bubonic plague! Such concepts are contrary to Bach's aesthetics just as much as the "*mezzoforte* plus-and-minus" system. Although it has been shown that final climaxes are not entirely alien to Bach (see p. 10, above), his architecture is nearly always of a kind in which the music is experienced by "viewing it from all angles," so to speak, in the same way one would circle a building; in this respect Bach's music resembles that of earlier generations. All in all, the dynamic plan of a Bach performance must avoid undue emphasis on the end (see below, p. 54).

It seems that to extend a gradual *crescendo* over an entire section or piece was not known, even as a possibility, to the musicians of Bach's time; otherwise, why would this type of *crescendo* have produced such a sensation about forty years later, in the time of young Mozart, when the orchestras of Mannheim and Paris were trained to achieve it? Bach, therefore, mostly had to resort to indirect procedures to realize swellings of sound in his keyboard music. One such device was the addition of voices. A perfect example is found in the *French Overture* (Ex. 63); at the end of a section marked *piano* (by Bach), additional parts marked *forte* are introduced one by one. Bach also occasionally adds a third voice for a *crescendo* effect at the end of his many dances in two-part writing (for example, in the Allemande of the Fifth French Suite

Ex. 63 *French Overture,* 1st Mvt., mm. 89–92.

*Czerny's well-known edition of the *Well-Tempered Clavier,* published in the 1830s (Schumann reviewed it in 1838), was probably the first to establish such practices. Czerny's claim that his dynamics were based on Beethoven's playing is hardly believable if one compares them with those that Beethoven carefully entered in his own scores.

in G major, ends of mm. 11 and 23). The last part of the *Chromatic Fugue,* too, is preceded by step-by-step sonority increases, beginning in m. 118, though without added voices (see Ex. 74e, below). It is obvious from the overall structure that at this point Bach must have wanted a *crescendo* effect. This can be achieved by playing very softly for four measures (mm. 118–21), then, as the musical pattern is repeated at the upper fourth, suddenly playing slightly louder for the next four measures (mm. 122–25), and playing the next four (mm. 126–29) *mezzoforte,* after which a final gradual *crescendo*—only here—would lead to *forte* at the return of the theme in m. 131.

F. W. Marpurg, in a letter dated February 2, 1760,[36] reports that Bach once criticized a fellow composer for failing to show "enough fire" to reanimate the theme by interludes. Such concern for variety is necessarily reflected in the dynamic shades used for thematic statements and interludes, the latter being played more softly than the former. Newcomers are easily misled by the fact that fugues begin with a single unaccompanied voice; they find it natural to start softly and produce fuller sounds as more voices join in. However, there is no doubt that in Baroque practice the exposition of a fugue, just like the exposition in any other kind of music, is meant to be *forte,* and nothing in Bach's scores indicates that he wanted that changed. The first rule of fugue playing is, therefore, that thematic statements are *forte,* episodes *piano.* The second, based on the A–B–A form of fugues, states that the beginning and the end—that is, the two sections in the tonic key—are *forte,* the middle section *piano.* The only trouble, obviously, is that the two rules are frequently incompatible! They agree only to the extent that (1) the subject and the accompanying voices* are to be played *forte* in the exposition and in the conclusion, and (2) episodes occurring in the middle section are to be played softly. Flexibility is needed in dealing with the two other possibilities: episodes *before* and *after* the middle section, and appearances of the fugue subject *during* the middle section.

The first episode usually occurs immediately following the an-

---

*Ever since Schweitzer's time, there have been discussions in the literature about the appropriate "voicing" of fugues.[37] However, no responsible pianist today would overemphasize the subject at the expense of any other voices sounding at the same time.

swer, during the exposition; here the general character of *forte* must be maintained. *Forte* is also called for when an episode occurs during the coda, as in the *Chromatic Fugue,* mm. 147–53, except that the episode itself should be just a little softer than the rest of the coda.

Thematic presentations during the middle section, on the other hand, occur frequently and cannot all be played at the same dynamic level. Especially when many thematic developments follow each other in quick succession, the choice of dynamics depends on the individual case. If a subject in the minor mode reappears in the major, for instance, it should be played *piano;* see the C minor Fugue, *WTC,* Bk. I (Ex. 64, where Schweitzer recommends *forte*); the E minor Fugue, *WTC,* Bk. II (Ex. 65); and the B minor Fugue, *WTC,* Bk. II (Ex. 66).* The character should be *dolcissimo* in these cases. As long as there is no overpedaling and no *rubato,* the music will not appear overromanticized. In fact, at the present time the opposite danger, of "underromanticizing," is greater. Although the instrumental works perhaps do not display the "affects" of vocal music in a deliberate way, each has its own specific character. Certainly, the subject of the E minor Fugue, *WTC,* Bk. I, is furious; those of the A minor Fugue and especially the G minor Fugue, Bk. II, are defiant and

---

*Here, the major mode does not exactly seem "happier," only perhaps tenderer than the minor. Conversely, the minor mode in Bach is not always an expression of tragedy. The supposed tradition, "minor equals sad, major equals happy," is of a later date. It was individually formulated by Goethe in a letter to Karl Friedrich Zelter dated March 31, 1831. Goethe, then over 80, had read that the major chord is supposedly "in Nature" while the minor, not being part of the overtone series, is not. This infuriated the old man. He wrote: "Nun erinnerst du dich wohl, dass ich mich der kleinen Terz immer leidenschaftlich angenommen und mich geärgert habe, dass ihr theoretischen Musikhansen sie nicht wolltet als ein *donum naturae* gelten lassen. Wahrhaftig eine Darm- und Drahtsaite steht nicht so hoch, dass ihr die Natur allein ausschliesslich ihre Harmonien anvertrauen sollte. Da ist der Mensch mehr werth, und dem Menschen hat die Natur die kleine Terz verliehen, um das Unnennbare, Sehnsüchtige mit dem innigsten Behagen ausdrücken zu können; der Mensch gehört mit zur Natur, und er ist es, der die zartesten Bezüge der sämmtlichen elementaren Erscheinungen in sich aufzunehmen, zu regeln und zu modifizieren weiss." ("Surely you remember that I have always been a passionate defender of the minor third and got annoyed at all you Toms, Dicks, and Harrys of musical theory who do not want to accept this interval as a gift of Nature. Yet, a gut or wire string certainly does not have such high standing that Nature would have entrusted her harmonies to it alone and exclusively. After all, a human being ranks higher; and it is to the human being that Nature has granted the minor third so that he can express with the most intimate delight the unnameable feelings of yearning; besides, Man is part of Nature, and it is he who knows how to absorb, regulate, and modify the most delicate relationships of all the manifestations of the Universe.")

Ex. 64   Fugue in C minor, *WTC*, Bk. I, mm. 11–12.

Ex. 65   Fugue in E minor, *WTC*, Bk. II, mm. 24–25.

Ex. 66   Fugue in B minor, *WTC*, Bk. II, mm. 36–37.

stubborn; and the F-sharp major Prelude and Fugue, Bk. I, is an ingratiating work. One can find all kinds of specific shapes of comedy and tragedy in these prelude-fugue combinations. It is especially in the middle sections of the fugues that it is possible to mold the dynamics so as to bring out the changing emotional aspects of the subject, because the performer is not obliged to play it at its full loudness, as in the beginning and the end.

Voice subtraction—which happens in dance pieces regularly (as between mm. 8 and 9 of the Allemande of the Fifth French Suite, after the statement of the opening theme)—produces a natural *decrescendo*.[38] On a piano, the performer is not supposed to try to compensate by using more pedal or playing louder than before; sometimes it may be appropriate to enhance the *decrescendo* by withdrawing the pedal, if it was previously used. In the G major Fugue, *WTC*, Bk. I (Ex. 67), the three-part texture thins out little by little after the end of the exposition, as it is replaced first by a duo of bass and treble, then (in m. 40) by the two upper voices, the softest possible voice combination. The entire section is episodic and written quite homophonically. For a guide to *diminuendo* structures over an extended period, one can

Ex. 67 Fugue in G major, *WTC*, Bk. I, mm. 38–40.

consult the passage preceding the cadenza in the opening movement of the Fifth *Brandenburg* Concerto, where Bach makes the
orchestra disappear in several stages with the same skill that
Haydn later uses in the *Farewell* Symphony.

Forms

A discussion of Bach's forms must deal not only with outlines
(two-part, A–B–A, etc.) but also with developmental features
such as intensification, extension, or contraction, which may
occur in both monothematic pieces (preludes and long fugues,
for example) and the different sections of concerto movements,
fantasias, and the like.

The term *section* needs to be defined. Although some of Bach's
short pieces, especially the dances, are sectional—each part ending with a full cadence stopping the flow of music—most of his
other pieces have no clearly audible separations between their
parts. Somewhere between these two extremes Bach also wrote
pieces which are *almost* sectional, except that they omit the full
stop after the cadence, usually by eliding one voice with the next
part. The E major Prelude, *WTC,* Bk. I, appears at first to be
unbroken, but close scrutiny reveals a pause after m. 8, in which
the dominant is reached. It would seem quite natural at this point
to repeat the piece from the beginning, and likewise, to make a
second repeat from m. 9 to the end.* Most of the Inventions and
Sinfonias contain similarly covered-up junctures. The C major
Invention, for instance, does not come to a total stop on the
dominant in m. 7 (Ex. 68); Bach delays the G in the bass by one
16th note in order to use that tone for the opening of the second

---

*As Busoni was the first to discover, the E major pieces of the two books are closely
related, as though those in Bk. II were a "rewrite" of those in Bk. I. It is therefore
interesting to note that the Prelude in Bk. II is one of the rare Preludes in two-part form,
with repeats.

Ex. 68   Two-Part Invention in C major, m. 6.

"section." (Cf. Mozart, C major Sonata, K. 545, first movement, m. 31, where the same device is used.)

The larger pieces are complex, and, therefore, each case must be analyzed separately. Bach has no general rules about the sharpness of the boundaries between parts. This is especially true of the opening movements of his dance suites, some of which are bipartite (e.g., the Fourth Partita) and some tripartite (e.g., the Second Partita and the *French Overture*), and even more so in the Toccatas, including the Toccata at the beginning of the Sixth Partita. Although there is an external separation between the fast part and the slow part preceding (and sometimes also following), some of the motives and patterns used are the same, even where the tempo is marked differently for each part. It is impossible, for instance, to play the opening of the Sixth Partita at a totally different speed from that of the ensuing fugue, for eventually both parts are fused in a most natural manner. See also the Sinfonia of the Second Partita and the Prelude to the Sixth English Suite.

If common motives and harmonic progressions transcend the limits of each part in a movement, they also often transcend the single movements themselves. Without exaggeration it is possible to state that the Toccatas and Suites are basically cyclic pieces. In the Second Partita, the second part of the Sinfonia, the Courante, and the Sarabande all begin with the ascending row G–C–D–E-flat (Exx. 69a, b, c). By using d'' as an *acciaccatura* in the opening chord of the *Grave,* one may—legitimately—introduce this row at the very outset of the Partita. The same piece also focuses on the dominant ninth as a melodic interval—for instance, in the last part of the Sinfonia (Ex. 69d) and the Courante (Ex. 69b). In the Rondeau, the A-flat is one octave lower, and the G one octave higher, but a clever harpsichordist, through registration, can probably project the descending seventh as a variant of an ascending ninth (Ex. 69e). In the First Partita, the ascending row F–G–A–B-flat (Exx. 70a, b) forms the melodic basis of nearly every movement. The Fifth Partita favors the descent from the fifth note of the scale to the first.

Partita No. 2

Ex. 69a Sinfonia, m. 8.   Ex. 69b Courante, m. 1.   Ex. 69c Sarabande, m. 1.

Ex. 69d Sinfonia, mm. 30–31.   Ex. 69e Rondeau, mm. 1–2.

Partita No. 1

Ex. 70a Praeludium, mm. 1–2.

Ex. 70b Allemande, m. 1–4, outline.

The cyclic character aids the type of architecture described on p. 47, above. It is almost the opposite of the "narrative" (or epic) character of multiple-movement pieces (symphonies, quartets, sonatas) by Haydn, Mozart, and Schubert, where, as in a story, one movement after another keeps "unfolding the plot," as it were. The Viennese listener could understand a first movement completely without knowing what would follow, but not a later movement on its own. However, in a Bach Concerto or Suite it is not possible to grasp a single movement, even the first, before hearing the whole work, because all the movements are interdependent, backwards and forwards. The same is true of the Preludes and Fugues of the *Well-Tempered Clavier,* Book II, and of quite a few in Book I; in all of them, Bach tries to provide the same beat for both the Prelude and the Fugue, a beat which can only be determined for the Prelude after one has also studied the Fugue.*

This interdependence does not, however, preclude occasional climactic final movements. For example, the last movement in the *French Overture,* entitled "Echo," epitomizes in a light style everything that went before. In this respect it is comparable in structure not only to the Badinerie at the end of the Orchestra Suite in B minor, but also to the famous Chaconne that concludes the D minor Suite for solo violin. All three pieces are preceded by a Gigue (the normal ending) and unexpectedly carry the music further to a climactic encore. (The supernumerary fourth movement of the First *Brandenburg* Concerto belongs to the same category; this Minuet, it seems to me, is the most brilliant and effective movement of the entire Concerto.) But, at the same time, all these pieces also retrospectively elucidate the buildup that precedes them; this is especially noticeable in the D minor Violin Suite, in which the Chaconne is anticipated several times during the dance suite itself.

As shown earlier (p. 10), in rare cases final climaxes also occur within each movement. Normally, however, Bach provides for a high point somewhere near the middle of the composition, and from then on "builds down." This happens especially in the first movement of the Fifth *Brandenburg* Concerto. The climax is reached in the middle of the "Supercadenza," about mm. 203ff. (Ex. 71a), where the music reaches the smallest note values (32nd notes); m. 209 then reverts to 16th triplets (Ex. 71b), followed in the second half of m. 214 (Ex. 71c) by the regular 16ths that are the basic melodic note value in the piece. After this, the tutti can reenter in m. 219. (Perhaps the same idea should be applied to the *Chromatic Fugue,* by placing the dynamic climax at mm. 140ff., not at the very end, despite the final octave doublings.**). Nowhere do Bach's forms constitute more of a *mimesis* of the forms of Nature than at the building-down of the music at the end of the cadenza in the Fifth *Brandenburg* Concerto, which is

---

*This was proven in a live performance of the entire Bk. II by my students and myself at the Peabody Conservatory in 1974. The only trouble spot was the Prelude and Fugue in G major; perhaps this is where Bach, as usual, made a single exception to a general, self-defined rule.

**If memory does not fail me, this is what d'Albert did in Berlin in 1922.

Brandenburg Concerto No. 5, 1st Mvt.
Ex. 71a m. 203

Ex. 71b m. 209

Ex. 71c m. 214

reminiscent of a river that, after a tremendous waterfall, soon returns to its previous smooth, vigorous flow.

The forms of long movements in Bach's Concertos and the Preludes and Fugues must be analyzed differently from those found in the works of the Viennese classics less than a century later. The Viennese masters' task, compared to Bach's, was relatively easy because by that time Bach's sons, among other composers, had invented sonata form. Sonata form could always be used, if not as a blueprint, at least as a starting point for the structure of large compositions. Audiences were sufficiently familiar with it so that, at any given moment during a performance, they knew approximately where in the piece they were. (If only one could say the same of today's audiences when a Haydn symphony is played!) Bach was less fortunate and was forced to think of *individual* solutions for each of his longer concerto movements and preludes or fugues, assisted only by the observance of the tonal scheme discussed earlier. Everything else was organized from case to case. The existence and order of themes, variants, episodes, development sections, strict and free recapitulations, and other details depended on the needs Bach recognized for each individual composition.

There are three tools of organization that Bach used regularly, however. The first was the *tying together of loose ends*. A motivic pattern never appears only once in a piece. For example, in the first movement of the *Italian Concerto,* the rhythmic figure that first appears in mm. 37–39 (Ex. 72a) is repeated in a new context

in mm. 67ff. (Ex. 72b). Furthermore, during the tutti of mm.
53ff. (Ex. 72c), Bach adapts the head motive to a sequential passage; this adaptation is not only recapitulated almost identically in
mm. 139ff. but is also used earlier in the left hand at m. 116 (Ex.
72d). In another instance, the ascending leap in m. 97 (Ex. 73a)
returns at m. 153 (Ex. 73b). There are also other instances of
motivic connections within the movement, beyond the overall
identity of the head motive.

Italian Concerto, 1st Mvt.
Ex. 72a m. 37   Ex. 72b m. 67

Ex. 72c mm. 53–55   Ex. 72d mm. 116–18

Italian Concerto, 1st Mvt.
Ex. 73a mm. 96–97   Ex. 73b mm. 152–53

Bach does not always pick up an earlier pattern before re-
capitulating a later one. In the *Chromatic Fugue,* for instance,
when the various auxiliary motives and episodes arising from
slight transformations of the fugue subject and its first
counterpoint—labeled A through F in the table below—appear
for the second time, no two of them are in the same order as
before!

Motive	Measure
A	46
B	49
A	64
C	76
D	85 (Ex. 74a)
E	90 (Ex. 74c)
B	97
F	118 (Ex. 74e)

Motive	Measure
D	126 (Ex. 74b)
C	140
F	147 (Ex. 74f)
E	154 (Ex. 74d)

Chromatic Fugue (slurs mine)
Ex. 74a mm. 85–87

Ex. 74b mm. 126–28

Ex. 74c mm. 90–91

Ex. 74d mm. 154–55

Ex. 74e mm. 118–19

Ex. 74f mm. 147–48

Another of Bach's primary tools in structural organization is *melodic variation*—a technique in the best Baroque tradition, especially employed by Boehm and Pachelbel in their chorale preludes. (Schweitzer devoted a chapter of his book to the study of these two masters and their influence on Bach.) When he composed with this tool, Bach was often quite audacious. The extreme thematic transformations during the four movements of the Trio of the *Musical Offering* (Exx. 75a, b, c, d) or the canons

Musical Offering
Ex. 75a Theme

Ex. 75b Trio Sonata, 1st Mvt., mm. 1–4.
Largo
continuo

Ex. 75c Canon No. 7, mm. 1–2.

Ex. 75d Finale, mm. 1–2.
Allegro
Flute
etc.

of the *Art of Fugue* (Exx. 76a, b, c, d, e[39]) exceed anything that theorists like Schenker or Reti could set forth! If one did not positively *know* from the context that these are indeed variants, one would be sure they were unintentional resemblances between heterogeneous themes!

Art of Fugue
Ex. 76a Theme

Ex. 76b Contrapunctus XI, mm. 1–4.

Ex. 76c Contrapunctus XIII, mm. 1–8.

Ex. 76d Contrapunctus XV, mm. 1–4.

Ex. 76e Contrapunctus XVI, mm. 1–4.

The entire slow movement of the *Italian Concerto* is (as Wanda Landowska remarked) the "double" of an implied, simpler melody (as in a Sarabande)—an "enigma" variation of a theme not given (Ex. 77a). To reconstruct such a "theme" one has to draw ascending and descending lines between the principal notes; the harmonies of the left hand indicate which notes these are. Nearly always, the reconstructed melody moves in diatonic steps (Ex. 77b). A special situation arises in mm. 22ff. (Ex. 77c) because the 16th notes are moving in a hidden triplet rhythm against the continuing regular 8th notes in the left hand, as a written-out *coulé* approximating two-part writing for the top part (Ex. 77d). (Cf. Ex. 22 above.)

Italian Concerto, 2nd Mvt.

Ex. 77a mm. 4–7

Ex. 77b Approximate outline

Ex. 77c m. 22

Ex. 77d Outline

The same kind of melodic decorations sometimes establish differences between the first and second parts of a sequence— differences which can seem so great that the sequential character of the passage is obscured. In mm. 33–35 of the same movement, Bach hides the second half of an otherwise simple sequence, which began on the second beat of m. 31 (Ex. 78a), behind artful decorations of the treble in which not only the melodic curve but also the rhythmic detail are altered. Ex. 78b shows how the second half would read in an exact sequential parallel; except for small modifications necessitated by the change from minor to major, the two halves could be identical. The melodic variants in the "echo" passages in the *Italian Concerto* and the *French Overture,* which are "blurred," as an echo is in nature,

Italian Concerto, 2nd Mvt.
Ex. 78a   mm. 31–35

Ex. 78b   Exact sequence of mm. 31–33.

belong to the same category (cf. *Italian Concerto,* first movement, mm. 65–68; *French Overture,* "Echo," mm. 4–5 and 22–25).

Finally, when Bach reworked any of this music, he liked to manipulate the size and proportions of his compositions by means of *insertion.*[40] This is most evident, of course, in the few works which have been preserved in different versions, such as the A minor Prelude and Fugue, BWV 894, which, about 15 years later, were reused as the first and last movements of the Triple Concerto in A minor, BWV 1044. For the concerto version, in which three soloists were to be accompanied by and alternating with a string orchestra, the pieces had to be lengthened. Bach "split open" the original score and inserted new variants and passages and a short cadenza, leaving the rest practically untouched. He must have figured out how many measures were needed in each instance, space-conscious as he was (see p. 17, above); the transitions, as Schweitzer was the first to observe, are so smooth that the uninitiated listener would never suspect that anything had been changed (see p. 30, above).

Another good example of basically the same technique, also for the purpose of enlargement, results from a note-for-note comparison of the C major Prelude of *WTC,* Bk. II, with its short precursor.[41] Bach transformed the original monothematic piece into a bipartite, almost sonata, form, including a regular recapitulation, again mostly by means of insertions.

When only one version is known, one may sometimes suspect that an earlier, shorter version was enlarged by way of such insertions. Such is the case in the first movement of the D minor Concerto, where, after a long cadenza (mm. 136–71), the final *tutti* begins. Originally it may have been planned as an immediate complete *da capo* of the first statement of the main theme, but Bach may have decided to "break the music open," interrupt the *tutti,* and insert an extra ten measures—as it appears now—not for the sake of variety but in order to "build down" the music gradually following the cadenza, after which the *da capo* begins once more and, this time, finishes.

A performer who has been alert to insertions of this kind may observe something curious just before the final *tutti* in the first movement of the *Italian Concerto;* mm. 157 and 162 (Exs. 79a, b)

Italian Concerto, 1st Mvt.
Ex. 79a m. 157   Ex. 79b m. 162

are identical, except that the former is one octave higher. Bach *could* have started the *da capo* in m. 158, but chose to insert four measures to transfer the music down one octave, in a kind of spiral motion, from the high register of the last episode to the medium register of the first *tutti.*

An eclectic accumulation of scholarly approaches has dominated this chapter. It is evident that the homeric character of Bach's music calls for such variety of analysis methods. Actually, those used here, far from exhausting the available choices, add up to no more than a first attempt at looking at this music by shaking it loose from that of Bach's elders and contemporaries. There is so much we have to learn about Bach *himself!* This means that the focus here is not on problems of performance practice—such as embellishments and instruments—which concern *every* composer of the period.

As for embellishments, as long as general rules are observed, in a majority of cases one way of realizing them is as good as another. In this field each era keeps developing fixed habits—as, for instance, in the question whether to begin a trill with the chicken or the egg—and these are then regarded as eternal laws.*

Undeniably, the use of the original keyboard instruments often yields wonderful insights. However, we cannot be certain that Bach would have wanted us to forego the advantages of the modern piano under all circumstances. For one thing, his piano music (to use the modern term) came into its own only when people followed the example of Beethoven, Mendelssohn, and others and began to play these works on the piano. I usually justify my choice of instrument by simply saying, "What was good enough for Beethoven is good enough for me." Indeed, the piano *was* good enough for him: Beethoven never saw it as a substitute for older instruments; and Brahms, too, with all his professional knowledge of the history of music, showed in his transcriptions that he felt this way. In this connection one ought to mention the well-known fact that Beethoven's writing for the piano was based more strongly on the textures of the *Well-Tempered Clavier* than on any other older keyboard music, even Haydn's and Mozart's. This would have been impossible, if he had not thought of Bach's music as *piano* music.

Thus we ought not to permit ourselves to be distracted by performance practice problems, important as they are, from the principal task, which is to concentrate our energies on illuminating what little of Bach's universe we can glimpse in his scores, where he sealed it.

---

*It reminds me of Latin pronunciation: If you were brought up pronouncing Caesar as "Seezar," suddenly to say "Kaesar" or "Tchaesar" seems anathema even if scholars have just "proved" that this is historically true.

Chapter II

HAYDN

Just about 20 years ago Haydn's piano sonatas finally began to appear regularly on the programs of several noted pianists, and thus, at last, they became known as an important part of the literature for the piano. Similarly, only a few years earlier, Schubert's large piano works had found their way into the standard repertoire after almost a century. What is still needed, however, is to get rid of some inherited prejudices and misapprehensions about these works, some of which date back to the early nineteenth century.

First of all, it was generally believed that because Haydn was not a concert pianist performing regularly in public, like Mozart and Beethoven,[1] he could not compose idiomatically for the instrument. It was said that, if anything, he was a harpsichord player, for he grew up before the modern pianoforte became fashionable. There is some truth to this. Occasionally—for example, at the very end of the B minor Sonata, Hob. XVI/32—one finds passages that are awkwardly written for the piano, and one misses those in which the pianist shines and at the same time enjoys the composer's glittering sonorities, as in the Mozart concertos. Moreover, the earlier sonatas were undoubtedly written for the harpsichord and probably even today sound best when played on that instrument.* But in his late years, when by

---

*The designation "for harpsichord," with which the Haydn sonatas, as everything else written for clavier, were published, is of no importance in identifying the intended instrument.[2]

63

himself, Haydn loved nothing better than to play the piano for joy and comfort. Furthermore, a genius like Haydn obviously does not have to be a public performer on an instrument in order to write well for it (witness the violin concertos of Beethoven and Brahms)!

Second, because Haydn was 24 years older than Mozart, it is commonly assumed that his piano sonatas—not only those for harpsichord—must be earlier in style, meaning closer to late Baroque music. Actually, not only was Haydn still writing his most important sonatas while Mozart was writing his, and even after Mozart's death, but also his compositions fit as well as Mozart's into the classical style.

In their piano output, the two masters were independent and never influenced each other, as they occasionally did in chamber, symphonic, and vocal music. Haydn's influence on Mozart's D major Quintet, K. 593, and Mozart's on the *Creation* are perhaps the most striking examples of such interdependence. Nothing similar occurs in the sonatas. However, Haydn's aim for an organic whole in the sonatas was as strong as Mozart's,* and this is what distinguishes both composers from Carl Philipp Emanuel Bach, who is often cited as Haydn's master in writing piano music.** Though the age difference in this case is smaller—C.P.E. Bach was only eighteen years old when Haydn was born—and though Haydn did copy some external patterns and attitudes from him, there is a true generation gap that is obvious when one looks at any of their sonatas as a whole. C.P.E. Bach's are essentially chains of improvisatory sections, held together perfunctorily by the "three unities" of meter, tonality, and motive. Haydn's sonatas, like all his other works, are organized so as to constitute a complete unit. They are structure-conscious to the point of often approaching cyclic form. No performance

---

*Kant, who was eight years older than Haydn, defined "organic" as a mutual dependence of the whole and its parts so that the latter cannot exist without the former and vice versa. Music "expresses the aesthetic idea of an indivisible whole of undefinable, full ideas generated by a theme that embodies the 'affect' of the piece" (*Kritik der Urteilskraft,* 1790, No. 53). This identification defines Classicism; Haydn, though not in the habit of reading, was affected by the same *Zeitgeist.*

**Hermann Abert, in a truly profound study of the Haydn sonatas as such, over 60 years ago, stated that Haydn's model was Wagenseil rather than C.P.E. Bach, but that Haydn learned from the latter to break up the traditional even bass notes into rhythmic, appealing subdivisions.[3]

suggestions applicable to C.P.E. Bach's music, except those regarding the execution of appoggiaturas, can apply to Haydn any more than suggestions about the performance of Handel's *Messiah* could be helpful to the conductor of the *Creation* or the *Missa Solemnis*. No scholarly search for antecedents is likely to provide the performer with the necessary ingredients of the spirit of any later composer with whom he has to deal.

A third fallacy stems, curiously, from the belief that one can understand Haydn's piano sonatas through his symphonies and quartets. In reality, Haydn's style of writing in each category is totally different, as are his modes of expression. It is not too much to say that in all aspects his composing for the piano is diametrically opposed to that for chamber and orchestral groups. The main reason is that, since no one sings or plays along with a piano sonata, Haydn is not bound to preserve a continuous flow over a steady pulse, as he must, and indeed does, in the symphonies and quartets. In nearly all the sonatas, especially the late ones, one finds fermatas, silences, and interrupted melodies; they are usually placed following the second subject in opening movements, all of which express moments of weakness and "fainting spells."* While the works for ensemble, particularly the symphonies, are objective, audience-conscious, and assertive, the piano sonatas are subjective, private, and deliberately tentative. The sonatas constitute a "musical diary," as it were, in which Haydn found refuge from the compulsion under which he had to compose his larger works. Because the stops are so striking, one easily overlooks the fact that these sonatas were put together with the same attention to form and unity as any quartet or symphony. Otherwise it would not have been possible for him musically to express his loneliness, devotion, and humility, and to falter, meditate, and often despair, as he does in the late sonatas.** He was also in a better position to experiment with

---

*Only the opening of the last Sonata, No. 52 in E-flat major, establishes an "official" symphonic continuity; but even here Haydn arrives at one of the typical "spells" before the exposition is over.

**The history of the slow movement of Sonata No. 49 in E-flat major, as reported by Geiringer,[4] biographically proves the truth of this assertion. That it took Haydn a full year to complete this movement is evidence of the compositional care with which he elaborated these inspirations.

sounds, metric irregularities, fine points of articulation, and other small eccentricities on his own instrument. The sonatas include emotional outbreaks of a kind which he would not have tolerated in ensemble music,* for example, in the coda of the F minor Variations and in the middle episode of the slow movement of the Sonata No. 49 in E-flat major.

Of course, on occasion he uses the same forms and the same types of material as in the quartets and symphonies. The devotional theme of the slow movement of Symphony No. 102 in B-flat major—which is derived from the F-sharp minor Trio, No. 26—in mood and melodic line resembles themes from piano sonatas Nos. 49 and 50 (see Exx. 6a, b and p. 74). Also, several of the final sonata movements are conceived in the same quick, vigorous vein as most of the finales of his late symphonies. Even here, however, there is a difference: Haydn's quartets and most of his symphonies have four movements, while the piano sonatas have two or three.** The scope of the finales in the sonatas reflects the fact that they are preceded only by an initial Allegro and a slow movement and not also by a minuet.

Finally, the neglect of Haydn's sonatas has something to do with the interpretive ethos of the late nineteenth and early twentieth centuries. As an indirect outcome of the intellectual advancement in the comprehension of music, as well as of the increased discipline of observing all details in a score—a training necessitated by the growing demands of orchestral and other ensemble music—pianists since Schumann's time have performed Haydn literally. But they have ignored the fact that more than any other composer of his time Haydn relied on the creative collaboration of performer and composer; that is the only way to

---

*It has often puzzled me that Haydn disapproved of Beethoven's C minor Trio, considering how progressive his own sonatas were. Perhaps he was offended by the subjectivity of Beethoven's style in a chamber piece—a genre in which he himself had always observed total objectivity. But one must also consider the possibility that his motives were not of the purest: While it is quite true that Beethoven cheated on Haydn, Haydn's own attitude and actions were anything but exemplary![5]

**Sonata No. 51, in D major, embodies two innovations generally attributed to Beethoven: it is a two-movement sonata (not of the pre-classic type) like Beethoven's op. 54, and it omits the repeat of the exposition in the opening Allegro. This combination is not found again in piano music until Beethoven's op. 90.

achieve the emotional directness and variety of character through which Haydn's music comes to life.*

The learning of a Haydn sonata best begins with the exploration of the *metric* units, *harmonic* rhythms, and *melodic* subtleties. More than in either Mozart or Beethoven, *asymmetric* correspondences are in the majority—at least in the late works. For instance, the second subject of the Sonata in E minor, No. 34 (Ex. 1), which is framed by two long pauses, is first stated in six measures; but the repeat carries an extension and intensification of the fourth measure so that its length reaches a total of seven measures.

Ex. 1   Sonata in E minor, Hob. XVI/34, 1st Mvt., mm. 29–42.

With most composers, as one learns a piece, questions of phrase length, melodic variants and intricacies, harmonic rhythms, etc., important as they always are, come up only after one has dealt with the obvious features, such as melodic line and overall harmonic and rhythmic scheme. To get into a minute analysis of the musical elements at this point would seem premature. Not so with Haydn. There is very little immediate impact of pretty melody, captivating chord progression, or imposing rhythmic definition. What matters, and what must be tackled immediately, are precisely the distributions of metrical periods, the subtle harmonic progressions and melodic fine points, and the structural ingenuities realized by slight modifications of returning patterns and motives.

Examine, for instance, the opening of the two-movement Sonata in D major, No. 51 (Ex. 2), written about 1794. Its first two measures are unusually definite, by virtue of the fanfare-like

---

*This was first revealed to me in a performance of the C minor Sonata by Horowitz at Salle Pleyel in 1936. He played it with tremendous freedom and intensity, in a style which was then utterly unheard-of.

Ex. 2 Sonata in D major, Hob. XVI/51, 1st Mvt., mm. 1–11.

rise of the chord-supported half notes in the right hand against a
strong syncopated bass, partly doubled at the octave, which
marches in the opposite direction. Motion in half notes, quarter
notes, and, at the end, triplet eighth notes is established at the
outset. Thus, one is curious to see whether Haydn will follow
this with contrasting new material or will continue along expected lines. But he leaves that open! Only the length is as expected: two more measures answer the first two. (If you know
Haydn, such regularity ought to make you suspicious of what is
going to happen later!) At first, one is inclined to see the second
half of the phrase as a contrast to the first and to play it *piano,* the
beginning being implicitly marked *forte,** thus producing
quasi–masculine/feminine dialogue. But *piano* is not marked at
the end of m. 2 in the original edition (the manuscript is not
preserved), and possibly this omission was intentional, for at the
end of m. 6, where it *is* prescribed, the situation is different. The

---

*According to eighteenth-century conventions of notation, a movement begins *forte*
unless otherwise marked. (See chap. 1, Bach, above.)

"feminine" (of the "masculine/feminine" contrast) in these measures lies in the graceful dotted rhythm of the new melody.

But soon one realizes that in many ways the music just continues what came before. The left-hand triplets of m. 2 are immediately imitated two octaves higher by the first four notes of the second half of the melody (three of them in the right hand, the fourth in the left)—deliberately, no doubt, as these notes are unaccompanied. Moreover, the fundamental melodic rise during the first two measures, from d' to f-sharp', is continued one step further to g' in mm. 3 and 4. The texture, finally, is even more evolved in the second half of the phrase than in the first, as the initial two-part writing is replaced by three-part writing.

The music then continues with a repeat of the first two measures, unchanged except for a mild decoration in the left hand. This time the answer is, by Haydn's own marking, soft. Also, it is now metrically irregular, despite its four-measure length, because its third measure (m. 9) is a rhythmic imitation of the second, in which the melody rises quite superfluously by one step (4 = 1 + 2 + 1). I say superfluously because the phrase makes sense melodically even without this extra measure.* In reality, of course, that measure is badly needed because of its subdominant harmony, by which the tonic 6–4 chord of the last measure (*forte*) is being prepared. This last measure (m. 10) then gives up the dotted rhythm of mm. 3, 4, 7, 8, and 9 and resumes the triplets which were briefly introduced in m. 2, left hand, and have not been used since. The triplets now lead into and continue as accompaniment during the second theme (m. 11), which is still in the tonic, yet embodies the forthcoming modulation to the dominant.

If we now look at the opening as a whole, we find that Haydn constructs it in ten measures, the first phrase occupying four and the second six. Mm. 1–6 are loud, as is measure 10; only mm. 7–9 are soft. The curious situation in which the *forte* phrase of mm. 3 and 4 is imitated softly in mm. 7 and 8 clarifies the fact that the first time it is more continuation than contrast, the second time more contrast than continuation. Finally, it is

---

*Like the measure Mozart inserts after the eighth measure of the recapitulation in the first movement of his Quartet in G major, K. 387.

significant for the large style in which this movement is conceived that the range of the theme is from F-sharp (the beginning
of the grace-note in m. 1) to b″ (in m. 9); that is, 2½ octaves, a
gamut larger than is the rule in classical music.

There is nothing in this analysis that does not at once become a
guideline for performance, although the resulting insights may be
materialized in different ways. For example, it is conceivable to
make a slight *decrescendo* from the end of m. 2 to the end of the
phrase in m. 4 in order to emphasize first the continuity and later
the inherent contrast. In m. 9 it might then be logical to play
slightly fuller than before, in deference to the added voice in the
left hand and in preparation for the cadencing *forte* harmonies of
m. 10. The left-hand triplets of m. 2 ought to have the same
articulation and exact same speed as those of m. 10.

One peculiarity of Haydn, which can be examined in the two
variations of the main section of his F minor Variations, is that he
only gradually gets around to varying a theme. His variations
usually start with a simple repeat of the theme, until the composer, as it were, gets bored with it, and starts to decorate the
melody. In Sonata No. 49 in E-flat major, at the end of m. 24
(Ex. 3a), the second thematic group begins exactly like the first,
except that it is in the dominant key. But in the following measure Haydn proceeds quite differently from the beginning,
thereby modifying the character of the opening theme just as
much as if he had invented a new motive. The advantage of this
technique is that the unity of the movement is safeguarded; this is
necessary principally because a little while later the music is dis-
rupted by a "fainting spell" (Ex. 3b).

Sonata in E-flat major, Hob. XVI/49, 1st Mvt.

Ex. 3a mm. 24–26

Ex. 3b mm. 50–52

Exposition, development, and recapitulation fill 190 measures;
the fact that a coda of 28 measures follows is so unusual (since
Haydn's codas, if any, are usually extremely brief) that it deserves an analysis. The coda is full of deliberate, in part humor-

ous, surprise reopenings. First of all, when the piece concludes
(Ex. 4a) with just as much finality as in the exposition, one cannot be sure that a coda will develop at all. Indeed, in the next few
measures, the music merely leads into descending sixth-chords
(nostalgically reminiscent of Mozart's last Piano Concerto, K.
595, in B-flat major, where the opening phrase of the slow
movement contains the same chords) to a hold, played softly on
a dominant-seventh chord in the melody register (m. 195; Ex.
4b). The next five measures make the music rise in pitch, harmonic intensity, and (presumably) tempo, until it is suddenly interrupted by a rest lasting almost an entire measure (m. 201).
Thereafter Haydn seems to want to end the piece with one particular phrase, which he repeats again and again. Futile E-flat
major chords, incompletely presented, appear at the beginnings
of mm. 203, 205, 207, and—after one longer preparation (like
hauling off from further back)—214. Here Haydn might have
ended the piece, but, for the second time, he goes on. Instead of
the root position of the dominant chord, he now uses its third
inversion and intensifies it by combining it with an ascending
chromatic scale in the right hand (mm. 215–16; Ex. 4c). Not
even this sounds final. Therefore, in desperation, he breaks the
music off in a brutal upward scale over harsh, loud chords in the
left hand (mm. 217–18; Ex. 4d). Beethoven learned from this
(see, for example, the last measures of the Finale of the *Pathétique*
Sonata and of the Scherzo of the Seventh Symphony), but his

Sonata in E-flat major, Hob. XVI/49, 1st Mvt.

Ex. 4a mm. 189–90   Ex. 4b mm. 193–95

Ex. 4c mm. 214–15   Ex. 4d mm. 217–18

procedure is differently motivated. When Beethoven slams the
door on a movement it is simply an indication that he has gotten
tired of it. Haydn, planning carefully here as always, with all the
deadlocked repeats just described, means to proclaim his frustration over the fact that, no matter how hard one tries, one cannot
cadence by using a succession of two chords, dominant and tonic, alone—a lesson which Beethoven *never* learned (see even the
final phrases of op. 111!). The two abrupt chords at the close—
again, nothing but dominant and tonic—are calculated to leave
us dissatisfied and tense.

Finally, the importance of analyzing motivic development in
Haydn's work can be shown by examining the Finale of Sonata
No. 32 in B minor. The head motive, unaccompanied when it
first appears, is a combination of five repeated key notes followed
by a descent of three notes landing on the key note. The lower
part, entering in the left hand after this, concludes with the same
melodic idea (Ex. 5a). During the modulation to D major (mm.
28–32; Ex. 5b), the opposite pitch direction is briefly realized;
this is necessary as contrast, for beginning in m. 39 (Ex. 5c), the

Sonata in B minor, Hob. XVI/32
Ex. 5a Finale, mm. 1–7.

Ex. 5b Finale, mm. 28–32.

Ex. 5c Finale, mm. 39–41.

second theme, in the right hand, reenacts the head motive in the new key,[6] simply replacing the three eighth notes of m. 2 by a figuration in sixteenth notes. At first, this figuration seems to be just a playful finger doodling on three notes, up and down; but in context, of course, it turns out to be a decoration of the descending notes of m. 2. This is very important for the articulation in the performance, since the pianist must always listen to the essentially *descending* character of this figuration (F-sharp″–e″–d″) as it is repeated over the next 18 measures. The left hand part is identical to an inversion of the original motive of the left hand, m. 6, but because of the monotony of the right-hand figure, it is automatically promoted from accompaniment to melody. Since that motive is basically an augmentation of what happens in the right hand, contrast and unity are achieved simultaneously. Logically (yet, if the music were lost, who else would be logical enough to think of it?), the coda of the movement presents the head motive in unison octaves, provides them with a "tail," and thus, abruptly but expectedly, concludes the Sonata. Looking back now, we discover that the germs of these scale motives and slower, motivic accompaniments already exist in the second movement, perhaps even in the first. The right-hand figuration in mm. 31ff. of the Menuet (Ex. 5d) is indeed identical with that of mm. 39ff. of the Finale (Ex. 5c).

Ex. 5d Menuet, mm. 31–32.

The careful articulation gained by such analyses does not by itself bring about a performance in which the piece comes to life. We must feel the composer's urge to express a specific "affect" (state of mind) when we play his music. In his sonatas, Haydn very obviously wants us to transmit what we receive from his music to those for whom we play it. At times, and especially in the slow movements of the late sonatas, a type of self-expression manifests itself which is not to be found anywhere in Mozart's music. Haydn's subjectivity in an epoch of classical moderation would perhaps shock us if it were not principally motivated by his well-known deep religious feelings.[7]

One particular phrase recurs in several slow movement themes from the last period. We encounter it in its purest incarnation in the F-sharp minor Trio (Ex. 6a), from which Haydn copied it exactly for Symphony No. 102 in B-flat major. The

Ex. 6a   Trio in F-sharp minor, Hob. XV/26, 2nd Mvt., mm. 1–4.

beat is subdivided into six (twice three) quicker notes, which are expressive rather than decorative here; this, in conjunction with downward-pointing figurations and gruppettos, dotted rhythms, and rests, evokes a suggestion of humility, loneliness, and suffering endured with courage and gentleness. In piano music, the themes of the middle movements of Sonatas Nos. 49 and 50 (Exx. 6b, c) are similarly formed and convey the same spirit.

Ex. 6b   Sonata in E-flat major, Hob. XVI/49, 2nd Mvt., mm. 1–4.

Ex. 6c   Sonata in C major, Hob. XVI/50, 2nd Mvt., mm. 1–2.

Through utterances like these Haydn's music becomes a solace and a source of strength in general: he fulfills music's noblest mission, that of giving help to those who suffer. If Mozart really said that Haydn "was the greatest of them all, for he can make people weep as well as laugh," this is what he must have referred to. Erich Hertzmann once said in a seminar at Columbia University that Haydn was "the most therapeutic composer of them all."

Karl Friedrich Zelter, Goethe's friend and Mendelssohn's

teacher, was apparently the first to formulate some of this feeling in print (1826):

> For the past fifty years, my own performing and listening have led me to a repeated total perception of Haydn's music to the effect that it made me subconsciously want to do something myself that would seem good and pleasing to God. But that feeling was and remains independent of reflection and free of passion. . . . Temperament, mindfulness, spirit, humor, flexibility, tenderness, vigor, and, last but not least, naivety and irony—those genuine twin signs of genius—must absolutely be conceded to Haydn.[8]

These words, though written in general, apply particularly to Haydn's piano music, his most private medium of expression.

Chapter III

MOZART

Only to an extremely limited extent is it possible to deal with the piano music of Mozart, that genius among all geniuses. While most composers' personal styles evolve gradually, like Beethoven's, or are inherently there from the start, like Chopin's, Mozart's was a combination of development and innateness. His idiom is unmistakable even in the compositions of his childhood, but his style continued to incorporate additional features until the end. He thus became the greatest inventor in the history of music. More than any other musician he reformed the size, the forms, and the language of music. Many aspects of music which we take for granted would simply not exist without him—the classical piano concerto, the clarinet as a member of the orchestra, the string quintet, the piano quartet—to mention only inventions in the field of instrumental music.

To Mozart are due today's standards of size, length, tempo, and idiomatic texture in nonvocal works. We are concerned here specifically with the ways in which he achieved the *enlargement of instrumental compositions* and with his exploration and *realization of the possibilities of the*—then brand new—*pianoforte,* * for solo works as well as for concertos. Although much of the credit for the genesis of other elements of classical style legitimately goes to Haydn and, earlier, to the two famous sons of Bach, in these two

*Today called "piano"—euphemistically so, considering the way people bang on it. "Forte" would be more appropriate: "The noted fortist XY. . . ."

fields it was Mozart who designed the definitive configuration of classical music.

Mozart's desire to create unity and his intuition for drama were two most helpful qualities in the accomplishment of these incredible feats. The impulse to unify—perhaps most ostensibly symbolized in the Finale of the *Jupiter* Symphony, with its marriage between the two principal traditional forms of sonata and fugue—corresponded to ideas prevalent at that epoch: the ethos of freemasonry (to which Mozart devoted many of his late works), the search for eternal peace by Kant, and natural law as formulated by the writers of the Enlightenment period, Rousseau, and others. Even though Mozart apparently did not read their works,[1] he was a child of his time, talked to people of all social strata, and was aware of the ideology in which rational unification was the supreme goal.[2] No other composer—not even Beethoven—had this strong wish to merge seemingly incompatible musical ideas, styles, forms, and modes of expression.

But without his theatrical genius Mozart would not have been able to implement these musical-ethical concepts. His was the dramatic secret of providing surprises and creating contrasts, suddenly and breathtakingly, without breaking the line of the music: what Edvard Grieg called the "seamless" quality of Mozart's music.* His personal behavior sometimes reflected this attitude. The writer and librettist Caroline Pichler tells in her memoirs of playing the Figaro aria "Non più andrai" while Mozart was visiting in her parents' home. Mozart first hummed the tune, then joined her at the piano and beat the rhythm on her shoulders. After a while he took over the treble and improvised delicious variations while she continued in the bass. But then all of a sudden he got up, began to jump over chairs and tables, miaowing like a cat, "as was his wont," and finally turned a series of somersaults—all this smoothly and without a moment's interruption![3]

---

*Grieg's, Tchaikowsky's, and Richard Strauss's understanding of Mozart must not be judged by their Mozart arrangements and transcriptions: Tchaikowsky's *Mozartiana*, Grieg's second-piano parts for solo sonatas, and Strauss's own recitatives provided for his performance, in Berlin (1932), of *Idomeneo*. They are absurdities which in no way reflect the genuine feeling these three composers had for Mozart.

I. THE ENLARGEMENT OF INSTRUMENTAL STYLE

It is not generally known that, compared to the output of his immediate predecessors and colleagues, Mozart's compositions are strikingly long. Saint-Foix[4] discovered that the Finale of his Violin Sonata in A major, K. 526, for example, is based on the Finale (called "Englese") of a violin sonata by Carl Friedrich Abel (1725–1787), also in A major.[5] But Mozart's piece is very much longer: Abel's movement, including the single repeat marked in the score, has only 66 measures; Mozart's, not counting the two repeats in the beginning, comes to 426 measures! The entire Abel piece serves only as the opening thematic group within a large sonata rondo; with the material Abel uses to build a house, Mozart plans and constructs a city.

Even when compared to Beethoven, Mozart is a composer of long pieces. The exactly 400 measures of the first movement of Beethoven's F major quartet, Op. 59, No. 1, must have seemed very long to the composer; for the first time in the history of the quartet, the repeat of the first part was omitted. Since the accompanying rhythm has about the same speed as that of Mozart's C major String Quintet, K. 515, one can compare the two pieces. The Mozart, written 19 years earlier, comes to 368 measures without the repeat; if the prescribed repeat is made, it totals 519 measures, considerably longer than the Beethoven movement. Obviously, this did not bother Mozart in the least!

However, length is an external characteristic when compared to the actual musical features. Mozart enlarged the scope of his keyboard music mainly by transferring his dramatic-vocal language to his sonatas and most of all to his concertos. The Swiss musician and writer Hans Georg Nägeli stated unequivocally that Mozart's instrumental writing had vocal character, and he criticized Mozart for mixing genres with his "false cantability," quite ignoring that here again Mozart's purpose was to create tools for the unification of music in general.[6]

There is no doubt that the melodic style of Mozart's keyboard works is indeed operatic and generally vocal. In particular, the "aria" character of the slow movements of his sonatas has been recognized by many.* It is important for performers to be aware

---

*In a recent telecast André Previn very effectively illustrated this by orchestrating part of the slow movement of the F major Sonata for piano duet, K. 497, and having a so-

of it, because otherwise these slow movements may easily sound puny and thin when they come on the heels of lively and massive first Allegros.* Occasionally, in a slow movement, Mozart copies the style of recitatives (I call them "finger recitatives"), for example, during the middle section of the Adagio of the D major Sonata, K. 576. Here, some degree of *rubato* is necessary for mm. 26ff. (Ex. 1); it must be based on the quasi-vocal rises, from

Ex. 1 Sonata in D major, K. 576, 2nd Mvt., mm. 26–27.

c-sharp' to e' (after the second beat, m. 26), d' to f-sharp', etc., just as a singer would do it. The vocal declamation also clearly reveals that while the left hand does not reach its peak until the third beat, the right hand arrives at its highest point during the second beat.**

Ex. 2a   Sonata in F major, K. 280, 2nd Mvt., mm. 9–10.

Sonata in D major, K. 311, 3rd Mvt.
Ex. 2b   mm. 69–70   Ex. 2c   m. 16

---

prano sing the melody line to an Italian text which had not been explained to the audience.

*If you improvise a short secco recitative in the style of a Mozart opera between the first two movements of a sonata such as K. 332, in F major, you can actually hear how much bigger the theme of the slow movement then seems to be; and you may even imagine Susanna or Pamina singing it!

**Both in aria-like and recitative-like passages, the observance of the traditional rhetoric figures is certain. See the sighs in the Adagio of the F major Sonata, K. 280 (Ex. 2a), and in the Rondo of the D major Sonata, K. 311 (Ex. 2b); the strategically placed fanfare in the same movement (Ex. 2c); the screaming in the slow movement of the A minor Sonata, K. 310 (Ex. 2d); and innumerable other, not immediately obvious, places. Mozart's use of rhetoric needs a special investigation.

Ex. 2d   Sonata in A minor, K. 310, 2nd Mvt., mm. 43–44.

The use of vocal melody lines is supplemented by the suggestion of orchestral tone colors. The tremolo in the right hand in mm. 13–16 of the so-called Dürnitz Sonata in D major, K. 284, first movement (Ex. 3a), corresponds exactly to the orchestral technique of the composers of the Mannheim School; see Johann Stamitz, Sinfonia a 8 in the same key, mm. 13–16 (Ex. 3b).[7]

Ex. 3a   Sonata in D major, K. 284, 1st Mvt., m. 13.

Ex. 3b   Johann Stamitz, Sinfonia a 8, m. 13.

Pedal should definitely be used here, even if we did not know of Mozart's letter to his father, dated October 17, 1777, in which he says that this sonata "sounds exquisite on Stein's pianoforte. The device, too, which you work with your knee; the knee-lever, functioning exactly as the pedal does, is better on his than on other instruments." Note that when Mozart thought of this sonata, he immediately also thought of pedaling. In this matter, I should like to refer to Paul and Eva Badura-Skoda's book *Interpreting Mozart on the Keyboard*[8] in which the legend of Mozart without pedal is once and for all put to rest. The authors state indeed that certain passages "in fact rely on a pedal effect." Contrary to the first movement of Haydn's C major Sonata, No. 50 (written shortly after Mozart's death), none of Mozart's piano music contains clear pedal marks. Indirect pedal marks may exist in the slow movement of the G major Sonata, K. 283 (Exx. 4a, b, c). The original, to the best of my knowledge, shows a quarter note on the first beat in the bass which is not followed either by a rest or by another note, although overeager editors have sometimes supplied the former. I read this as an indication to sustain the harmony by pedal instead of keeping the fifth finger on middle C for another beat.

Sonata in G major, K. 283, 2nd Mvt.

We do not know exactly how Mozart produced the *alla turca* effect on which the entire Sonata in A major, K. 331—not just its Finale—is dependent. Pedal played a big role here; probably he had the use of special pedals, among them the "Janitscharen-zug,"[9] which had been created precisely for such purposes. On the modern piano, the tone color must be suggested by a combination of all the pedals at our disposition and a great variety of touches, inspired by orchestral pieces such as the Overture to the *Entführung aus dem Serail,* with its triangles, etc.*

In the solo works, the orchestral imagination of the pianist will be a principal help in finding the appropriate pedaling. Pedal, in Mozart, is not needed either to amplify the sound in general or to sustain special tones beyond their written value. But it can, and

---

*I would not consider it a crime to play the right hand of the F-sharp minor episode (mm. 32–40, Ex. 5, and 49–56, with their initial upbeats) of the Rondo *alla turca* one octave higher than marked, at least at the repeat. Mozart might well have done the same thing himself, had this high register been available to him, for the passage certainly smacks of piccolo flutes.

Ex. 5 Sonata in A major, K. 331, 3rd Mvt., mm. 33–35.

often must, provide the same kind of rhythmic organization as is
achieved in concertos by an accompanying string body in sometimes short, sometimes sustained chords on principal beats. (This
is also true for the unaccompanied solo passages in the concertos,
as, for example, in the second theme of the A major Concerto,
K. 488, first movement.) In the opening of the F major Sonata,
K. 332—which consists of a miniature prelude and fugue followed by a scherzo-conclusion in ten remarkable "seamless"
measures—the downbeat pedal in each of the first four measures
ought to last only through the end of the second beat, thereby
suggesting an orchestral half note followed by a rest (Ex. 6).

Ex. 6 Sonata in F major, K. 332, 1st Mvt., mm. 1–4.

This example leads into a general discussion of Alberti basses
in Mozart. Their function becomes clear wherever a concerto
theme accompanied by an Alberti bass is subsequently repeated
by the orchestral tutti with a more differentiated underpinning.
The last movement of the B-flat major Concerto, K. 595,* is a
case in point (Ex. 7). Beginning in m. 9, the broken chords of the
Alberti bass, used in the first eight measures, are replaced by repeated notes in the winds and are further supplemented by a new
rhythmic pattern in the bass. In mm. 11, 13, and 15 there are
tones on each of the two beats while in the other five measures
there is music only on the downbeat. It is feasible and—I
think—advisable to transfer this rhythmic idea to the first eight
measures, by giving discreet accents to the lowest tones of the

---

*Its rondo theme, by the way, excellently illustrates the "vocal" character of Mozart's
melodies, since he immediately reused it for the song "Sehnsucht nach dem Frühlinge,"
K. 596.

Ex. 7 Concerto in B-flat major, K. 595, 3rd Mvt., mm. 1–8 (unaccompanied piano solo).

Alberti bass at the corresponding places; especially by placing two accents in m. 5 and one in m.6. This illustrates the need to differentiate between outwardly identical Alberti basses according to the musical situation as one sees it. In the absence of other indications, harmonic rhythm is an important factor.[10] It is also important to remember that the common Alberti bass in 4/4 (as it is found in the beginning of the Easy Sonata in C major, K. 545) does not really consist of four-tone groups, undivided, but of subdivided units, mostly 2 + 2, but sometimes also 1 + 3. Attention to these subtleties keeps the long line alive, especially when the Alberti bass goes on for a good long time, as in the slow movements of the same Easy Sonata and the F major Concerto, K. 413.

Thus, quite often, it is up to the left hand to safeguard the flow and continuity. For this purpose Mozart occasionally introduced a secondary theme with some metrical independence in the left hand alone. See the first movement of the Easy Sonata, m. 13 (Ex. 8a), and some earlier works: the first movement of the Sonata in C major, K. 309, mm. 33–34 (Ex. 8b); the Finale of the C major Sonata, K. 330, mm. 35–36 (Ex. 8c); and the slow movement of the F major Sonata, K. 332, especially mm. 12 (Ex. 8d) and 32, third beat (Ex. 8e).

Ex. 8a   Sonata in C major, K. 545, 1st Mvt., m. 13.

Ex. 8b   Sonata in C major, K. 309, 1st Mvt., mm. 33–34.

Ex. 8c   Sonata in C major, K. 330, 3rd Mvt., mm. 35–36.

Sonata in F major, K. 332, 2nd Mvt.
Ex. 8d   m. 12

Ex. 8e   m. 32

In addition to Alberti basses, and with the same intention—
that is, to create orchestral effects—Mozart used the recapitulations of sonatas to extend the use of the keyboard by a most
primitive and ingenious device. In the mature piano concertos the
recapitulations were more than mechanical repeats of the (partly
transposed) exposition. They usually constituted the climax of
the entire sonata movement.[11] In the sonatas he achieved this
goal by the manner in which he transposed the second thematic
group into the tonic key. Whenever such a transposition from the
dominant happens, the composer has the obvious choice of going
up a fourth or down a fifth. But Mozart oscillated between up

and down! By this method he made the music appear to be in
two registers, instead of the single register used in the exposition,
and thereby he widened the scope of the presentation; to the
imaginative listener the music could now suggest the fuller orchestration that might occur in a symphony. In the G major
Sonata, K. 283, for instance, the second group begins in m. 90 at
a fifth below its original presentation (Exx. 9a, b), but four
measures later it rises by an octave (Ex. 9c); the same happens
again after mm. 102 and 107 (Exx. 9d, e). The confrontation of
registers is narrower in the following passage (mm. 110–11; Ex.
9f); here, the music starts in the higher register and continues an

Sonata in G major, K. 283, 1st Mvt.

octave lower. The concluding phrase (mm. 112ff.), finally, begins (Ex. 9g) and ends below, after an intervening skip to the
upper register (Ex. 9h). The total effect of these constant
switches is that the music appears much bigger in the recapitulation than in the exposition.

In the long-range organization of the rendering of a Mozart
piece, in addition to the manipulation of accompaniment figures
and attention to the change of registers, the sensitive performer
will gradually develop an acute awareness of alternating *tensions
and releases* in the music. This structural rhythm permeates all of
Mozart's works, and its observance is what principally holds performances together. The tensions sometimes consist of dissonances which resolve, sometimes of modulations that arrive at a
new key, or of sharp rhythms out of which a continuous flow is
formed, but especially of polyphonic densities which dissolve
into homophonic textures, sometimes in the style of simple folk
songs. In the first movement of the F major Sonata, K. 533, after
a section spiced with daring, almost Wagnerian dissonances and
deceptive cadences (Exx. 10a, b) and additionally weighted by
the use of fugued style (mm. 66–89; Ex. 10c), relaxation is provided at the end of the exposition by a coda of simple arpeggios
(Ex. 10d). Two other important examples may be quoted from
the sonatas: In the slow movement of the C major Sonata, K.
330, an extraordinary dissonance in m. 39 precedes the return of

Sonata in F major, K. 533, 1st Mvt.
Ex. 10a   mm. 21–22

Ex. 10b   mm. 28–30

Ex. 10c mm. 67–70

Ex. 10d mm. 89–90

the theme (see chap. 4, Beethoven, Ex. 34); and in the Andante
of the B-flat major Sonata, K. 333, tension is at once created by a
sharp dissonance at the close of the exposition, which, though
prepared melodically, is harmonically unexpected (Ex. 11a). The
tension is then gradually dissolved by modulation in which the
subdominant (mm. 40–43; Ex. 11b) plays a soothing role; all this
in perfect unity throughout. See also the Violin Sonata in A
major, K. 526, second movement, and the String Quintet in D
major, K. 593, second movement.[12]

Sonata in B-flat major, K. 333, 2nd Mvt.
Ex. 11a mm. 31–32

Ex. 11b mm. 40–43

The examples show, moreover, that Mozart was inclined to
reserve certain musical techniques (in this instance, sharp dissonances or modulations to remote keys) for specific situations arising at certain places in the music (here, the developments in slow
movements). I call this the "locus" principle, of which further

applications will be seen later. It is essential for the pianist, at the
moment of performing, to experience the tensions in Mozart's
music as well as their subsequent releases in his or her own person; an attitude opposite to what one ought to experience during
the playing of a perpetuum mobile of the kind sometimes composed by Haydn (Finale of the E-flat major Sonata, Hob. XVI/
52) and Beethoven (the finales of his F major sonatas, Op. 10
No. 2, and Op. 54), or during the toccata movements of
Schumann, Ravel, Prokofieff, and others. It is surely no coincidence that Mozart did not write these types of movements.[†]

In certain structural situations Mozart resolved the tensions
more abruptly. For instance, the sudden modulation in the slow
movement of his G major Concerto, K. 453, brings the lyrical
main theme back to C major after a rhapsodic excursion to the
remote key of C-sharp minor (mm. 83–90), rendering the return
of the theme more emphatic. See also the Finale of the Sonata in
C major for piano, four hands, K. 521, mm. 141–42.

The principal locus, where these breathtaking switches serve
structural ends, is in the middle of a rondo finale in a piano concerto or piano quartet. Here Mozart breaks new ground inasmuch as he does not write a single central episode in either the
relative minor or the subdominant but uses both keys, one after
the other, in extreme dramatic juxtaposition and emotional opposition.[*] In the A major Concerto, K. 488, for example, the
F-sharp minor episode of the Finale is more agitated and tragic
than could normally be expected in a last movement in the major
mode (mm. 230ff.). All of a sudden, the mood completely re-
verses itself, and the sweetest, most lyrical passage of the entire
concerto follows in a theme played by the clarinets (mm.
262ff.[**]). The four measures in the orchestral tutti which precede
this theme constitute a bare minimum of harmony connections

[†] In the Guglielmo aria in *Così fan tutte* the perpetual motion has purely dramatic functions.

[*] In the E-flat major concertos, K. 271 and 482 (the latter being an obvious attempt to
duplicate certain formal features of the former and regain its youthful extremes of mood),
the final rondo has only a single central episode, consisting of a slow section in the subdominant major key, but in both works this episode is preceded by an abortive modulation in the direction of the relative minor! See K. 271, Finale, mm. 208–23 and K. 482,
Finale, mm. 202–12.

[**] The appoggiatura written as a quarter note in m. 265 (clarinets) and m. 273 (piano) is
usually played incorrectly. Leopold Mozart[13] makes it absolutely clear that the small note
a″ must be held for a dotted quarter and the half note g″ for an eighth.

so that the emotional switch is complete. The negative reaction
of a traditional, orthodox theorist to Mozart's extremism is fully
expressed by Girdlestone.[14] He sees what is happening, but by
no means approves: "Such a juxtaposition, not only of keys but
also of moods for which they stand, is something of a shock. The
unprepared substitution of a waggish tune [!] for a passionate and
earnest one seems to us to savour of frivolity. . . ." Even more
extreme are the corresponding sections in the Finale of the big C
major Concerto, K. 503 (which ought to be called the "Jupiter"
Concerto). The wild A minor episode beginning in m. 145 is
connected with the ensuing dreamlike, almost surrealistic, F
major theme by nothing but three quick, loud chords (m. 162).
Slightly more gradual is the transition in the E-flat major Piano
Quartet, K. 493, from the C minor episode, which begins in m.
170, to the A-flat mirage of mm. 200ff. The sudden switch from
the relative minor to the subdominant is also found in the one
piano sonata whose Finale contains features of a concerto, the
B-flat major Sonata, K. 333; see mm. 65ff. (G minor) to mm.
76ff. (E-flat major).

It is mostly in these final concerto movements that the student
of Mozart's music can observe how the master, while respecting
traditional forms — for he never wanted to be a revolutionary — managed to use them in novel ways by exploiting the
opportunities for opposing tensions and how he was thereby able
to create unprecedentedly long lines of music. In these rondos the
most spectacular phenomenon — and also the most convincing
proof of Mozart's locus principle — is what invariably happens,
from K. 456 on, at the end of the first statement of the theme by
soloist and tutti. In the final rondos of *all* later piano concertos,
of the two piano quartets, and of the Clarinet Concerto (his last
instrumental work), Mozart, almost audibly, says as soon as the
first group ends, "Let's get on with it," as the soloist embarks on
the *same* three-tone scale ascent, from the third to the fifth tone:
B-flat major Concerto, K. 456, m. 58 (Ex. 12a); D minor Concerto, K. 466, m. 63 (the ascent is in the top voice of the left
hand; Ex. 12b); Piano Quartet in G minor, K. 478, m. 44 (Ex.
12c); A major Concerto, K. 488, m. 62 (Ex. 12d); and, almost
identically, Clarinet Concerto, K. 622, m. 57 (Ex. 12e); E-flat
major Piano Quartet, K. 493, m. 47 (the only time that the as-

cending motive appears directly in the dominant key; Ex. 12f); C major Concerto ("Jupiter"), K. 503, m. 49 (Ex. 12g); and B-flat major Concerto, K. 595, M. 65 (Ex. 12h).

The usefulness of Mozart's device can be detected by comparing any of these rondos with the Rondo of Beethoven's early B-flat major Concerto, op. 19 (Ex. 12i), where, between the end of the first group (mm. 21–22) and the opening of the transition to the second (m. 23), an embarrassing gap opens up at the precise point where Mozart would put the ascending scale motive. (All in all, Beethoven's use of the sonata rondo form was, and remained, more conventional than Mozart's.) A recapitulation of this standard motive usually takes place where Mozart wants to say, "Let's get on with the recapitulation," as it were; that is, directly after the end of the central (double-) episode, at the place where in the conventional sonata rondo the main theme reappears. Mozart thus saved one repeat of the main theme and made it possible for him to conclude the rondo with its last appearance.[15]

The need for the unification of the music in a long movement and the establishment of a long line make it necessary for the performer to concentrate on questions of tempo.*

1. Whatever the tempo is, a *steady beat* must be maintained throughout a movement. This includes slow introductions to an allegro and fast middle sections in slow movements. In the Introduction to the Violin Sonata in B-flat major, K. 454, the half note of the Allegro must equal the eighth note of the Introduction; that may cause some unavoidable adjustments in the speed of one or the other. The middle section of the Romance forming the second movement of the D minor Concerto, K. 466, is to be played at exactly the same beat as the main section; this becomes abundantly clear at the end, where Mozart builds the gradual return to the beginning on precisely that relationship.

The continuity of the tempo is never interrupted by *rubato,* because rubato affects only the declamation of the melody. In Leopold Mozart's words, "an experienced accompanist . . . will not give in to a good, solid virtuoso, for if he did, he would ruin

---

*What little I know about tempo in Mozart I owe to Fritz Busch, the great Mozart conductor whose explanations and demonstrations were of immeasurable value.

Ex. 12a   Concerto in B-flat major, K. 456, 3rd Mvt., mm. 58–61.

Ex. 12b   Concerto in D minor, K. 466, 3rd Mvt., mm. 64–67.

Ex. 12c   Piano Quartet in G major, K. 478, 3rd Mvt., mm. 44–47.

Ex. 12d   Concerto in A major, K. 488, 3rd Mvt., mm. 62–65.

Ex. 12e   Clarinet Concerto in A major, K. 622, 3rd Mvt., mm. 57–60.

Ex. 12f   Piano Quartet in E-flat major, K. 493, 3rd Mvt., mm. 48–51.

Ex. 12g   Concerto in C major,
K. 503, 3rd Mvt., m. 48.

Ex. 12h   Concerto in B-flat major, K. 595,
3rd Mvt., mm. 65–66.

Ex. 12i   Beethoven, Concerto in B-flat major, Op. 19
3rd Mvt., reduction of tutti, mm. 21–23.

that man's tempo rubato."[16] And Mozart, in his letter of October
23, 1777 to his father, said, "They all are astonished that I keep
playing accurately in time. The tempo rubato in an adagio—that
the left hand does not know about it—they cannot grasp." The
only places where the music gets slower are at *fermatas* and *calan-*
dos. When a long note is held by a fermata, the note is approached in free, relatively slow recitation. Such a ritard was
implicit and did not have to be specially marked; occasionally,
however, one finds *a piacere* ("as you like it") written by Mozart
before such fermatas; see the C minor Sonata, K. 457, third
movement (Ex. 13). The principal locus for a calando (which in

Ex. 13   Sonata in C minor, K. 457, 3rd Mvt., mm. 228–32.

Mozart simply means "weakening")[17] occurs in the recapitulation
of a first movement following the restatement of the first theme. A
short fainting spell here precedes the transition to the second thematic group. In the A minor Sonata, K. 310, Mozart marked this
in mm. 94–95 (Ex. 14a); in other places an experienced performer
will sense that the same nuance is to be used; see the G major
Sonata, K. 283 (Ex. 14b) and the B-flat major Sonata, K. 333
(Ex. 14c).

2. The *correct choice* of tempo is necessary to assure the maintenance of continuity and long musical line in Mozart.

a. The opening Allegro of a sonata or concerto, in the terminology of Mozart's elders and contemporaries, was usually
classified as *Allegro moderato* when relatively slow, as *Allegro maës-*
toso when somewhat faster, and as *Allegro con spirito* when fast.
The attributes *maëstoso* and *con spirito* here did not refer to the
character but to the speed of the music. To give a general idea of
the speeds involved, here are approximate metronome marks in
4/4: *Allegro moderato* ♩ = MM 100–104 (the B-flat major Violin
Sonata, K. 378, for example), *Allegro maëstoso* ♩ = MM 108–112
(the classic example being the C major Concerto, K. 503), and
Allegro con spirito ♩ = MM 132–138 (as in the D major Sonata, K.
311). In addition to these three established categories Mozart also

Ex. 14a Sonata in A minor, K. 310, 1st Mvt., mm. 94–95.

Ex. 14b Sonata in G major, K. 283, 1st Mvt., mm. 81–83.

Ex. 14c Sonata in B-flat major, K. 333, 1st Mvt., mm. 108–10.

used, for a specially fast allegro, *Allegro di molto* or *Allegro assai.* However he frequently abstained from any qualification and simply wrote *Allegro,* leaving it to the performer to figure out which kind he meant. A fine distinction has to be made between the freedom of the individual to find the tempo which is absolutely right for him (but may not be right for another performer) and his freedom to change such tempo from day to day depending on hall acoustics, piano action, or simply on moods. The first kind of freedom is always justified, the second only very exceptionally. An alla breve meter (₵) in an *Allegro con spirito* or *Allegro assai* does not change the tempo much. The conductor Peter Hermann Adler once remarked very aptly that "a true Mozart allegro is precisely too fast to be conducted in 4, and too slow to be conducted in 2."

If the meter is 3/4, the tempo must be approximately 9/8 faster in order to be felt as equally fast by the listener; that is, two measures of 4/4 equal three measures of 3/4.* For instance, if the

---

*This rule is not mentioned in today's literature, but the *Brockhaus Riemann Musiklexikon* article "Allegro" quotes James Grassineau's statement of 1740: "It is to be observed, the movements of the same name as Adagio, or Allegro, are swifter in triple than in common time."[18]

opening movement of the C major Concerto, K. 503, is played at
♩ = MM 112, to produce the same sensation of a moderate allegro one would have to play the opening movement of the C
minor Concerto, K. 491, at ♩ = MM 126. In a faster type of
allegro, if one played the opening movement of the C major
Trio, K. 548, at ♩ = MM 128, one would have to play the opening of the E major Trio, K. 542, at ♩ = MM 144 to produce the
same tempo effect. A similar relationship exists between the
opening movements of the two piano sonatas in B-flat major, K.
333 and K. 570.

  b. The slow middle movements of the sonatas and concertos
demonstrate even better how the various Mozart tempi developed into *tempo giusto* (meaning a regular, normal tempo), setting
the pace for all later generations. Basically, these movements are
marked either *Andante* (for example, Sonatas in G major, K. 283;
F major, K. 533) or *Adagio* (Sonatas in F major, K. 332; D major,
K. 576); if the former, the quarter note constitutes the beat, if the
latter, the eighth note is the unit of counting. (This tradition had
been firmly established by Quantz in his *Essay on How to Play the
Traverse Flute* of 1752.[19]) If one accepts a speed of 1 second per
beat (♩ = MM 60) as average for a Mozart andante, his *giusto*
tempo for an adagio would be about ♪ = MM 80, making
adagio one-third slower than andante. Nearly all of Mozart's
slow movements fall unmistakably into one or the other category; an exceptional borderline case is the capriciously decorated
slow movement of the C major Sonata, K. 309, marked *Andante,
un poco adagio.* Other qualifications of the tempo mark of andante, such as *con espressione* (K. 311), *cantabile* (K. 330), and
amoroso (K. 281; cleaned up in the Schirmer edition as *espressivo!*),
do not affect the tempo but refer to the character of the movement.

  c. In final movements there is a great variety of speeds, of
meters, and therefore of tempo marks. The traditional, inten-
tionally sentimental *Tempo di Minuetto* for a Finale was still used
by Mozart on rare occasions (see Piano Trio in B-flat major, K.
254; Concerto in F major, K. 413). It is faster than a minuet
proper in the middle of a sonata (like that of the E-flat major
Sonata, K. 282), quartet, or symphony. Its beat approximates ♩
= MM 108–112. In variation movements at the ends of sonatas

and concertos, or which constitute an individual set, the adagio
variation, which is usually next to last, does not interrupt the
beat; it is to be played exactly at half speed. The final variation,
even if not specially marked, is meant to be about one-third
faster than the rest. The Presto in the Finale of the A minor
Sonata, K. 310, refers to the half note or—what amounts to the
same thing—to the full measure as the conductor's beat. However, here, too, "in 1" is too fast and "in 2" too slow.

A device occasionally utilized by Mozart to unify a mul-
timovement composition, such as a piano sonata or piano concerto, consists of a thematic connection between movements, a
structure that is usually called *cyclic*.[20] Open cyclic writing, in
classical times, was frowned upon—probably because in that
epoch of melodic primacy, in which instrumental music had been
freshly impregnated with the spirit of Italian opera by composers
such as J. C. Bach, a composer was supposed to show his imagination in inventing ever new melodies and motives. To use the
same theme in successive movements, as Bach had still openly
done in the C minor Partita, the Trio Sonata from the *Musical
Offering,* and the D minor Toccata, would have seemed a sign of
poor invention.*
This may explain why the classical composers, when they did
use cyclic devices, did so surreptitiously. In Mozart's B-flat
major Sonata, K. 333, the cyclic construction is perhaps a little
less hidden than in the other sonatas. In the opening measure of
both the first and the last movements, the last note in the left
hand, g', is in exactly the same harmonic configuration (Exx.
15a, b); and the transitory motive in mm. 15f. (Ex. 15c) of the
first movement is resumed, almost identically, at the corresponding place in the Finale (mm. 24–27; Ex. 15d). Shortly before the
conclusion of the second movement of the D major Sonata, K.
576, the end of mm. 61 and 64 (Ex. 15e) is repeated identically a
few seconds later in m. 8 of the Finale (Ex. 15f)!

*In the first edition of Six Haydn Sonatas (1780), Haydn made the publisher, Artaria,
apologize to the public for the similarity between the main themes of the C-sharp minor
Sonata (Hob. XVI/36), second movement, and the G major Sonata (Hob. XVI/39), first
movement, "in order to forestall the criticisms of any witlings" (Haydn, letter of February
25, 1780).[21] They are not even part of the same composition!

Sonata in B-flat major, K. 333
Ex. 15a   1st Mvt., m. 1.

Ex. 15b   3rd Mvt., m. 1.

Ex. 15c   1st Mvt., m. 15.

Ex. 15d   3rd Mvt., mm. 25–26.

Sonata in D major, K. 576
Ex. 15e   2nd Mvt., m. 64.

Ex. 15f   3rd Mvt., m. 8.

More significant, perhaps, for Mozart's unifying intentions is the fact that when he incorporated the previously composed F major Rondo, K. 494, into the F major Sonata, K. 533, as its Finale, he found it necessary to insert a long cadenza (mm. 143–69) in which he employed some of the poignant harmonies as well as the fugato style of the rest of the sonata. These features were not in the Rondo in its initial, small-scale form (Mozart had originally called it "ein kleines Rondo").[22]

Finally, a word about the *fantasias*—a form Mozart apparently cherished, to judge from the relatively high number of them among his piano works. The challenge, for him, was in achieving cohesion without the three usual quasi-Aristotelian unities of time signature, key signature, and monothematic structure.* The challenge for the performer, correspondingly, is to float along with the music without getting lost in the drift. Most characteristic in this respect is Mozart's C major Prelude–Fantasia, K. 394. After a slow introduction of eight measures, the music goes

---

*I have mentioned before the importance of the three unities of Aristotle's drama, as used by the French classicists of the seventeenth century, for the classical style in music.[23] I keep hoping that someone will look for the historic connections between the two schools. But, even without actual investigative evidence, it is clear that the aesthetics of French drama were consulted by the Viennese composers in their endeavor to create classical musical forms.

on for 34 measures without key and without motive. It is then interrupted by a cadenza, after which it continues in partial recapitulation for another twelve long measures. All this time, repeated notes—at first in 16th triplets, later (from m. 23) in 8th note octaves—are the only mortar that Mozart employs to hold the music together. Instead of themes and tunes, a few exclamations express the agitated feeling of the piece. They occur first in the left hand, partly while crossing the right, and later in the right hand. As the music gets more and more excited, it modulates through D minor (m. 11), A minor (m. 15), C minor (m. 19), B-flat major (m. 21), from there sequentially through various neighboring keys finally to B-flat minor (m. 31), back to C minor (m. 33), D minor (m. 34), G minor (m. 35—a half measure), and, with innumerable changes of key literally in every measure, to A minor (mm. 39–47), the key of the cadenza. After this, the modulations resume but one cannot properly call them that, since Mozart never stops long enough anywhere for a full key establishment by cadence.

The famous Fantasia in C minor, K. 475, has an essentially identical structure; it especially shows the same programmatic omission of a key signature (with the exception of the episode in B-flat major). The difference between the two fantasias is that Mozart gave the one in C major a minimum of metrical unity but instead provided the one in C minor with some degree of thematic construction, especially by writing a free *da capo* at the end. Also, several of the latter's episodes are definitely in a single key, even if not always so marked. The performer who is aware of the essential difference between a fantasia and a sonata will not try for "improvisational" liberties of tempo, dynamics, and expression—they would be nonsensical in a fantasia—but for performance unity with the help of the individual devices used by the composer in each instance.

II. THE REALIZATION OF THE POSSIBILITIES OF THE PIANOFORTE

While Bach only rarely concentrated on the actual sonorities of a composition (as in the First *Brandenburg* Concerto, where the use of a *violino piccolo* was an afterthought), for Mozart the real sound was an element in music as important as any other. Deutsch[24] does not believe the story that Mozart, on his deathbed, asked to hear Papageno's first aria from the *Magic Flute* once more. The conductor(?) Roser allegedly sang it for him, bringing tears to Mozart's eyes. Even if this story is not true, it holds an *internal* truth: Mozart needed the live sound. Although in his mind he could have heard the aria with perfection, far surpassing anything Roser could produce for him, the imagined sound was not enough for Mozart at this supreme moment. His sensitivity to sound as a child made him terribly afraid of solo trumpets, and, as the trumpeter Andre Schachtner—who had known Mozart all his life—stated after Mozart's death, "Just to hold a trumpet against his chest was for him like a gun."[25] These anecdotes indicate that he wanted full, "real," lovely sonorities, with no excessive noise.

Under the influence of today's emphasis on Baroque performance practice, many Mozart players do not realize that the delicate, detached sonorities of the typical harpsichord piece were alien to Mozart as well as to his immediate predecessors J. C. Bach and J. S. Schröter.[26] In many ways Mozart was more robust than we are inclined to admit, just as his humor, as expressed in *Ein Musikalischer Spass* ("A Musical Joke"), K. 522, and in some letters, is anything but delicate! Even though the textures of his piano works are more transparent and less thick, on the whole, than Haydn's and Beethoven's, they should not sound less full; it is just that Mozart was raised in a different, Italian-style tradition (Padre Martini, Johann Christian Bach), in which clustery writing was excluded for the sake of better-sounding top voices.

1. Mozart's *melody writing* for the piano gains its vitality by exploiting the contrast between *diatonic and chromatic lines,* by centering the principal melodies around the *fifth tone of the scale,* and, finally, wherever needed, by *wide leaps.*

a. The theme of the Finale of the B-flat major Sonata, K. 570 (Ex. 16a), illustrates some of the melodic functions of *chromati-*

Ex. 16a   Sonata in B-flat major, K. 570, 3rd Mvt., mm. 1–4.

cism in Mozart's piano music. Chromatic and diatonic elements
are juxtaposed here so that mm. 1 and 3 offer chromatic rises,
while mm. 2 and 4 react to them with diatonic descents. The
same antiphonal texture is found in the theme of the A minor
Rondo, K. 511 (Ex. 16b), except that the chromatic rise occurs in
the middle (mm. 2 and 3), between the diatonic descents (mm. 1
and 4). In the slow movement of the C minor Sonata, K. 457
(mm. 6 and 7; Ex. 16c), it is the chromatic line which falls, the
diatonic which ascends (mm. 9, 15; Exx. 16d, e). These measures
explain, in retrospect, the construction of the second phrase in
the first movement (Ex. 16f), in which the diatonic answer to a
chromatic descent (mm. 9–12) is given by a brief diatonic fanfare
(m. 15 with upbeat), the importance of which is often ignored in
performances.

Ex. 16b   Rondo in A minor, K. 511, mm. 1–4.

Sonata in C minor, K. 457, 2nd Mvt.
Ex. 16c   mm. 6–7

b. The *immediacy* of sound which Mozart clearly wanted to
establish from the start includes an antigravitational element: the
music at once "lifts you off your feet." To this end Mozart used
the melodic device of starting the opening theme in the region of
the *fifth tone of the scale* on top of a tonic chord. What causes such
a psychological boost remains a mystery. But it may be helpful
to remember that a great many nursery rhymes center on the
dominant tone;* and that, to my knowledge, the Kodaly system
of teaching young children starts from the assumption that they
will sing and hum the fifth of the tonic chord before attempting
the keynote.

---

*See also Brahms's folk-like three-note theme of the Intermezzo in C major, Op. 119
No. 3.

Sonata in C minor, K. 457, 2nd Mvt.
Ex. 16d m. 9

Ex. 16e m. 15

Ex. 16f Sonata in C minor, K. 457, 1st Mvt., mm. 9–16.

Some of Mozart's sonatas begin *on* the fifth tone of the scale (such as the E-flat major, K. 282, Ex. 17a; G major, K. 283, Ex. 17b; A minor, K. 310, Ex. 17c; C major, K. 330, Ex. 17d; F major, K. 533, Ex. 17e). Others move *toward* this tone during the opening phrase (for instance, all three D major Sonatas, K. 284, Ex. 17f; K. 311, Ex. 17g; and K. 576, Ex. 17h; and Sonata in B-flat major, K. 570, Ex. 17i). The opening of the C minor Sonata, K. 457 (Ex. 18), is not really an exception, since the initial "rocket," which leads only up to the third of the scale in mm. 1–2, is continued to the fifth during the next phrase (m. 3), a fact that one ought to be aware of at the moment of performance. Finally, in a related design, the ten measures of the opening theme of the B-flat major Sonata, K. 333, repeat the first five notes of the scale in a descending order in every other measure, that is, five times altogether.

These beginnings constitute a Mozart specialty, as any comparison with Haydn and Beethoven sonatas will confirm. Beethoven's op. 7 in E-flat major (Ex. 19a) and op. 10, no. 2, in F major (Ex. 19b), for instance, seem to begin the same way, but in the former (as Hugo Riemann was the first to state in print[27]) the phrase is directed beyond m. 3 (in which the fifth is reached) to the upper octave (m. 5); while in the latter the initial rise from a' to c″, by itself quite Mozartian, is retroactively invalidated by the smaller rise from a' only to b-flat', in m. 3.

Ex. 17a Sonata in E-flat major, K. 282, 1st Mvt., mm. 1–4.

Ex. 17b Sonata in G major, K. 283, 1st Mvt., mm. 1–4.

Ex. 17c Sonata in A minor, K. 310, 1st Mvt., mm. 1–2.

Ex. 17d Sonata in C major, K. 330, 1st Mvt., mm. 1–2.

Ex. 17e Sonata in F major, K. 533, 1st Mvt., mm. 1–2.

Ex. 17f Sonata in D major, K. 284, 1st Mvt., mm. 1–3.

Ex. 17g Sonata in D major, K. 311, 1st Mvt., mm. 1–2.

Ex. 17h Sonata in D major, K. 576, 1st Mvt., mm. 1–2.

Ex. 17i Sonata in B-flat major, K. 570, 1st Mvt., mm. 1–4.

Ex. 18 Sonata in C minor, K. 457, 1st Mvt., mm. 1–4.

Ex. 19a Beethoven, Sonata in E-flat major, Op. 7, 1st Mvt., mm. 1–6.

Ex. 19b Beethoven, Sonata in F major, Op. 10, No. 2, 1st Mvt., mm. 1–4.

c. In moments of great intensity Mozart sometimes resorted to *wide leaps* in the melody. A prime example is the intensified recapitulation of the tragic Siciliano constituting the slow movement of the A major Concerto, K. 488 (m. 65; Ex. 20a); or the passionate conclusion of the agitated Finale of the C minor

Sonata, K. 457 (mm. 301ff; Ex. 20b), where the leap, achieved
by crossing hands, is so extraordinary that the first publisher
diminished it by one octave. This type of writing is related to
Mozart's use of the wide range of the dramatic soprano (for
example, Fiordiligi's aria-rondo "Per pietà," in *Così fan tutte,* No.

Ex. 20a   Concerto in A major, K. 488, 2nd Mvt., mm. 65–68.

Ex. 20b   Sonata in C minor, K. 457, 3rd Mvt., mm. 301–305: first print and autograph.

25; Ex. 20c), and of the clarinet (for example, Clarinet Concerto
in A major, K. 622, second movement; Ex. 20d). The difference
is that, unlike singers, pianists do not dispose of a gliding portamento, nor can they, as both clarinetists and singers do, modify
the loudness and color of a tone after it has been sounded. To
enhance the projection of the leap, most pianists in a live concert
will therefore resort to visible gestures to express the distance
over which the sound has to travel. But the leap can also be directly suggested in the music, simply by stressing the preceding
tone so that a diminuendo results in which the leap becomes

Ex. 20c   Rondo, "Per pietà ben mio perdona," *Così fan tutte,* No. 25, mm. 16–20.

Che   ver go gna e or - ror - mi fa,   che ver go gna;   che ver go   gna

Ex. 20d   Clarinet Concerto in A major, K. 622, 2nd Mvt., mm. 89–90.

plainly audible (cf. Beethoven, Sonata in E major, op. 14, no. 1, second movement, end of main section).

2. The vitality of Mozart's *rhythmic* patterns is expressed, most of all, in his favorite marching pattern—four quarter notes the third of which is preceded by a sixteenth note upbeat.[28] Its rhythmic function is usually enhanced by the repetition of a single note; see, for example, the main theme of the F major Concerto, K. 459, and its development in extraordinary unisons played by the orchestra in mm. 149–61 and 316–27. In these measures nothing else is played but this motive in unison, over and over again! The Concertos in D major, K. 451, G major, K. 453, and B-flat major, K. 456, also begin with it. In many other places Mozart alludes to this pattern, for example, in the first movement of the C major Sonata, K. 330 (Ex. 21a), and in the opening movement of the A major Concerto, K. 488 (Ex. 21b). The motive is by no means restricted to piano music. It dominates the Minuet of the A major Symphony, K. 201, the second *Idomeneo* March (Act. 2, No. 14), and the Wedding March in *Le Nozze di Figaro,* "Ecco la marcia." A similar motive, in which the sixteenth note is effectively split into two 32nd notes, appears dramatically during the overture to *Idomeneo* to enhance the heroic character of the music. Wherever this motive appears it bears the stamp of Mozart's personal signature tune. In keyboard performances care has to be taken to play the downbeat sharper and heavier than the third beat, lest the Morse Code effect of the pattern be obliterated.

Ex. 21a Sonata in C major,
K. 330, 1st Mvt., m. 27.   Ex. 21b   Concerto in A major, K. 488, 1st Mvt., mm. 99–102.

The execution of a related pattern requires equal care and total accuracy in timing. After a dotted or double-dotted note Mozart frequently subdivides the succeeding short note into several even shorter ones. Examples of this pattern occur twice during the D minor Fantasia, K. 397: first in the Adagio (Exx. 22a, b), and then in the Allegretto (Exx. 22c, d), juxtaposed with a group of ordinary sixteenth notes; and also in the main theme of the opening movement of the B-flat Trio, K. 502, m. 6.

Fantasia in D minor, K. 397
Ex. 22a Adagio, mm. 12, 14.

Ex. 22b Allegretto, mm. 58, 72.

Sonata in C major, K. 330
Ex. 22c   1st Mvt., m. 38.

Ex. 22d   2nd Mvt., mm. 3, 6.

Ex. 22e   3rd Mvt., m. 61.

In the C major Sonata, K. 330, the pattern gains the force of a cyclic motive. As such it pervades each of the three movements (Exx. 22c, d, e). In the second movement compare m. 6 with m. 3! This sonata also gives authentic clues for the performance of the pattern. There are very few dynamics markings in the piece, but in the first movement, Mozart specifies *sf* for the beginning and *p* for the end of m. 38 (Ex. 22c); and in the second movement, he again marks the end of m. 6 *p* (Ex. 22d). Many pianists might be inclined to do exactly the opposite! However, through these dynamics Mozart ensures that the very short notes end with surprising lightness on the new beat—this is another case of his antigravitational trend.

Though this ought to go without saying, it is perhaps prudent to remind performers that the dotted or double-dotted note preceding this grouping must be held for its entire length. This is especially important where various types of subdivisions are close together, as in m. 58 of the D minor Fantasia, K. 397 (Ex. 22b). To bring in a group of quick upbeat notes as late as possible is always a Mozart trademark,* to be observed in different constellations as well. The opening measure of the Clarinet Trio in E-flat major, K. 498, presents a typical case. Most other com-

---

*Although this is similar to Baroque double-dotting, I do not see it as historically related, but as a personal preference of Mozart's.

posers would simply have subdivided the third beat into four 32nd notes, but Mozart dots the downbeat note so that the quick notes, starting in the middle of the third beat only, become 64th notes. Since this must be played accurately, the tempo cannot be as fast as it is sometimes taken.

3. Mozart's *use of registers* is a deliberate exploitation of the novel sonorities of the pianoforte (see above, p. 76), and just as in the confrontation of Sarastro and the Queen of the Night, symbolism may have been inherent in Mozart's occasional going to extremes, especially in the Finale of the C minor Sonata, K. 457 (see chap. 4, Beethoven p. 125). On at least three different occasions, a rondo ends extremely low and soft: in the C major Sonata, K. 309, Finale; D major Rondo, K. 485; and F major Rondo, K. 494. Instrumentally speaking, these places probably reflect an attempt by Mozart to create a type of sonority which was not attainable on any other instrument (not even the harpsichord) or instrumental combination.

At the same time, these coda sections exemplify how one may be able to set a mood through the appropriate use of registers. Occasionally Mozart went further. In the C major Sonata, K. 330, each successive movement penetrates more deeply into the low pitches. In the first movement, which is deliberately small-scaled and "moderate," the entire bass line, except for a three-note interjection in mm. 18 and 105, is within violin and viola range. In the serious Andante cantabile which follows, as early as m. 2 the bass reaches down a fifth further, to F. The active, boisterous Finale, from m. 9, provocatively accompanies the rondo theme in the lowest available register, starting with a thickly placed C major arpeggio. Such evolution within the same work, establishing a character progression between movements, is daringly anti-Baroque; and Mozart's subtle realizations of textural nuances are utterly effective.

4. Only a few authentic pieces of information exist about pianistic details of performance practice, such as *legato, slurs, appoggiaturas,* and *trills.* Most of the rules being taught and published rely on guesswork or musical intuition—unreliable guides, both of them![29]

We must begin with a strange remark by Beethoven about Mozart's playing, quoted by Czerny to Jahn.[30] According to this verbal quotation, Mozart "had a fine but choppy [*zerhackt*] way of playing, and no *legato*." If Beethoven said this—and it is indeed doubtful whether he ever heard Mozart play—he cannot have meant it quite that way, for it is obvious that Mozart, master of the "singing" piano style, must have commanded a perfect *cantabile* legato touch in his playing. The observation only makes sense if Beethoven referred here to Mozart's relatively light, unemphatic touch as compared to what he himself needed for his own adagio movements (see chap. 4, Beethoven, p. 159). That Mozart's playing was "choppy" I simply refuse to believe, nor do I believe that Beethoven ever said it.

In groups of two-note slurs, Mozart was very careful to distinguish between those in which the second note is held throughout its entire length and those in which it is snapped off. To hold was the rule; to shorten, the exception. In the opening movement of the C major Sonata, K. 309, the second theme at first comes with such a snap, marked by a rest (Ex. 23a); the second time, the second note of each group, despite the slur, is connected to the first note of the next (Ex. 23b). One must conclude from such differentiated notation that the more-recent habit of shortening the second note of a two-note slur, as in the opening of Beethoven's *Tempest* Sonata, was normally incompatible with the Mozart articulation. This is also true for the ending of the opening movement of the D major Sonata, K. 311 (Ex. 23c): not only are the second eighth notes in each group of two unabridged but also it is necessary to hold the very last chord in the right hand for its full value of a quarter.

Sonata in C major, K. 309, 1st Mvt.
Ex. 23a m. 37   Ex. 23b m. 41   Ex. 23c Sonata in D major, K. 311
                                                                        1st Mvt., mm. 111–12.

It is well known that Mozart used dots as well as vertical dashes to establish his two basic forms of staccato. The difference between the two kinds lies not so much in their heaviness as in their length, the vertical dash indicating a half-staccato, the dot indicating a very short duration. Instances like the early B-flat major Sonata, K. 281, first movement, m. 17, prove that the dash-staccato is not usually heavier than the dot-staccato: Mozart would certainly not have wanted the single upbeat note, preceding four repetitions of that identical note, to carry an accent. Hermann Abert, whose analysis of the musical language of the solo part in the piano concertos has never been equaled,[31] established that Mozart's relatively rare *portamento* marking—dot plus slur—always indicates a heightened expression.[32] Abert cites examples from the F major Concerto, K. 413 (first movement, mm. 172–83; second movement, m. 25; third movement, mm. 87ff.). Another very important portamento passage is the subsidiary motive in the slow movement of the C minor Sonata, K. 457, mm. 5f., where the portamento applies to a descending chromatic scale, implying a crescendo during these four tones, but *subito piano* on the fifth note (not marked portamento), which belongs with the left-hand chord that follows.

In the last years of his life Mozart began to write *slurs* which extended over more than one measure, against the custom of his epoch, as a means of clarifying large metrical divisions. The center of the Finale of the C minor Sonata, K. 457, for example, is divided into double measures by such slurs (mm. 46f., 146f., 287f., etc.), making it necessary to count "*One*–two" for alternate downbeats here. Mozart notated the rondo theme in the F major Sonata, K. 494, with a three-measure slur for the opening when he wrote the incipit in his private diary; that means one must begin the fourth measure as a new thought. In other places, however, if he could assume that pianists would know the length of the metrical period, and if the divisions of the music were in accordance with the division into barlines, he conformed to the standard notation and did not draw slurs over barlines. In the concertos and piano quartets, the phrasing of certain themes can best be discovered by studying the slurs in the string parts. A good example is found in the Finale of the Piano Quartet in E-flat major, K. 493, mm. 167–70. In this instance, while the piano is to play with less articulation, much louder, and altogether differently from the strings, the basic structure of antecedent (action) and consequent (reaction) must be the same, meaning that the first upbeat will consist of one quarter, and the second upbeat of three quarters. This can only be discovered through Mozart's markings for the string parts.*

---

*The Neue Mozart Ausgabe (Kassel: Bärenreiter) is the only edition known to me which prints the correct markings.

As for *embellishments,* Mozart was very much his father's child, which is to say that one can find most answers by studying Leopold Mozart's *Gründliche Violinschule.* The informal and elastic approach of both father and son—very different from the rigid rules of Bach's time, which were also used by C.P.E. Bach—is clearly stated in chap. 9, no. 9. In discussing whether to play an appoggiatura long or short, one reason Leopold Mozart gives for playing a normally long appoggiatura short is the avoidance of harmonies "that would insult the ears." He is concerned that one not "take away the liveliness" of a piece by using long appoggiaturas; and he ends with examples "in which the performance, if it included long appoggiaturas, would sound much too sleepy." This view seems to indicate that when in doubt, play the appoggiatura short rather than long, and is applicable to the D major theme of the G minor Piano Quartet, K. 478, Finale, m. 60, quoted in the D major Rondo, K. 485. Where triplets and dotted-eighths-plus-sixteenths coexist, contrary to Baroque practice, they must be played exactly as written, that is, polyrhythmically. This applies to the slow movements of the C major Concerto, K. 503, and of the Violin Sonatas in C major, K. 296, and B-flat major, K. 378.

Although trills and embellishments in Mozart's time normally still began with the upper note and were played *on* the beat, some flexibility, especially about the second of these rules, must be applied in instances where bad voice-leading would result from an orthodox application, for example, in the opening of the Clarinet Trio in E-flat major, K. 498. In m. 4, parallel octaves with the bass would result from doubling d on the downbeat; also, in m. 35 of the Adagio of the E-flat major Sonata, K. 282, the playing of the appoggiatura on the downbeat (instead of before) would lead to parallel fifths with the inner voice.*

Trill chains must be smoothly connected, with no accent given to the new trill tone at its entrance. Mozart gave a special exercise to Hummel when Hummel studied with him as a child; when he recorded it later in his four-volume School of Piano Playing, he

---

*Two types of embellishments were possibly played *before* the beat: three-note grace notes, as at the opening of Mozart's A minor Rondo, K. 511, and in m. 16 of the trio section of Haydn's F minor Variations; and two-note slides leading up to a beat note, as in the example from the Clarinet Trio.

gave Mozart ("Mozart himself") credit for it. The exercise consists of trilling the same two white keys, changing fingers but
without interrupting the flow: 1–2, 1–3, 2–3, 2–4, etc.[33]

Finally, Mozart's interest in *fingerings* is clearly in evidence in
the Finger Exercises, K. 626 b/48, which have at last been published.[33] They demonstrate, in mm. 4, 9, 14, etc. (Ex. 24), that
Mozart thought of the final cadence IV V I as entering, in the
treble, *detached* from what precedes it: Using Mozart's fingering
there is no way to connect the first and second beats in these
measures; most later editors of similar passages would have provided smooth, legato transitions by fingering them differently.

Finger Exercises, K. 626 b/48
Ex. 24a   m. 4   .Ex. 24b   m. 14

Coming to the end of this chapter, I feel compelled to repeat
here what I wrote almost forty years ago in a program booklet:

Musical children generally have a direct approach to Mozart's music, being able
to enjoy it completely, as far as their understanding goes. Later on, when they
hear his works again, they feel that after all they did not understand this music
quite as well as they do now. And as long as the development of our mind and
our soul continues, this experience repeats itself. We shall always be led to believe, when listening to Mozart, that we have grasped his music entirely, and
shall always be undeceived the next time we listen to it. This music not only
seems to be, but actually *is* complete at any stage of our receptive capacities; and
as these capacities increase after new inner experiences, we may find that these
experiences, too, are included in Mozart's music.

Chapter IV

BEETHOVEN

I. THE PHENOMENON OF BEETHOVEN

Individualization

If Beethoven, unlike Bach and Mozart, has not yet found his definitive biographer and analytical theorist, it may be because, in many essential ways, he belongs to the *present* epoch of music. There are unresolved ingredients in the complex substance and aesthetics of his music that make Beethoven truly as controversial as today's avant-garde composers. This viewpoint differs from the traditional opinion, according to which our period of musical history begins with Beethoven—the alleged prototype of a Classical musician—and with his alleged epoch-making innovations. If this were true, it would have been possible to assign him a definite place in musical history long ago. Romain Rolland,[1] W. J. Turner,[2] J.W.N. Sullivan,[3] other writers, and even Nazi politicians tried to do this, to label him, each in his rather divergent way. However, such efforts are still premature. A genius of such impact can only be assessed objectively long after his own time.

Most of the innovations themselves must be credited to earlier composers, from Bach's sons to Mozart; what Beethoven did was to integrate all of them into his brand new musical "world view" (*Weltanschauung*), thus making them function in new ways. This is one reason why, in over 150 years, his music has not been fully absorbed or superseded; and also why it has sometimes stood in the way of the appreciation of certain Haydn and Mozart works. People (including great musicians) would "praise" Mozart for the C minor Sonata as "almost Beethovenian." Schubert, especially, was never regarded as his own man, but was compared step by step with Beethoven (see chap. 5, Schubert). Indeed, Beethoven became and remained the most influential of all composers for the piano, once the hegemony of Hummel and Weber diminished during the last third of the nineteenth century. Even Chopin, who disliked Beethoven, could not always escape the power of his personality.*

Beethoven's "world view" has many facets, but its essence is the *individualization* of musical compositions. He refused to submit to the categorization of music, as his predecessors had done.** Beethoven's sonatas, quartets, and symphonies, unlike those of Mozart and Haydn, are meant to be perceived singly, not as parts of a series or as examples of a generic type (which is true for both Mozart and Haydn despite tremendous differences in musical detail). Beethoven's piano sonatas, for instance, are in no way interchangeable. It is true that some of them resemble each other, as a father and son might show a family resemblance—op. 7 and op. 106, for instance. But, like Mozart's operatic characters—Figaro and Donna Anna—each sonata has an identity of its own. Beethoven put the sonatas together individually without any other music or musical types in mind; they are *functionally* incomparable. To achieve this, he used various compositional techniques; notably, he always sought new ways of using sonata form or forms. Even his very last composition,

Ex. 1a Sonata in F major, op. 10, no. 2, 2nd Mvt., mm. 1–4.

Ex. 1b Chopin, Ballade No. 4 in F minor, mm. 8–9.

---

*A curious example of subconscious influences exists in the retrograde relationship between the motive of the Allegretto of Beethoven's Sonata in F major, op. 10, no. 2 (Ex. 1a) and that of Chopin's Ballade No. 4 (Ex. 1b).

**One manifestation of this attitude was his refusal to acknowledge a *tempo giusto* for the Allegro and Adagio in a sonata or symphony.[4]

the Finale of the B-flat major Quartet, op. 130, presents yet another unprecedented twist.

Beethoven's aesthetic corresponded exactly to his personal philosophy. It is well known that Beethoven was not only an indi-
vidualist himself but also a champion of the general independence
of the individual, which included composers' rights and their
place in society. Consequently, early in life he liberated himself
from patronage, believing as he did in enlightenment and reason
as successors to class, wealth, power, and general establishment.
When Beethoven saw his brother's calling card: "Johann v. Beethoven, Real Estate Owner," he promptly wrote: "Ludwig v.
Beethoven, Brain Owner." He wanted each person to be himself,
different from all others, not typecast and class-bound. Similarly,
he worked to make his compositions absolute, i.e., different
from and independent of each other. It is remarkable and
paradoxical that, in addition to the individuality of each work,
Beethoven wanted to assert his own individuality in his compositions, not in an unconscious manner, as with one's handwrit-
ing, but as a deliberate gesture of personal identification. This is
most noticeable in works of an improvisatory character, like the
Fantasy, op. 77, and in works built on other composers' music,
such as his cadenza for the first movement of Mozart's D minor
Concerto (Ex. 2). In the opening of the cadenza, Beethoven uses
a low E-flat major chord, followed by a bass descent to D-flat
beneath an augmented sixth chord, to establish himself deliberately, as if to say, "This is now Beethoven speaking!" The dual

Ex. 2 Cadenza for Mozart, Concerto in D minor, K. 466, 1st Mvt., mm. 1–7.

assertions of individuality—the composition's and the composer's own—always coexist peacefully without distorting the
deeper human purpose of Beethoven's music.

Thematic Invention

For the past hundred years, textbooks and college courses have
repeated the stock phrase that musical material has no value in
itself, that, aesthetically, the only thing that matters is what the
composer does with it. At times, all the Classical composers used
those more-or-less trite motives that, as Paul Henry Lang has
said, "were in the public domain" (compare the opening of
Mozart's C minor Sonata, K. 457, with that of Beethoven's op.
10, no. 1). But for Beethoven, certainly more than for Haydn
and Mozart, the musical material *does* matter; part of Beethoven's
genius lay precisely in his ability to invent the exact motive that
would hold a composition together and give it its unique identity. It would have been unthinkable for him to do what Mozart
did in the Finale of the String Quintet in D major, K. 593: to
change the main motive after the piece was finished by substitut-
ing a "criss-cross" scale for a straight chromatic scale (Exx. 3a,
b).[5] Since Beethoven's Fifth Symphony is often used to advance

Mozart, String Quintet in D major, K. 593, 4th Mvt., m. 1.

Ex. 3a   original version   Ex. 3b   final version

the argument that thematic content is nothing and development
is all, let us substitute the lower semitone for the second of the
three tones in the first upbeat, wherever this motive occurs (Ex.
4). Even without changing anything else in the movement, the
music becomes ridiculous! It is precisely because Beethoven understood the importance of the thematic substance for his oeuvre,
and was aware that the individualization of a new work takes
time and effort, that he was constantly making sketches. Most of

Ex. 4   Symphony No. 5 in C minor, 1st Mvt., theme with alteration.

them did indeed serve to shape the ideal principal motive, hence the miracles of the opening measures of the first movement of the B-flat major Sonata, op. 22 (Ex. 5); the Finale of the D major Sonata, op. 10, no. 3 (Ex. 6),* or the first movement of the Cello Sonata in D major, op. 102, no. 2 (Ex. 7). Thus the performer must concentrate at the very outset on achieving an immediate, delicate, and thorough presentation of the piece's musical essence—something quite unnecessary in a Haydn or Mozart sonata.

Ex. 5 Sonata in B-flat major, op. 22,   Ex. 6 Sonata in D major, op. 10,
1st Mvt., m. 1.   no. 3, 4th Mvt., m. 1.

Ex. 7 Cello Sonata in D major, op. 102, no. 2, 1st Mvt., mm. 1–3.

Conversely, Beethoven occasionally dramatized the search for the main motive by starting vaguely or, rather, pretending to start vaguely, improvising, and letting the listener participate in the process of concretization (see below, p. 126).

The "Three Styles"

Beethoven's three styles were established by Wilhelm von Lenz[6] not very long after the composer's death. In 1912, Paul Bekker[7] corrected Lenz's divisions with his discovery of a fourth style centering on the late quartets (and, in the piano music, on the *Diabelli* Variations and the last Bagatelles). Some writers have denied the validity of Lenz's categories, but at least in terms of attitude there does exist a marked difference between the early, the middle, and the late and very last epochs.

In the early style, Beethoven cultivated the image of a pugnacious revolutionary by making certain deliberate changes in tradition. For instance, he was the first composer of distinction to write classical sonatas (op. 2) and piano trios (op. 1) in four

---

*Note the opposing directions here, as in op. 14 no. 2!

movements instead of three. He also utilized his vibrant energy, which had made him famous as a pianist, to establish a deliberate extroversion.

After that, the spirit of the times—the French Revolution and the Napoleonic wars—moved Beethoven toward Handelian attitudes in his middle period. He sent out messages of encouragement and spiritual strength, as well as promises of a forthcoming liberation, to the common men of all lands, through pieces like the Third and Fifth symphonies, the *Egmont* music, the big "titled" piano sonatas, and, most of all, *Fidelio.* After 1814, when Beethoven was almost completely deaf and was to get increasingly lonely and politically isolated under the reactionary Metternich regime, he finally sought religious expression in pure music. He explored musical depths of unprecedented emotional communicativeness, with such big textures, harmonies, and deviations of form that it will take several more generations of musicians and music lovers to understand and enjoy them fully.* In this respect, these works can be compared to the second part of Goethe's *Faust,* which was written at exactly the same time but which Beethoven never saw. Whereas Goethe created from a serene and optimistic state of mind, Beethoven was moved by the urge to overcome tragedy and despair. Evidence of Beethoven's spiritual strength is that in total effect his late oeuvre is even more positive than Goethe's.[9]

II. "TWO PRINCIPLES"

In a series of conversation book entries, now proven to have been forgeries,[10] Anton Schindler attributed two extremely significant comments on the early sonatas to Beethoven. The first refers to the Sonata *pathétique,* op. 13: "*Two principles* [italics mine] also in the middle movement of the *Pathétique.* Thousands do not grasp this."[11]** The second stems from the following (forged) entry: "Do you remember when I was permitted a few

---

*Carl Dahlhaus,[8] states that Beethoven uses more singable types of themes in his late works than in the earlier ones, but does not ask why. In my opinion it was the urge toward religious expression that compelled him to change his melodic style.

**August Halm,[12] one of the greatest musical thinkers of the early twentieth century in Germany, unjustly forgotten until recently ("schmählich vergessen," according to Adorno[13]), was probably the first to draw attention to this remark.

years ago to play the Sonatas, op. 14, for you?—now everything clear.'' This remark must be taken together with a conversation—also probably apocryphal—between Beethoven and Schindler on these two sonatas, which was supposed to have taken place in 1823 and which Schindler reported in the first edition of his biography of Beethoven (1840).[14]* According to Schindler this is how Beethoven analyzed these sonatas:

First of all he declared that when he wrote the Sonatas, op. 14, about 24 years earlier, the spirit of the times was more poetic than it was "now" [1823]. In the earlier period listeners "automatically recognized in the two sonatas, op. 14, a struggle between two principles, or a dialogue between two persons because that was quite obvious." The two principles are described as "pleading" and "resisting." "In the second sonata, this dialogue, as well as its significance, is expressed more tersely, and the opposition of the two voices (the two principles) is even more noticeable than in the first sonata. Right from the beginning, the opposition of the two is evident in the contrary motion [Ex. 8]; at the end of the exposition the two voices (or principles) come somewhat closer together, and their mutual understanding can be felt in the cadence of the dominant immediately following. Unfortunately, right after this, the struggle begins again.''**

It is not an overstatement to say that these remarks are a key to the understanding of all of Beethoven's music, at least his piano music, and not just of op. 14. Indeed, their substance is so

Ex. 8   Sonata in G major, op. 14, no. 2, 1st Mvt., m. 1.

---

*This report was ignored and finally forgotten because Beethoven's first German biographer, Adolf Bernhard Marx, objected to it.[15] (His objections will be discussed below.) In recent history only William S. Newman has even mentioned it.[16] Even though this exchange probably did not take place in this form, there is much inner truth to it. As Peter Stadlen has stated,[17] the fact that so many of Schindler's reports proved to have been put in later by Schindler himself, to give his statements the ring of authenticity, does not necessarily mean that their musical substance is inaccurate. In this instance, it is most likely that at some time or other Beethoven said exactly what Schindler attributed to him.

**Schindler is quoted by Marx[18] up to this point. What follows—about the development and about the third movement—smacks more of Schindler than of Beethoven.

elementary that, like Dr. Watson, we fail to comprehend how we could have missed this clue. Beethoven analyses in biographies, liner notes, textbooks on form, etc., have all missed it, to our everlasting shame. The meaning of the remarks is valid even if it turns out that the conversation was entirely spurious.

To the unbiased observer, this entire statement, as attributed to Beethoven, makes good musical sense. From the very start, and in the most obvious manner, right hand and left hand are brought into rhythmic and melodic opposition. *Rhythmically:* until m. 8, the left hand is deliberately and ingeniously prevented from playing on the downbeat and, from m. 5 on, on the second beat as well, so that the right hand plays most of its melody unaccompanied, and the establishment of a tangible beat is postponed until m. 8. The same technique is applied not only to the second theme (Ex. 9) but also, with modifications, to the main theme of the Finale. The squarely established beat of the theme of the second movement, therefore, is probably meant to serve as a contrast. *Melodically:* the beginning of the first theme is an embellished descending G major triad in the right hand; its answer in the left hand is an unadorned ascending G major triad. In the second theme, the left hand (mm. 26–27) ascends by three octaves; then the right hand, unaccompanied, descends in step-wise motion. At the end of the exposition (Ex. 10), the alternation of right- and left-hand melodies resumes, but the directions

Ex. 9   Sonata in G major, op. 14, no. 2, 1st Mvt., mm. 26–28.

Ex. 10   Sonata in G major, op. 14, no. 2, 1st Mvt., mm. 47–50.

are now complementary rather than antagonistic, so that a "truce" seems to be expressed, in conformity with Beethoven's remarks.

Perhaps the clearest and most specific utterance by Beethoven is his description of the one side as "pleading" (obviously the right-hand opening), the other as "resisting" (which challenges the performer to convey this character without unduly emphasizing the left hand). Marx did not understand this because he thought in the academic categories of melody and counterpoint. To him, the left-hand motive could not be a resisting principle—or any principle—because it was just an accompaniment. The second theme, he explained, could not embody a struggle between *two* principles because the right hand, starting in m. 26, plays in parallel thirds, and thus there exist not two but three voices in all! Marx did not see—did not want to see—that when Beethoven thus expressed himself he was referring to melodic directions and rhythmic functions, not to independent voices as in a fugue. Characteristically, Beethoven himself spoke only of "opposing motions." It is illuminating to study what poor imagery Marx—and unfortunately many, many later writers—put in the place of Beethoven's precise and sober analysis of the main motives. The first movement, according to Marx, is

a pure picture of tenderness and grace, lightly and naively drawn as though by the hand of a girl genius. Thus, the first subject walks along in light motion, like a plea [!] fleetingly expressed in caressing flattery—certain that it will be impossible to resist [!] the plea. And the sweet child approaches with such eloquent speech (second subject) that one can almost hear the actual words, as in a delicate scene from Paisiello in Rossini's time.

That similar descriptions of the movement can still be read in responsible publications of our own time is due to Schindler;[19] when he amended his report in the third edition of his biography of Beethoven, Schindler, no hero, endorsed Marx's comments as "undoubtedly valid." True, he did correctly state that Beethoven simply meant two opposites, not "predominant voices," as Marx had understood it. Nevertheless, his retraction killed the report, which, to my knowledge, is revived here for the first time.

After using this compositional technique in the Sonatas, op. 14, Beethoven permanently adopted opposite directions between the top and bottom of the musical texture as a structural principle. Now the listener would be aware of a basic construction, where heretofore he had only been able to feel a vague excitement while academically tracing the development of motives. Here are a few characteristic examples from various periods of Beethoven's piano music:

In the first movement of the Sonata in E-flat major, op. 27, no. 1 ("quasi una fantasia"), with quiet, generally even note values in the right hand, the first melodic step descends (m. 1) and the second ascends (m. 2) back to the beginning (Ex. 11). As if hastily wanting to interrupt this quietness, quick notes in the left hand first ascend from B-flat to A-flat, then descend to E-flat (downbeat of m. 3); though the last note falls on a downbeat both times, it is so brief and unaccented that, as in op. 14, no. 2, it does not establish a settled metrical frame for the bass. Again, as in op. 14, the contrast of the two principles is directional and functional rather than motivic (although Beethoven reuses the bass motive later, particularly in mm. 3 and 4 of the Finale).

Ex. 11 Sonata in E-flat major, op. 27, no. 1, 1st Mvt., mm. 1–2.

The first movement of the Sonata in D minor, op. 31, no. 2 ("Tempest"), has been analyzed in the German literature of the early twentieth century more often than any other composition by Beethoven. Paul Bekker[20] falls victim to the Marx type of poetic imagery, though he mixes occasional bits of solid musical analysis into the descriptions. Halm, in an analysis of over 40 pages,[21] takes Bekker to task for his approach, in an attempt to get to the bottom of the "Two Principles" idea. Albert Hensel,[22] in a striking analysis based on Halm, concludes that Beethoven's two principles must have referred to the contrast of slow and fast elements. In reality, however, the type of contrast established here is, again, one of direction. The composer makes it very obvious: in the very first measure of the Allegro (Ex. 12), he has the bass go up precisely when the treble goes down, in what would have been considered rather crude counterpoint by his teacher

Haydn. The same kind of opposing directions occurs again, particularly at the end of the exposition (mm. 75–84; Ex. 13), where it is followed by a "truce" resembling the one at the corresponding place in op. 14, no. 2.

Ex. 12   Sonata in D minor, op. 31, no. 2, 1st Mvt., m. 3.

Ex. 13   Sonata in D minor, op. 31, no. 2, 1st Mvt., mm. 75–78.

In the late sonatas, the idea of two principles helps unify the sonata, transcending single movements. The opposing directions are now often successive rather than simultaneous. An example is the E major Sonata, op. 109. Its opening movement begins with a *diatonically descending bass* (Ex. 14a) beneath a freely floating melody. This bass line occurs on the off beats, as in op. 14, no. 2. The two hands play alternately, and the left hand does not have a downbeat until the third measure of the Adagio espressivo section. Directly following this alternation is a slow section with a *chromatically descending treble* from a'' to f-sharp'' (Ex. 14b),* which is subsequently repeated in a decorated variant at the upper octave (Ex. 14c).[23] The opening bass descent becomes clearer in the recapitulation (mm. 48–52) because its notes are held over so that they still sound *on* the beat.

The cyclic importance of these descending lines reveals itself in the two remaining movements.[24] The *diatonic descent* in the bass at the beginning of the second movement (Ex. 15a) is identical to that of the first movement, except that it is in the minor mode

---

*Only the g-natural is provided by the left hand at the lower octave (m. 10).

Sonata in E major, op. 109, 1st Mvt.

Ex. 14a   mm. 1–4

Ex. 14b   mm. 10–12

Ex. 14c   mm. 13–14

and played on the beat. During the middle section (which is like the trio section of a scherzo) the direction of the bass is reversed, for the first time, into a *diatonic ascent* in C major, the submediant of E minor (Ex. 15b).* In the recapitulation of the main section, the descent returns at the top in reversed counterpoint. As if fulfilling a prophecy expressed by the ascending bass of the middle section, the bass of the Finale theme, with its soothing melody, rises noticeably over an octave and a half (Ex. 15c).** However, the *chromatic descent* in the right hand first featured in mm. 10ff. and mm. 60ff. of the first movement is maintained to

Sonata in E major, op. 109

Ex. 15a   2nd Mvt., mm. 1–8.

Ex. 15b   2nd Mvt., mm. 83–90.

Ex. 15c   3rd Mvt., mm. 1–4.

---

*This kind of "floating tonality"[25] between E minor and C major is dear to Beethoven (see op. 14, no. 1, second movement: and op. 59, no. 2, Finale).

** The prophetic character of the Trio of the fast middle movement in relation to the Finale is the same here as in the Ninth Symphony.

the end, and repeated in disguises in the other movements, especially in mm. 43–46 of the Prestissimo (Ex. 16a) and mm. 9–10
(after the second ending of the first half) of Variation 4 of the
Finale (Ex. 16b). When comparing these measures in Variation 4
with the totally diatonic corresponding measures of the Finale
theme, one cannot doubt that Beethoven brought in the quotation from the first movement deliberately to recall the earlier opposing directions, even after this opposition had been overcome.

Sonata in E major, op. 109
Ex. 16a   2nd Mvt., mm. 43–46.

Ex. 16b   3rd Mvt., Var. 4, mm. 9–10.

III. SYMBOLISM

The "two principles" mean, first of all, that compositional
unity is achieved by *contrast,* instead of—as in early classicism—by a single *affect* lasting throughout an entire sonata or
symphony. But, beyond that, Beethoven's description of the
opposing directions in op. 14 makes it clear that directions
symbolize ideas. All too often we miss this implication in
Beethoven's music—an implication which he must have considered obvious—because nowadays we take basic elements of
music too much for granted.

To begin with, this is the case with certain harmonies. For
example, quite often the music alternates in quick succession between *major and minor intervals.* Twice in the first movement of
the E major Sonata, op. 14, no. 1 (Ex. 17a), following the second
subject, a melodic minor sixth (g') is replaced in the next mea-

Ex. 17a Sonata in E major, op. 14, no. 1, 1st Mvt., mm. 46–49.

sure by a major sixth (g-sharp'), with all four tones marked *sforzato*. In the first movement of the Sonata in B-flat major, op. 22 (Ex. 17b), flat and natural supertonic alternate in a quasi major/minor oscillation. At one point in the opening movement of the Sonata in G major, op. 31, no. 1 (Ex. 17c), Beethoven substitutes B major for B minor (B major had been the key of the preceding second subject) to settle all the more firmly in B minor, confirming it over and over again. Most listeners take these alternations—there are a few more instances—so much in stride that they play and listen to them mechanically, oblivious to their symbolism. Yet, in *Fidelio,* where a similar exchange of different melodic sixths occurs (Trio no. 5; Ex. 17d), the symbolism is unambiguous, since the *minor* sixths are sung to the words "bitt're Thränen" (bitter tears) and the *major* sixths are sung to "süsse Thränen" (sweet tears)!

Beethoven is supposed to have said that the diminished-seventh chord always engendered fear and trembling in him

Ex. 17b Sonata in B-flat major, op. 22, no. 1, 1st Mvt., mm. 59–62.

Ex. 17c Sonata in G major, op. 31, no. 1, 1st Mvt., mm. 98–108.

Ex. 17d *Fidelio,* Trio, no. 5, Allegro molto, mm. 64–71.

whenever he heard it. One may doubt whether this statement is
authentic, for he is also alleged to have said, "One does not talk
about religion and harmony [*Generalbass*]." At any rate, the
diminished-seventh chord, according to Bekker, in reference to
the opening of the Sonata in C minor, op. 111, is "the most
poignant dissonance in Beethoven's vocabulary."[26] Although the
term "dissonance" is technically correct, the sensitivity of the listener to the dissonant quality of this chord has decreased almost
to the zero point, making it hard to feel it in passages like the
opening of op. 111 and the *Pathétique* Sonata, op. 13,* or the third
measure of the *Appassionata* Sonata, op. 57. However, if the
listener-performer will focus again on the emotional impact of
these diminished-seventh chords, their effect can be as shattering
as in Beethoven's time, and their almost motivic function in the
Pathétique Sonata** can again become obvious.

The best-known rhythmic pattern used symbolically is the dotted rhythm which Beethoven applied to marchlike movements in
order to express heroic convictions and impulses. In addition to
the obvious examples, such as the second movement of the A
major Sonata, op. 101, these rhythms are found in such unexpected places as mm. 27–29 of the first movement of the *Appassionata* Sonata, op. 57, and the opening measures of the slow
movement of the *Waldstein* Sonata, op. 53, where, in 6/8 time, the
features of a military rhythm are combined with the motion of a
slow solemn march. The character of a slow march is more recognizable in the main theme of the middle movement of the *Emperor* Concerto, op. 73, especially when one consults Beethoven's
sketches for it. Unfortunately, this piece is but rarely performed
in a way that allows its heroic nature to emerge.

Not only single chords and chord progressions, but entire sections of movements, movements in their totality, and whole
multi-movement works become symbols of Beethoven's poetic
ideas. In most cases, verbal explanations are not available; yet it is
important to understand that, although it is absolute music,
Beethoven's music was written to express concrete poetic ideas.
For instance, in March 1827 (the last month of his life), Beethoven is alleged to have had a conversation with Schindler in which
he must have mentioned Euripides' *Medea* (apparently as an in-

*The pianist Richard Goode states that at the age of six "I felt the vibrations of these
chords throughout my whole body. I was thrilled, frightened, fascinated."[27]
**See the slow movement, mm. 48–49, and the Finale, m. 5.

spiration for the *Archduke* Trio), for Schindler answered, "but Euripides' *Medea* is no longer present to my mind."[28] Later in the same conversation Schindler proposed his own conception of the basic "story" of the *Archduke* Trio. But there is no reason to assume that Beethoven agreed with Schindler's interpretation. On the contrary, Schindler wrote, "I am most curious about the characterization [obviously Beethoven's own] in the B-flat Trio." It may be recalled that the Trio was written thirteen years earlier!

The opposition of ascending and descending melodic lines, discussed above, is typical of the kind of symbols Beethoven used in his piano works. It is not a technique of shaped leitmotifs or musically elaborate structures—comparable to the motives used by Beethoven in the same compositions with such skill and finesse—but a primitive device that appeals to the subconscious of even the uneducated music lover, historically unrelated, I think, to the "anabasis" and "katabasis" of musical rhetoric.

Other symbols frequently seen in Beethoven's piano works are the opposition of registers, polyphonic writing, the contrast of major and minor, and the counterplay of scalar and arpeggio motives:

The *opposition of extemely low and high registers* is a device Beethoven used especially on the piano, where these registers naturally blend. He may have derived this idea from Mozart's extraordinarily low and high tessituras for Sarastro and the Queen of the Night respectively, symbolizing their antithetical ethical stands. Characteristic examples are found in the slow variations of Beethoven's so called *Eroica Variations*, op. 35 (for example, Variation 15; Ex. 18a*), and in the second subject of the opening movement of the Sonata in C minor, op. 111 (Ex. 18b). The significance of this opposition varies, but, as in

Ex. 18a *Eroica* Variations, op. 35, Var. 15, m. 22.

Ex. 18b Sonata in C minor, op. 111, 1st Mvt., mm. 48–50.

*The downbeat staccato makes a sound gap between low and high necessary. Similar cases (usually played incorrectly) are found in the *Pathétique* Sonata, first movement, last measure of the last Grave; and *Waldstein* Sonata, second movement, mm. 8 and 16. The left hand and the pedal have to be off in these places before the right hand plays.

Mozart, it indicates a special intensity of the spirit, something outside the field of normal lyrical or dramatic expression.

In his late works, Beethoven sometimes used *polyphonic writing* to symbolize conflict and turmoil in contrast to peace of mind and equanimity. The best example is found in the Finale of the Sonata in A major, op. 101, where a cheerfully energetic, contredanse-like Allegro is suddenly interrupted by a colossal fugato in the minor mode. This never fails to confuse and upset listeners—which is just what Beethoven planned, I think.

Like everyone else at the time, Beethoven used *major and minor modes* for the expression of positive and negative moods, as already stated. But he used them more abstractly and deliberately than did most composers. In several cases, he programmatically combined major mode and ascending line, as well as minor mode and descending line. The opening movement of the *Appassionata* Sonata, op. 57, has a descending F minor arpeggio as its first subject and an ascending A-flat major arpeggio as its second (Ex. 19a). The first of the two movements of the Sonata in E minor, op. 90, begins with three descending tones (g′–f-sharp′–e′) of the E minor scale; the second movement begins with the same three tones, but in E major and ascending (Ex. 19b).

Ex. 19a Sonata in F minor, op. 57, 1st Mvt.   Ex. 19b Sonata in E major, op. 90
1st subject   2nd subject (m. 36) 1st Mvt., m. 1.   2nd Mvt., m. 1.

In some bigger works, it is possible that Beethoven also used *scale motives* in the first movement and *arpeggio motives* in the last to symbolize the progression from tight, closed music to open and inviting music. The Violin Concerto, op. 61, is the prototype of this kind of structure. A similar purpose may have been the basis of the themes of the *Emperor* Concerto in E-flat major, op. 73, and for the earlier G major Concerto, op. 58.

Some beginnings of movements reflect his mysticism, for if Beethoven does not immediately jump into the ring—as in the C major Sonata, op. 2, no. 3; the B-flat major Sonata, op. 22; the G major Sonata, op. 31, no. 1—he likes to open, as Haydn did in the *Creation*, with initial Chaos and with a vagueness that only gradually becomes crystallized into thematic substance. The D minor Sonata, op. 31, no. 2, and the *Appassionata,* op. 57, are prototypes of this extremely evocative procedure. It is interesting to note that, in his urge to validate such mystic passages in retrospect, Beethoven usually includes them in his recapitulations, where they then seem comparatively integrated and orderly.*

The statements above are made with caution. Obviously, in the absence of authentic explanations, the various symbols cannot be explained with any degree of precision or even plausibility—a consideration that earlier writers, from A.B. Marx to Edwin Fischer, tended to overlook. All we know is that, in his later years especially, Beethoven was preoccupied with moral values—with the strengthening of free will, with human dignity, and with religious humility. Almost certainly, rising pitches were meant to express the gaining of freedom. Conversely, descending pitches may have been meant to suggest the blows of fate and injustices. Beethoven's most beautiful melodies (for instance, the two E major tunes in op. 90 and op. 109) convey a sense of peace. His sharper dissonances (especially those happening during the trill that concludes the middle movement of the G major Concerto, op. 58) seem to symbolize futile struggles and despair; their power of suggestion is so strong that even in our era of dissonant music and decreased sensitivity we cannot fail to respond. What makes such dissonances musically different from those later used by Wagner in *Tristan und Isolde* is that they do not point to a triadic resolution.

All Beethoven's symbols are quite simple, in keeping with his character and upbringing. How do you suggest liberation in music? By going up in pitch. Fatality? By going down. Struggle? By dissonant writing and/or polyphony. And so forth. One is reminded of the signs in the Chinese I Ching and their manifold, yet simple, translations into concrete applications. As a person, Beethoven was equally direct. He himself mentioned his "unbuttoned" moods, and some of his visitors described him as totally uninhibited (*ungebändigt* was Goethe's word for him), almost primitive, despite his being exceptionally well-read in poetry, philosophy, and religion. Beethoven's reading resulted entirely

---

*A curious example of this inclusive type of recapitulation can be found in mm. 287–94 of the Finale of the *Waldstein* Sonata, op. 53, where mm. 23–25 of the slow movement are recalled in the same mysterious *pianissimo.*

from his own efforts, not from a well-rounded childhood education, such as most of his fellow musicians had had.[29]

Beethoven's musical symbols were communications from person to person. They were meant to ignite a "divine spark" in the listener but certainly not to move anyone to tears (as Beethoven steadfastly emphasized). If we are now too over-educated, numb, or shallow to react to Beethoven's symbolic language intuitively, it is our own fault. But perhaps it is possible to resensitize ourselves to his language. Never was there an artist of any kind who more closely united the personal and the universally human, who could jump more directly from the individual level to transcendental awareness.

Certain other symbols are less important and are conjectural; for instance, the waving good-bye which seems to animate so many coda sections, from the Finale of the Sonata in E-flat major, op. 7, and the Sonata in G major, op. 14, no. 2, to the last Sonata, op. 111.

IV. VIBRATION

What I tentatively call the *vibration* in Beethoven's music, especially the piano works, is the physical counterpart of his symbols. At the very beginning of many of his piano compositions Beethoven creates a regular tremor of the strings of the keyboard instrument. Such an intention is undeniable in the D major Sonata, op. 28, and the *Waldstein* Sonata in C major, op. 53. The repeated quarter notes in the first measure of the D major Sonata (Ex. 20) are neither a rhythmic head motive nor a fixation of tonality. Nowhere are these notes further developed—as a motive would be—and the tonality of D major is briefly questioned in the very next measure, where c-natural in the treble disrupts the D major scale.* On the other hand, they provide more than a

Ex. 20 Sonata in D major, op. 28,
1st Mvt., mm. 1–2.

---

*Harmonically, this is in the best tradition; cf. the opening of Bach's C major Prelude, *WTC*, Bk. II, and the opening of Mozart's Sonata in F major, K. 332.

simple rhythmic pattern by which to establish a beat. (They do
establish it, but that is not all. Why is it necessary to give the beat
in advance of the melody?) By isolating the bass, Beethoven
creates a vibration of the instrument of such communicative
power that it will stay in the listener's mind throughout the
entire movement, just as if the vibrating basses were continued
from beginning to end. The physical impact of this opening
proves how much Beethoven lived with the sound of the piano,
regardless of the specific kind of piano he used. The reverberat-
ing sound of the low D brings the piano to life in its pulsating
sounding board.* By playing these bass tones one becomes as
much a part of the instrument as by striking a gong; it feels almost as if the vibration were passing through the pianist's torso
down to his feet. I am convinced that the intense effect of
Beethoven's piano music on the listener—an effect recognized by
everyone since Beethoven's time, but never quite explained—is
caused, in considerable part, by this ongoing vibration, which
creates spiritual excitement at the same time as bodily involvement.

A more complex situation arises in the opening movement of
the *Waldstein* Sonata. Beginning with the decorated repetition of
the second subject, the vibrating eighth notes of the beginning
(Ex. 21) are temporarily replaced by eighth-note triplets (Ex. 22).
However, the initial vibrations, doubly exciting because of their
low register and low dynamic level, are so strong that the triplets
are heard as a polyrhythmic counterpoint to the inwardly con-

Ex. 21   Sonata in C major, op. 53, 1st Mvt., mm. 1–2.

Ex. 22   Sonata in C major, op. 53, 1st Mvt., m. 42.

---

*When I am asked to help select a piano, I often use the beginning of this sonata to find
out if the instrument is capable of a lively vibration across the board.

tinuing regular eighth notes.* As an unobtrusive link between
the two types of beat subdivision, Beethoven reuses the bass syncopation from m. 11 (Ex. 23), with its strong accent, in mm.
50–53 (Ex. 24).** August Halm is very critical of this passage.[30]

Ex. 23   Sonata in C major, op. 53, 1st Mvt., m. 11.

Ex. 24   Sonata in C major, op. 53, 1st Mvt., mm. 50–53. (Original written in C major with accidentals.)

He says it leads nowhere; apparently he is not aware of its function in establishing a common denominator between the two
subrhythms. Nor does Halm realize the motivic justification of
the syncopation motive, which returns once more at the very end
of the movement (Ex. 26) to stop the music just before the three
final chords. It does not bother Beethoven a bit that, as two-part
writing, mm. 50–53 are such poor music that in Bach's and even
in Haydn's time a music student would have been thrown out for
writing them! They are nothing but broken chords in one hand
and repeated tones as syncopation in the other; nothing but an
unending alternation of tonic and dominant. Yet, in the context
of the piece, just as the triplet motion is going to be retransformed into eighth notes, they make perfect sense. They are a

---

*The situation is different in this respect from the opening movement of the Violin
Concerto, where, though triplets appear at the same place in the first movement, they are
unopposed by the memory of any preceding eighth notes.

**In m. 11, the syncopated bass *sforzato* serves as a preparation for the *Magic Flute*
quotation, which begins in the following measure (Ex. 25a). This quotation should be as
obvious to the listener as that which Beethoven identified in Variation 22 of the *Diabelli*
Variations. It refers to the dramatic moment in the first Finale, in which Tamino, approaching the temples, is confronted by the exclamation "Zurück!" by the priests (Ex.
25b).

Ex. 25a Sonata in C major, op. 53, 1st Mvt.
mm. 12–13   mm. 167–68

Ex. 25b Mozart, *Magic Flute,* 1st Act, Finale, *Allegro assai,* mm. 13–15.

Ex. 26 Sonata in C major, op. 53, 1st Mvt., m. 300.

shining example of Beethoven's priorities. What mattered to him first and foremost was vibration becoming motion; to produce interesting musical detail ranked second.

Vibration, though a favorite structural device, is by no means used constantly. The first movement of the A-flat major Sonata, op. 110, for instance, has a steady beat but nothing in the nature of a vibration; neither does the Adagio of the Sonata in F minor, op. 2, no. 1. In other cases, the vibration is there, although not always immediately apparent, and comes to the attention of the listener or student gradually. For example, in the *Archduke* Trio, op. 97, the quietly undulating figure in the left hand at the beginning (Ex. 27a) resumes during the presentation of the second subject in G major (Ex. 27b); its quasi-pastoral nature resembles

Trio in B-flat major, op 97, 1st Mvt.
Ex. 27a mm. 1–2
Allegro moderato   Ex. 27b m. 60

the rhythms of the slow movement of the Sixth Symphony. (See below, chap. 5, Schubert, p. 169.) In the first movement of the *Appassionata* Sonata, op. 57, the vibration, consisting of repeats of low C, appears only at the recapitulation; yet it has the retroactive effect of illuminating not only the very beginning but especially the transition to the second theme. The sensitive listener will immediately be struck by the inevitability of these repeated tones.

The pulsating vibration ties the music together beyond all distinctions between contrasting motivic ideas. If this phenomenon has been overlooked, it is because of Beethoven's other skill, that of establishing and developing motives. Motivic development became the cornerstone of German musical aesthetics;* consequently the overriding structural importance of a unifying vibration was not realized. In the Fifth Symphony, where the main motive is first presented alone, theorists and biographers usually focus exclusively on its further development; they consequently overlook the fact that the same motive also serves as an ongoing vibration in iambic eighth notes ("and–two–and–one, and–two–and–one") from the bass entrance in m. 28 (Ex. 28).

Vibration, to Beethoven, is a spiritual experience; and the long trills in the late works must be understood in this light. A trill, as Artur Schnabel put it,[31] is a "vibration of the main note." The end of the E major Sonata, op. 109, is the best-known example

Ex. 28 Symphony No. 5 in C minor, 1st Mvt., mm. 28–33.

---

*In a letter to Ferdinand Hiller, dated January 24, 1836, Mendelssohn reproaches Hiller for not logically developing his symphony motives. He argues that, while the melodic inspiration for the motives is of divine origin, their development is a moral duty for the composer: "Just as I believe that a person of beautiful talents has the obligation to develop these (so that, if he turns out less well than expected, he himself is to blame), I am also convinced that the same thing applies to any piece of music." This attitude analogizes dealing with motives and dealing with money; both are to be invested sensibly and not wasted.

of this: at first (in the beginning of Variation 6) the dominant tone B (doubled two octaves above) carries the vibration in slow, bell-like beat notes. Then the speed and intensity of these repeated tones gradually increase until single tones are replaced by trills. They begin as measured trills but become unmeasured when they reach top speed. The music flies to outer space, as it were, and brings to mind Beethoven's famous quotation from the Conclusion of Kant's *Kritik der Praktischen Vernunft* of 1788: "The moral law within us, and the starry sky above us!"[32]

V. VIBRATION AND INSTRUMENTAL RHYTHM

Beethoven's vibrations constitute more than just a steady accompanying rhythm of the kind found in Schubert's songs or in the first movement of Mozart's C major String Quintet, K. 515. The distinction is subtle, and borderline cases are not infrequent. In the *Archduke* Trio, as we saw, the accompaniment pattern also serves as a genuine vibration, because it encapsulates the essential character of the piece. The effect of a vibration may be soothing, exciting, passionate, proud, or a great many other things; a vibration may be descriptive, epic, or personal. Its attributes are impossible to verbalize completely, just as were the "affects" in the lists drawn up by Mattheson. In Beethoven's music, vibrations constitute the basic form in which instruments, as such, share in the creation of a musical atmosphere. Largely through their use, Beethoven removed the music from everyday expressions of joy and sorrow, providing the specific sound quality—at once tranquil and intense—through which the listener might enter the Beethovenian world of the spirit.

In the strictly musical domain, vibrations are possible partly because of Beethoven's *melodic rhythms*. In nature, all vibrations happen in even time intervals, though these intervals are sometimes too rapid to be consciously perceived. The beats of sound waves, the trembling of a sounding board, and similar happenings combine animation with tranquility of an even and (in theory, at least) unending motion. The vibrato of the human voice, of a violin string, etc.—wanted or not—also belongs to the natural vibrations. These are the vibrations which the genius of Beethoven succeeded in conveying in his piano music. He

sometimes used "man-made imitations," like trills and tone repeats, and sometimes enlisted the support of actual vibrations
engendered by the sonorous playing of bass notes or by the
pedal. Beethoven's vibration rhythms are totally different from
speech rhythms, which are the product of musical declamation in
speech and song. Speech rhythms are found in all of Bach's and
Mozart's works, including their instrumental pieces, since both
men were primarily vocal composers. This means that even in
piano music the minimal inflections of timing and shading, of
pausing and starting, of grouping of syllables and separating of
sentences—nuances too fine to be notated—are subconsciously
derived from language, that is, from Western languages.*

Beethoven is different. Eloquent as his music is in expressing
ideas and feelings, it does not actually "speak." Bach's and
Mozart's speech rhythms, because they are mathematically irregular, are incompatible with the periodicity of vibrations as we
find them in Beethoven. His instrumental rhythms are strict in a
particular manner. Not only do they rely on the intrinsic vibrations of the instrument—of the piano especially—more than any
vocal or string music could ever rely on the natural vibrato, but,
in essence, they are *evenly timed.* Beethoven's dislike of odd
shapes brings to mind Hercule Poirot of the Agatha Christie
stories. Beethoven made several attempts, for instance, to do
away with seven-tone scales, either by eliminating the second
scale tone (as in the A major Sonata, op. 2, no. 2, first movement, m. 32, and the first Allegro of the Piano Quintet in E-flat
major, op. 16, mm. 131f.), or by adding an eighth tone between
the fourth and fifth tones (as in the C major Concerto, op. 15, m.
162, and in the G major Rondo, op. 51, m. 9), putting the fifth
tone squarely on strong beats every time.

If vibration rhythms are not identical with accompaniment patterns, neither are they in any way *dance rhythms.* On the contrary,
they *de-*emphasize the metrical accents and the rhythmic motives
characterizing Beethoven's dance tunes. (See the contredanses in
the G major Sonata, op. 31, no. 1, first movement, second subject, and in the A major Sonata, op. 101, Finale, mm. 99ff., and
the waltz in *Diabelli* Variation 25.)

---

*This can be a handicap for Oriental musicians, if they are unfamiliar with the cadence
of Western languages.

One can understand Beethoven's delight when the metronome was invented. It was not only a means of securing a particular tempo. The possibility of repeating sounds at strict time intervals was the fulfillment of a wish for Beethoven, as shown by his Maelzel canon, which he subsequently transformed into the second movement of the Eighth Symphony.*

Thus, Beethoven's way of writing is worlds apart from Mozart's vocal style. It is more natural to sing a Mozart melody than to play it (one of the difficulties in his piano music!), but it is more natural to play a Beethoven melody than to sing it, because it is not built on language rhythms. This accounts for the trouble that singers have even with Beethoven's simplest tunes. Significantly, the "Ode to Joy" is introduced by the orchestra before it is sung. Beethoven specifically scored the instrumental recitation so that it would be played "in strict time"[33] and put that request in the score at m. 9.

In his early years, Beethoven developed these instrumental rhythms, which were his principal addition to the classical style of Haydn and Mozart, but he apparently never made an effort toward a vocal style of his own. Later, for instance in the recitatives of the *Tempest* Sonata, op. 31, no. 2, he seems to have been struggling for vocal declamation. But did he succeed? These recitatives are still conceived in a fixed meter and must be played thus (*semplice*), despite some hesitations and ritards.** In the introduction to the Finale of the A-flat major Sonata, op. 110, Beethoven tried even harder to achieve a real rubato, hence the name *Recitativo* and the frequently changing tempo markings for these measures. But this passage is very different from a genuine vocal recitative in a Mozart *opera seria*. The first measure of the recitative (Ex. 29), in which the beat is the eighth note, naturally divides itself into 2 + 8 + 4 = 14 beats, in a slightly changing—first slackening, then quickening—elastic beat. The

---

*This transformation is a musical reality despite Schindler's forgery mentioned in n. 10.

**The second recitative is preceded by a fermata. The first is not, and there is no *pianissimo* marking near it, as there is in the second. It is hard to see how the recitatives can be played *espressivo* if they are nothing but a whisper. One ought to begin the first recitative strictly in time, in a full *piano* (not *pianissimo*) dynamic. The second recitative, since it begins later because of the fermata, is manifestly intended to be weaker. It seems therefore appropriate to continue the *pianissimo* prescribed for the two preceding Largo measures. But even here, the expression must be more than a faint echo, except that at the very end the music disappears.

Ex. 29   Sonata in A-flat major, op 110, 3rd Mvt., m. 4.

continuation, as can be seen from the notation of the left hand, is exactly twice as long and consists of 14 beats of a quarter note each (8 + 5 + 1), ending in the middle of m. 7, just before the vibration leading to the *Arioso dolente* begins.*

Beethoven's reliance on even, vibrationlike reiterations is of great importance in performing, for it transforms playing in strict time from a mechanical accuracy into an interpretive goal. Just imagine playing the opening of the *Waldstein* Sonata (see Ex. 21), or the last few measures before the repeat sign in the second movement of the E-flat major Sonata, op. 31, no. 3 (Ex. 30), in an elastic, approximate rhythm! The slow triplets of the first movement of the *Moonlight* Sonata, op. 27, no. 2, also belong to this category. In practically all of Beethoven's early works and in many of his later ones, the perfectly even timing of each note is an important part of the interpretation itself, especially of the melodic line. It is not enough to establish a solid beat through basses and accompanying broken chords. The instrumental rhythm is centered in the details and small values of the melodic line itself.

Ex. 30   Sonata in E-flat major, op. 31, no. 3, 2nd Mvt., mm. 58–59.

---

*The subdivisions of the right hand in m. 5 must be timed so that the two whole notes in the left hand have exactly the same length. As in the first three variations in op. 111, Beethoven was more concerned with the big than with the small time divisions. For details of the right hand, see the facsimile of Beethoven's two autographs in the Schenker analysis of op. 110[34] and the footnote in the Schnabel edition of the sonata. The rising octave a'–a" in the beginning of m. 5 is an imitation of the f-flat'–f-flat" on the second beat of m. 3. Whatever its notation, it is not meant to sound like an appoggiatura.[35]

It is precisely in this respect that Beethoven took an unprecedented leap. Because of the vocal origin of melody, Italian Baroque string melodies, French keyboard music, and even the compositions of Mozart and Haydn were not conceived with the top voices as part of the overall metrical framework, especially in slow pieces. It was the duty of the accompanist to keep the soloist in line, as Leopold Mozart expressly stated. When Mozart's melodies are played without accompaniment the count is hardly ever clear; Beethoven's, however, are different. An unaccompanied opening of the entire main theme, such as occurs in Beethoven's A major Cello Sonata, op. 69 (Ex. 31), far exceeds

Ex. 31 Cello Sonata in A major, op. 69, 1st Mvt., mm. 1–6.

Mozart's style, whose longest unaccompanied opening was the first two beats of the D major String Quintet, K. 593.* Although the opening melody of the Adagio of Beethoven's first Piano Sonata, op. 2, no. 1, in F minor (Ex. 32), has no accompaniment

Ex. 32 Sonata in F minor, op. 2, no. 1, 2nd Mvt., m. 1.

for the duration of the first upbeat, the beat is totally clear. It is instructive to compare this opening with the beginning of the first Allegro in Mozart's B-flat major Sonata, K. 333, where, because of the quick tempo, the beat ought to be even easier to grasp. But that is not the case. Although the melody is accompanied immediately after the first downbeat, Mozart fails to give the ear a clue as to where that downbeat is.** Beethoven may have relied on melodic beats because he did not have a real

---

*Beethoven's opening, in the second part, is derived from that of Haydn's Quartet in G major, op. 76, no. 1. One may consider Haydn as Beethoven's forerunner, although he did not go the whole way. Mozart's E-flat Quartet, K. 428, has a tutti opening.

**When Beethoven did the same in the G major Sonata, op. 14, no. 2 (see above, p. 117), he meant to create a situation that was exceptional for him, for a poetic purpose.

rubato.* In the rare instances in which Beethoven put explanatory words to an instrumental phrase—in his piano music this only happened once, in the beginning of the E-flat major Sonata, op. 81a—they are given in strict time, subject to a time signature.

The requirement of playing strictly in time becomes a challenge in passagework, particularly during the first movements of Beethoven's piano concertos. These brilliant passages at the ends of expositions and recapitulations are to be treated differently from Mozart's. The latter were fashioned after coloratura virtuosity, and therefore their timing depends on flexibility of articulation and breathing. Also, in true Baroque tradition, their structure is iambic. As a result, when the music is in 4/4 time, in the best Mozart style, the third beat might sometimes be played a little early, since the whole phrase tends to reach toward the next downbeat. Not so in Beethoven. The slightest anticipation of the third beat would interfere with the continuing rhythmic vibration of the whole piece. Each measure is split exactly in half. This applies, for instance, to the uninterrupted sixteenth-note passages in the opening movements of the First and Third concertos, and to Beethoven's *perpetuum mobile* movements, such as the finales of the G major Violin Sonata, op. 30, no. 3, and of the piano sonatas in F major, op. 10, no. 2, and op. 54. The more excited the music gets the more its vibrating pulse must be protected by the performer, who has to create excitement precisely by *resisting* the temptation to accelerate in the middle of the measure. It is therefore sound practice to play third beats as late as possible and to reach the next measure from there.** Beethoven's pupil Ferd-

---

*In this respect, Beethoven is the true predecessor of Liszt. It was probably because, as a pianist, Liszt did not match Chopin's natural rubato that he wrote so much about it. This may, in part, be explained historically. Unlike Chopin, Liszt was never fully exposed to Baroque performance practice, since Czerny was his teacher during his most sensitive boyhood years. Liszt thus resembles Beethoven, whose main teacher had been Neefe, a classicist Mannheim composer.

**Curiously, the same principle is helpful in playing Beethoven's rhythmic motives, in which several sixteenth notes (usually four) are followed by a longer note on the next beat. The four sixteenths here are like a microcosm (in quadruple diminution) of the four beats in concerto passages. Again, by making a new start on the third sixteenth (as the concerto passages do on the third beat), the rhythmic clarity of the entire motive is secured, as the entire group of four notes is thus propelled into the next metric unit. This works for the openings of the C major Sonata, op. 2, no. 3 (Ex. 33a); the B-flat major Sonata, op. 22 (Ex. 5); the A major Violin Sonata, op. 30, no. 1 (the last two tones of m.

inand Ries reported that Beethoven himself went even further: "Now and then he would hold the tempo back during a crescendo, creating a crescendo with ritardando, which had a beautiful and most striking effect."[36] This practice is analogous to the emphasis Beethoven put on single notes. They are usually marked *sf*, and, according to Schindler,[37] they may be held longer than their notated value even in the absence of a fermata sign. (See below, p. 151.)

VI. HARMONIC LANGUAGE

The establishment of autonomous instrumental rhythms also influenced Beethoven's harmonic style, mostly by restricting it. One can learn from his music how much harder it is to avoid monotony when using a limited number of harmonic progressions than to create a superficial interest by employing plentiful and colorful chord combinations. In the many phrases in which Beethoven operates exclusively with dominant-seventh chords and their resolutions, one is never even aware of any limitation of the harmonic vocabulary unless one happens to analyze the passage for statistical purposes. The first phrase of the C major Sonata, op. 2, no. 3, has such alternations throughout its first six measures. All the Beethoven sonatas, including the late ones, abound with examples of this kind. Yet, Beethoven's economy is usually richer than most other composers' variety. Even when he does go into the subdominant, Beethoven often proceeds with an analogous sequence, by first adding a flat seventh to the tonic chord. (See the A-flat major Sonata, op. 110,

Ex. 33a Sonata in C major, op. 2, no. 3, 1st Mvt., m. 1.

Ex. 33b Violin Sonata in A major, op. 30, no. 1, 1st Mvt.. m. 1.

---

1 leading into m. 2; Ex. 33b); and the D major Cello Sonata, op. 102, no. 2 (Ex. 7). However, this is not a general performance rule; it pertains to Beethoven's music in particular. For instance, it would distort the music if it were applied to the Finale of Schubert's B-flat major Sonata, op. posth., m. 9 (and many places later in the same movement).

first movement, m. 9, where he adds a G-flat to the bass before using the first inversion of a D-flat major chord.)

In the alternation of tonic and dominant, the fifth step of the scale is often featured as the common denominator of the two chords. When this tone is found in a middle register, as in the second half of the variation theme of the *Archduke* Trio, third movement, or in mm. 76ff. of the D major Sonata, op. 10, no. 3 (where the accent marks refer specifically to this tone*), the gravity of sound must be right there (that is, with A in the *Archduke* Trio example). In his later years, this emphasis on the fifth step of the scale as a "harmonic connection" sometimes enabled Beethoven to omit the dominant chord altogether in normal cadences and let the tonic 6–4 be followed directly by the same chord in root position. There is no better example of this practice than the very end of the last sonata (C minor, op. 111).**

Beethoven generally did not share Bach's and Mozart's love of startling dissonances and abrupt modulations. His dissonances, as well as his enharmonic changes (for example, in the beginning of the development of the first movement of the *Pathétique* Sonata) are structurally justified. For instance, he copies Mozart's introduction of a poignant dissonance at the end of the middle section of the slow movement of the C major Sonata, K. 330 (Ex. 34), by using chromaticism in the middle movement of his own F major Sonata, op. 10, no. 2, in the same place (m. 114, sharpening a chord previously used in m. 90; Ex. 35). However, Beethoven's dissonance appears tame compared to Mozart's. Another famous dissonance in the piano sonatas is meant not

Ex. 34   Mozart, Sonata in C major, K. 330, 2nd Mvt., mm. 37–39.

---

*See also the E-flat major Sonata, op. 81a, first movement, mm. 12 ff.[38]

**An early example, at a strategic juncture, is found in the first movement of the D minor Sonata, op. 31, no. 2, between the last of the three arpeggios opening the development section—an F-sharp major chord in 6–4 position—and the ensuing F-sharp minor chord, mm. 97–99.

Ex. 35 Sonata in F major, op 10, no. 2, 2nd Mvt.
mm. 89–90   mm. 113–14

only structurally but also programmatically—the tonic-dominant clash at the end of the first movement of the E-flat major Sonata (*Les Adieux*), op. 81a (Ex. 36).

Ex. 36 Sonata in E-flat major, op. 81a, 1st Mvt., mm. 231–35.

The only consistent exception to Beethoven's avoidance of harsh dissonances is his habit of anticipating the resolution of an appoggiatura by simultaneously putting it into a lower voice (this can be found in his first as well as in his last sonata!). See the Minuet of the F minor Sonata, op. 2, no. 1 (Ex. 37a), m. 4 and especially m. 8 (d-flat' together with c'!); and the first movement of the C minor Sonata, op. 111, m. 119 (c'' with b, in the same hand; Ex. 37b). Perhaps the reason for this idiosyncrasy was that Beethoven wanted to get away from the slightly effeminate character of appoggiaturas of C.P.E. Bach's time.

In the accompaniment of serene, peaceful movements, especially rondos, Beethoven sometimes liked to alternate harmonic notes with their lower semitones as a mild enhancement of a mood of tenderness. In C major, C could alternate with B, or D with C-sharp, or E with D-sharp. The violin sonatas offer lovely examples of this practice; see the first movement of the D major Sonata, op. 12, no. 1 (Ex. 38a), and the Finale of the *Spring*

Ex. 37a Sonata in F minor, op. 2,   Ex. 37b Sonata in C minor, op. 111, 1st Mvt., m. 119.
no. 1, 3rd Mvt., mm. 4 and 8.

Sonata, op. 24 (Ex. 38b). These nuances are best brought out by
not bringing them out. (See also the Violin Concerto, first
movement, mm. 10 and 11.) Similarly, in the late works, the
recapitulation of the main theme of an opening movement shows
a richer harmonization, achieved with the help of tones taken
from the subdominant region, and a quicker harmonic rhythm.
(See especially the A major Sonata, op. 101, and the *Hammerklavier* Sonata, op. 106.) In earlier works, for instance, in the
Emperor Concerto and still in the *Archduke* Trio, Beethoven had
been satisfied with coloring the harmony just by using appog-
giatura-like decorations in the melody.

Ex. 38a   Violin Sonata in D major, op. 12, no. 1, 1st Mvt., mm. 58–60.

Ex. 38b   Violin Sonata in F major, op. 24, 4th Mvt., mm. 1–3.

VII. MELODY AND TEXTURE

The instrumental character of Beethoven's melodies (see
above, pp. 133–38) generally does not influence his use of
melodic intervals and directions—except in that they are more
conservative than Mozart's wide skips and Haydn's melodic dissonances because his primary emphasis was on musical values of
a different character. However, Beethoven apparently had an exceptional fondness for the interval of a rising fourth. That is obvious in the first movement of the E major Sonata, op. 14, no. 1,
and the first movement and final fugue of the A-flat major

Sonata, op. 110, but the interval occurs elsewhere as well.[39] The first melodic interval of his First Sonata is a rising fourth! In the Third Sonata a rising fourth appears in m. 2; and in the Fourth Sonata the same melodic progression is particularly striking over the barline from m. 4 to m. 5. In the second and third movements of the *Pathétique* Sonata, op. 13, the rising fourth serves to establish the opposing key of A-flat major. The first interval in the bass and the second interval of the melody at the opening of the Adagio are rising fourths; and the A-flat major episode in the middle of the Finale consists almost completely of rising fourths, for as long as its quasi-fugato continues. Beethoven's reason for relying on this interval so much (probably an unconscious one in the beginning) may have been that it corresponds to the most elementary harmonic progression—dominant to tonic.* When Beethoven set an outburst of intense feeling to music, the ascending interval is often widened to a major sixth, from the dominant to the major third of the scale. Examples of this are found in the openings of the slow movements of the First Sonata (see Ex. 32), the *Waldstein* Sonata, op. 53 (Ex. 39a), and the variations from the String Quartet in A major, op. 18, no. 5 (Ex. 39b).

Ex. 39a   Sonata in C major,
op. 53, 2nd Mvt., m. 1.

Ex. 39b   String Quartet in A major, op 18, no. 5,
3rd Mvt., mm. 1–2.

In scale formations and scale-based patterns, Beethoven sometimes liked to make use of written-out mordents or inverted mordents, although they are not always immediately recognizable as such. A good example occurs during the Trio section of the Minuet of the First Sonata, op. 2, no. 1, in F minor, where the written-out mordent covers a hidden dotted rhythm at the start (Ex. 40a) and especially during the progression in sixth chords (Ex. 40b). In retrospect, mm. 25–28 (in the main section;

---

*However, when the same interval occurs in the opening theme of the Violin Sonata in G, op. 96, it has a different harmonic implication—namely a rise from the third to the sixth tone of the scale.

Ex. 40c) may be understood in the same manner, although other interpretations are possible. See also the Finale of the A major Sonata, op. 101, mm. 248–51 (Ex. 40d), and the first movement of the *Spring* Sonata for violin and piano in F major, op. 24, mm. 26–27 (Ex. 40e).

Sonata in F minor, op. 2, no. 1, 3rd Mvt.
Ex. 40a   mm. 41–44

Ex. 40b   mm. 60–63

Ex. 40c   mm. 25–26

Ex. 40d   Sonata in A major, op. 101, 4th Mvt., m. 248.

Ex. 40e   Violin Sonata in F major, op. 24, 1st Mvt., mm. 26–28.

In his early years, Beethoven frequently used orchestral accompaniment patterns in his piano music; the broken octaves in the first movement of the *Pathétique* Sonata are typical. Sometimes he also established part writing in string-quartet fashion, for example, at the last return of the theme in the slow movement of his Second Sonata in A major, op. 2, no. 2. Such textures appear natural in light of his late transition to the composition of actual quartets and symphonies. For a long time Beethoven's piano music was his principal outlet for *all* compositional urges. As has often been stated, his attention to pianistic style began with the Sonatas, op. 31, and the Variations, opp. 34 and 35, after he had established himself in the other instrumental fields. The Variations, op. 35, are of particular interest because they use the same material as the Finale of the *Eroica* Symphony, but cast in typically pianistic sonorities. The pianistic style of Beethoven's late years—and also his quartet style—became concise almost to the point of being mannered. This had nothing whatever to do with his deafness. It stemmed from his determination to be utterly precise and succinct, both horizontally and vertically.

At a certain point Beethoven must have realized that sticking to the same number of parts throughout an entire phrase was an old-fashioned convention that was unnecessary and could make the music obtuse. Consequently, in the late works, he freely changed the number of parts from chord to chord according to the need of the moment. See mm. 4 and 5 of the left-hand accompaniment to the varied theme of the Finale of his last Violin Sonata, op. 96, in G major (Ex. 41). To the eye, there is a single voice, followed by two, then three voices, and finally a single voice again. To the ear, of course, the third and fourth eighth notes in m. 4 form a three-voice chord that is resolved by the three-voice chord on the following downbeat. Even more typical of Beethoven's later style are mm. 7 and 8 of Variation 30 of the *Diabelli* Variations, op. 120 (Ex. 42). After the first two chords, the number of parts increases from three to four, then to five on the third beat; and at the end of the measure it falls back to four. In the next measure, while the left hand remains in strict two-part voice-leading, the right hand switches from three to two to one, back to three, and finally to two voices.

Ex. 41   Violin Sonata in G major,
op. 96, 4th Mvt., mm. 4–5.   Ex. 42   *Diabelli* Variations, op. 120, Var. 30, mm. 7–8.

These fine gradations of texture testify to Beethoven's keen
musical ear. Beethoven always knew what was going to be audible and was not fooled by notation on paper. There are two
other examples of the acuteness with which he heard music, one
from his early days and one from the late works. At the very end
of the Finale of the G major Sonata, op. 14, no. 2 (Ex. 43), after
no fewer than four successive "good-bye wavings" on the notes
C–A–G, the very last instance, in the bass, is changed to A–
F-sharp–G for harmonic reasons. Beethoven obviously knew
that, despite the change, the conclusion would still be heard as a
perfect imitation of the preceding measures; magically, the final
G would still be heard as the lowest note in actual sound, despite
the preceding F-sharp.

Ex. 43   Sonata in G major, op. 14, no. 2, 3rd Mvt., mm. 249–54.

Whenever the main motive of the opening movement of the A
major Sonata, op. 101, is played, the second half of the first
measure consists of a quarter note followed by an eighth, while a
lower part either moves in even eighth notes throughout (as in
m. 1; Ex. 44a) or fills the gap created by the quarter note with a
syncopated note (as in mm. 38 and 41; Exx. 44b, c). Only once is
the presentation different: in the second half of m. 35 (Ex. 44d)
the motivic top voice also contains three eighth notes (the second
of which is in unison with the lower, syncopated part). This
baffling change can be explained as an example of Beethoven's

Sonata in A major, op. 101, 1st Mvt.

Ex. 44a m. 1   Ex. 44b m. 38   Ex. 44c m. 41   Ex. 44d m. 35   NB

awareness of what is really heard. While normally the lower voice is a fifth or sixth below the upper, on this occasion they are only a major third apart. Beethoven knew that even if he had written the e just for the lower voice, it would still be heard as part of the upper.* Therefore, he wrote what would actually be heard in any case, foregoing exact motivic identity on paper.

It can be assumed that Beethoven followed strict melodic rules—rules he had gradually established for himself over the course of time. It is well known, for instance, that he objected to Diabelli's waltz theme for the Variations, op. 120, on the grounds that it was full of sequences in ascending seconds, of the kind called—by him and others—"cobbler's patches" or "rosalias."[40] Whenever he needed sequences, Beethoven proceeded to dissimilate the identity of the links by changing the figurations, very much as Bach had done, since he also was aware of the danger of melodic monotony. This can be seen particularly in the *Diabelli* Variations, especially the second halves of Variations 7 and 26, in which this technique is used almost to exaggeration, leading to noticeable differences between basically identical phrases. Even in the absence of sequences, Beethoven was always so afraid of repeating a melodic figure that he would go to any length to create small differences each time. This is very clear throughout Variation 2 of the Finale of the E major Sonata, op. 109, and in certain figurations in the first movement of the *Appassionata* Sonata in F minor, op. 57 (as in mm. 203–208; Ex. 45).

Beethoven essentially defied history in his melodic writing, in accordance with his general political and social rebelliousness. The best evidence of this attitude is delivered by the long cadenzas to the first and second piano concertos, written many years after the concertos themselves were composed. He not only de-

---

*A lesson that Schubert, to the dismay of all pianists, failed to learn when he wrote m. 4 of the B-flat Sonata, op. posth.

Ex. 45   Sonata in F minor, op. 57, 1st Mvt., mm. 203–206.

parted abruptly from the style of the concertos for the cadenzas but even used the recently added high notes (beyond f''') of the pianoforte for them. Nevertheless, Beethoven loved to play games with stylistic details of older music. Thus, the *Grazioso* Finale of his Second Sonata (A major, op. 2, no. 2) is a profile of the tender music in the *Empfindsamkeit* style of last movements, which was in favor two generations earlier. The Thirty-two Variations in C minor are a deliberate evocation of the Chaconne form as practiced by Bach; one even finds here the tripartite outline minor–major–minor with somewhat similar proportions to Bach's D minor Chaconne for violin.* The solemnity and dotted rhythms of the introduction to the C minor Sonata, op. 111, first movement, followed by the fast and fluent Allegro, may have been conceived as a modern revival of a French Overture, as the pianist Linda Kobler has suggested. Melodically, the Trio section of the Scherzo of the D major Sonata, op. 28, consists exclusively of the same four-measure phrase with alternate endings (Ex. 46), comparable to the "clos–overt" melodies of ancient French secular songs. Most peculiarly, the two main themes of the Prestissimo movement of the E major Sonata, op. 109, bear distinct resemblances to *cantus firmus* tunes of the Renaissance: the first one, in the bass at the opening, to the "La sol fa re mi," on which Josquin wrote a Mass; and the second one (mm. 57ff; Ex. 47a) on the best-known motet tune, "L'Homme armé" (Ex. 47b), with which it is practically identical, though in the minor

Ex. 46   Sonata in D major, op. 28, 3rd Mvt., mm. 71–78.

*Bach: 131—76—50 mm; Beethoven: 96—40—128 mm. Beethoven's last part is considerably longer than Bach's, and, in addition, it is followed by an extended coda.[41]

Ex. 47a Sonata in E major, op. 109, 2nd Mvt., mm. 57–60.   Ex. 47b L'homme armé
   Prestissimo

mode.[42] Certainly, most of Beethoven's fugues lean on features
of late Baroque music, though perhaps more on Handel than on
Bach.[43]

The question arises whether these are coincidences or whether
Beethoven really knew the old forms and tunes. The correct answer is that he probably did know them. As a boy he had served
as court organist;[44] and at the same time as he was composing the
late sonatas, he was actively searching for old music in preparation for writing the *Missa Solemnis*.[45]

VIII. PROBLEMS OF PERFORMANCE PRACTICE

Anatole France once made the ironic statement[46] that a histo-
rian is well off only as long as there exists a single source of
information; as soon as a second source on the same topic turns
up, most likely it will contradict the first.* The situation is
exactly the same with regard to the way Beethoven wanted his
piano works played. Czerny and Schindler are our two principal
witnesses, and they are diametrically opposed to each other on
nearly every point of importance. Unfortunately, it is impossible
to prefer one to the other on general grounds since their claim to
authenticity is about equal, or—one might say—equally imperfect.

Czerny was an important pianist and pedagogue. He first performed many of Beethoven's works under the master's supervi-
sion, and, as a long-time pupil, he based his own pianistic teaching, as well as his Bach editions, on what he had personally
learned from Beethoven. Moreover, he wrote a book on Beetho-

---

*"Il est extrêmement difficile d'écrire l'histoire. . . . Quand un fait n'est connu que par
un seul témoignage, on l'admet sans beaucoup d'hésitation. Les perplexités commencent
lorsque les événements sont rapportés par deux ou plusieurs témoins car leur témoignages
sont toujours contradictoires et toujours inconciliables." [It is extremely difficult to write
history. . . . When a fact is only known by a single testimony one accepts it without
much hesitation. The troubles begin as soon as events are reported by two or more witnesses, for their testimonials will always be contradictory and always be incompatible.]

ven's piano music. Schindler, on the other hand, was a frequent house companion in the master's later years, at a time when Czerny had ceased to be Beethoven's pupil, and became an important early biographer of Beethoven. At first, one is inclined to believe Czerny, the accomplished professional musician, rather than the musical amateur Schindler. But precisely because of his own preeminence, Czerny underwent other influences in his later development, especially in accepting some of Hummel's smoothness and elegant virtuosity. By this evolution he inevitably broke to some extent with Beethoven's more idealistic standards, although Czerny was certainly not aware of this. He was so scrupulous in his intention to record Beethoven's views faithfully that, in 1850, he revised the metronome markings he had given to the movements of the piano sonatas in 1842, fifteen years after Beethoven's death.[47] On both occasions he was simply trying to state correctly what he knew of Beethoven's own tempo choices, especially in the early works. But it is significant that in the later markings the prescribed speed was faster in nearly all instances.

Schindler, on the contrary, not being a professional pianist, was obsessed by the idea that everyone was playing Beethoven's music much too fast. This criticism applied not only to Czerny but also to Mendelssohn, Liszt, and Clara Schumann.[48] In some cases Schindler's attitude is manifestly untrue, in view of some excessively fast metronome markings by Beethoven himself (for example, the first movement of the *Hammerklavier* Sonata, op. 106, and the Finale of the A minor Cello Sonata, op. 102, no. 1). From these one must generalize that Beethoven intended fast movements to be very rapid indeed. In other cases, especially slow movements, Schindler was probably right in criticizing Czerny's middle-of-the-road markings, in that they made it virtually impossible to do justice to the concentrated expression and inwardness of these works.

Even in the early works Beethoven sometimes wanted extreme contrasts of tempo, as in the C minor Sonata, op. 10, no. 1, in which an Adagio Molto is followed by a Prestissimo Finale. Schindler found the first movement (Allegro molto e con brio) to be a prime example of Beethoven's agogic liberties for expressive purposes. Czerny not only insisted, with rare exceptions, on keeping the same tempo throughout a piece but also emphasized that a single beat could not be prolonged except when marked "rit." or provided with a fermata. Schindler, on the other hand, claimed that when Beethoven played expressive pieces—even fast ones, like this first movement—he would sometimes hold fermatas longer than the ordinary fermata sign would normally permit, and would even add fermatas wherever the musical expression made them desirable.

The length of a Beethoven fermata actually depends on its function. In the coda sections of the G major Rondo, op. 51, no. 2 (Ex. 48a) and the opening movement of the F major Sonata, op. 54 (Ex. 48b) the fermatas at the beginning and at the end of these segments lead directly into the next melodic tone and must therefore be rather short.*

Ex. 48a   Rondo in G major, op. 51, no. 2, mm. 220–22.   Ex. 48b   Sonata in F major, op. 54, 1st Mvt., mm. 135–36.

*The c″ in the Henle edition for the first of these three notes is presumably a misprint.

Schindler knew, perhaps better than Czerny, the spirit in which Beethoven's piano music must be presented. Conversely, Czerny was surely more familiar with musical detail. This is particularly true of his interpretation of the two-note slur in the Finale of the C major Concerto as an appoggiatura notation, and of the "tie" over the initial right-hand notes in the Scherzo of the Cello Sonata, op. 69, as a slur in which the second note is very soft and short.[49] Most of his explanations ought to be known by every music teacher.

Tempi

As to Beethoven's tempo markings and their application to individual movements, the investigations, first by the great vio-

Ex. 49   Symphony No. 5 in C minor, 1st Mvt., mm. 1–5.

---

*In the much-quoted opening of the Fifth Symphony, Beethoven tried to achieve more precision by writing the first hold within a single measure (m. 1) and the second as a tie across two measures (mm. 4–5). Thus, the phrase is asymmetrically notated in five measures (Ex. 49).

linist Rudolf Kolisch[50] and then by William Newman,[51] are so complete and stimulating that there remains nothing much to say with respect to both general principles and the judgment of individual cases. However, it is worth emphasizing that Beethoven's tempo, more than most composers', depends largely on the acoustic circumstances created by the hall or the room as well as by the piano; and that the tempi for the various movements of a piece—sonata, variation set, etc.—are in subtle ways interdependent. Thus it may be that because one is going to play a Finale faster, one will also have to speed up the preceding Scherzo, as could happen in the D major Sonata, op. 28. Conversely, after a very swift rendition of an opening movement, the ensuing slow movement ought to be more deliberate, not only to provide more contrast but also to preserve the approximate length of the whole work.

Beethoven clearly left these artistic decisions to the pianist's own judgment. How else could one explain why Beethoven, who was always ready to utilize the metronome for symphonies and quartets, mostly refrained from giving metronome markings to his piano works? One must indeed assume that he saw the piano primarily as an instrument of improvisatory qualities, in which the personality of the performer is interposed between the composer and the listener. However, nearly all this is speculation; for instance, there is no evidence to help us decide whether it is permissible in variation sets, such as the one in C minor, to change the tempo noticeably between variations.

Dynamics

In Beethoven's early works, as in the music of Haydn and Mozart, dynamic contrasts consist mostly of sharp alternations between loud and soft, while intermediate grades of loudness are admitted only during *crescendi* and *decrescendi*. *Mezzo forte* remains an exception and must be used only if so marked, for Beethoven grew up in this tradition. Hans von Bülow was the first of many nineteenth-century editors to obscure the visual aspect of the score by adding innumerable opening and closing "hairpins," indicating small *crescendi* and *decrescendi*, as well as *mf* and similar marks. In the later works, Beethoven himself carefully marked quite a few small dynamic nuances. This definitely means that where no such nuances are noted, Beethoven, in the interest of

the long line of the music, is asking for long, uninterrupted
stretches without change and development, especially when the
dynamic is *piano*. This applies to the first eight measures of *The
Absence* (op. 81a, second movement), and to all of Variation 2 of
the *Diabelli* Variations. Beethoven's *crescendo* passages have the
same tendency to serve the musical structure rather than the details of harmonic rhythm. Normally, a seventh chord resolving
into a triad is played louder than its resolution. This is the case in
mm. 9–13 of the theme of the *Diabelli* Variations (Ex. 50a),
which is marked *forte* and given extra *sf* marks on the various
seventh chords. But in many of his variations, Beethoven
changes these dynamics and proceeds in a gradual build-up by
crescendo. In Variation 3 (Ex. 50b), for instance, any melismatic
diminuendo in the top voice on the second beats in mm. 9–13
would utterly ruin Beethoven's structural design. Another good
example occurs in the first movement of the G major Violin
Sonata, op. 96 (Ex. 50c). Here Beethoven's markings are meant
to exclude any *diminuendo* between downbeats and second beats
in the top voice until m. 87, where the phrase ends in a *piano
subito* in which the *lower* octave of the melody is emphasized by
slurring, producing a G-string kind of sound.*

Ex. 50a *Diabelli* Variations, op. 120, theme, mm. 9–13.

Ex. 50b *Diabelli* Var. 3, mm. 9–13.

Ex. 50c Violin Sonata in G major, op. 96, 1st Mvt., mm. 85–88.

---

*This challenge is beautifully met on the recording of Szigeti and Schnabel playing this
sonata.[52]

In all the instances of such *piano subito* after *crescendo,* which are found in nearly all of Beethoven's later works, the *piano* must be felt as the climax to which the *crescendo* has been leading; in other words, the *piano* must not be separated from the *crescendo* by a "dramatic" pause to enhance an alleged surprise effect. The melody of the Finale of the E minor Sonata, op. 90, illustrates this well; at the end of m. 7 the *crescendo* flows so beautifully into the last two notes that they emerge as the high point of the entire melody. Beethoven highlights this ending by understating it.

Beethoven's *sforzato* markings are determined by their context. In many cases they simply indicate a shifting of the accent from the strong beat to the off-beat, as in the second half of Variation 4 of the Finale of the E major Sonata, op. 109 (Ex. 51). In other cases they represent the intense expression of the moment, often combined with a stress in time, as in m. 57 of the first movement of the *Tempest* Sonata, op. 31, no. 2.[53] The quality of the accent here depends on the amount of sound needed to play much louder than the listener expects, yet without interrupting the continuity of the music, which is to be reestablished immediately. It is not always easy to gauge the exact quantity of sound needed, nor will it always be necessary to play all notes in a *sf* chord equally loud and equally long. Regardless of the type of instrument used to play Beethoven's works, *una corda* and similar markings (including *mezza voce* and *sotto voce*) have to be translated into simple dynamic indications, since neither the instruments nor the concert halls exactly reproduce the conditions for which Beethoven made these markings.*

Ex. 51   Sonata in E major, op. 109, 3rd Mvt.,
Var. 4, m. 11 (Schenker edition).

---

*The slow movement of the A major Sonata, op. 101, and Variation 30 of the *Diabelli* Variations do not have to be played *una corda* throughout; and Variation 31, marked *tutte le corde,* may in part be played with the left foot down. The method can vary as long as the performer achieves Beethoven's purpose of establishing a more distant sound in Variation 30 than in Variation 31.

Pedaling

It is hardly necessary today to repeat that Beethoven's pedal marks must be obeyed to the letter, at least in using half-pedal. We may assume that audiences are no longer shocked by the blur effect which Beethoven intended in these places. This applies particularly to the opening of the slow movement of the C minor Concerto, op. 37, which Czerny heard Beethoven play in 1803. Czerny remarked that "Beethoven continued the pedal during the entire theme, which, on the weak-sounding pianofortes of that day, did very well, especially when the shifting pedal [*una corda*] was also employed."[54] One may be skeptical, then, of Czerny's advice to change pedal "at each important change of harmony" as "the instruments have acquired a much greater body of tone," seeing that Beethoven himself marked certain pedal changes and non-pedalings in the course of the theme. One can agree with Czerny, however, when he concludes the discussion by stating—less literal-mindedly than usual—that "the whole theme must sound like a holy, distant, and celestial harmony." Beethoven extends the pedal from the opening chord of the second movement—E major, with g-sharp on top—to the chord in m. 4—G-sharp major with the same g-sharp on top—to establish a "superprogression" of the principal harmonies (I to III), facilitated for the ear by the identity of the top note (Ex. 52).* The intermediate V chord and VI chord on the first and last beats of m. 2, and the inverted f-sharp chord in m. 3, are hereby reduced to secondary importance, a mere "foreground," in Schenkerian terms.

Ex. 52 Concerto in C minor, op. 37,
2nd Mvt., harmonies, mm. 1–4.

---

*It is well known that Beethoven often progressed by changing the tonality underneath an identical melody note, especially between movements. Thus, both Finales of the Quartet in B-flat, op, 130 (including the *Great Fugue,* op. 133), begin with the same illogical note, G, unaccompanied, simply as a continuation of the last melody note of the preceding Cavatina. Especially in the Fugue, which immediately modulates to B-flat major, this is simply a transition, with no structural meaning at all.

Another type of pedaling dear to Beethoven in his later years is usually overlooked. He marked certain soft chords with individual pedals, not to prolong them but simply to establish a certain tone color. Examples are found at the very last chord of the Finale of the E major Sonata, op. 109 (in which the theme was first heard without such pedaling) and in mm. 95–98 of the first movement of the A major Sonata, op. 101. The implication is that these chords must be played lightly and ethereally. Even in the rare cases when they are marked *forte* (as in the concluding chord of the last *Diabelli* Variation), the same character should be achieved. Even the slightest percussiveness would be wrong here, where the pedal is supposed to open all available overtone resources to a chord which otherwise would not vibrate enough. The effect is comparable to the sympathetic vibrations on a viola d'amore or an Aeolian harp.

Technique

In this field, on the whole, one can trust the reports by Czerny, not only because he was a genius in teaching piano technique himself but also because he consciously based his technique entirely on what he had learned from Beethoven. Indeed, most of Czerny's etudes and studies were written to provide the necessary tools for mastering the technical difficulties of the Beethoven sonatas and concertos. Beethoven was very concerned with piano technique. Nottebohm was the first to publish several of Beethoven's early piano studies, which were possibly written for publication, for they contain short explanations.[55] It is interesting to note that in one exercise Beethoven's caption reads, "the hand being held together as compactly as possible" (I do not agree with Gerig's translation, "contracted"); another exercise is defined as a study "for exercising the fist." Still in the same context is Beethoven's remark about *jeu perlé,* in a letter written to Czerny in 1817: "One sometimes wishes for some other kind of jewelry."[56]

From all indications, Beethoven used a strong, quiet, round, "pycnic"* hand, from which the fingers fall quite easily and

---

*A term used in the well-known book *Körperbau und Character* (1921) by the German scientist Ernst Kretschmer. *Pycnic* ("bottlelike") designates people of the "cobbler" type, who are compact and sturdy.

deeply into the keys, to produce a full-sounding, singing legato. According to his student Therese Brunswick, "he never wearied of holding down and bending my fingers, which I had learned to stretch up and hold flatly."[57] If this seems normal to us, it is because we have forgotten that Beethoven was the first pianist to insist on round fingers at the keyboard! Schindler agrees with this technique and quotes a rule Beethoven often repeated during lessons: "Place the hands over the keyboard in such a position that the fingers need not be raised more than necessary. This is the only method by which the player can learn to *generate* tone and, as it were, to make the instrument sing." But when it comes to J. B. Cramer's Etudes, our two primary sources contradict each other again. While Schindler claims that Beethoven considered them the principal basis for solid playing, Czerny quotes Beethoven as saying that the Etudes make the playing sticky, and that one cannot learn staccato and leggiero from them[58]—a comment that is quite plausible.

Describing the extraordinary qualities of Beethoven's own pianism that distinguished him from his rivals, Czerny mentioned, first, that Beethoven had a unique facility in negotiating quick leaps without disturbing the flow of the music or its beat (that explains many passages in his works, such as the end of the Scherzo in the C major Sonata, op. 2, no. 3, and the *Diabelli* Variation 10); and, second, that he "knew to an astounding degree how to play a progression of full chords perfectly legato without pedal." Czerny points out that this type of legato was different from the finger legato applied to fugue playing.* Beethoven furthermore greatly developed the playing of all types of scales over several octaves in both hands, as some of his studies show; one could consider the coda of the Finale of the G major Violin Sonata, op. 96, as another such exercise (mm. 261–68), further complicated by the necessity of coordinating the piano part with that of the violin.

Obviously, Beethoven was also interested in fingerings. Once when he had to accompany his Horn Sonata, op. 17, and found that the piano was a semitone flat, he was immediately able to

---

*For example, see the beginning of the coda of the first movement of the E major Sonata, op. 109 (Ex. 53a), and the opening of the Adagio of the A-flat major Sonata, op. 110 (Ex. 53b).

Ex. 53a Sonata in E major, op. 109, 1st Mvt., mm. 78–82.

Ex. 53b Sonata in A-flat major, op. 110, 3rd Mvt., mm. 2–3.

play in F-sharp major instead of F major.[59] This proves that he would use the same fingerings for both tonalities and therefore would not hesitate to use the thumb on black keys.*

Beethoven's attitude of not being interested in *jeu perlé* but in techniques of expression, and his approach of the compact hand, are quite different from those of his pupil Czerny. Obviously, pearly playing is not possible when the thumb and fifth finger are regularly used on black keys. On the other hand, many of Beethoven's passages are easier to play with his five-finger position than if one had to avoid using the outer fingers on black keys. (One may try this in the second half of Variation 23 of the *Diabelli* Variations.) Paradoxically, Beethoven's round fingers and compact hand are also of help in the difficult, wide-spread left-hand accompaniments of the Finale of the *Emperor* Concerto (especially in the coda) and in the second theme of the first movement of the E minor Sonata, op. 90 (Ex. 54). The tendency

Ex. 54 Sonata in E minor, op. 90, 1st Mvt., mm. 55–57.

---

*Perhaps von Bülow knew this when he stated, in the introduction to his selection of Cramer's Etudes, that a good pianist must be able to play the *Appassionata* Sonata in F-sharp minor at an instant's notice, without changing a single fingering.

to spread the hand and flatten the fingers in such passages is to be resisted. Eugen d'Albert, whom this author heard twice, in 1922 and 1923, played everything with this Beethovenian technique and, as no one else then or since, always achieved the audience reaction that "Beethoven must have played this way." Occasionally—as in the Finale of the E-flat major Trio, op. 70, no. 1, or in Variation 8 of the *Diabelli* Variations—Beethoven worked out specific, complicated, acrobatic fingerings; these are always worth studying, because they always shape the sound.

Finally, and most importantly, Beethoven's individual, expressive legato, very different from Mozart's, is best explained as a technical innovation by referring to his use of the word *pathétique* for op. 13. The German word *pathetisch* does not at all mean "tragic" or "pathetic"! It implies a heightened tone and emphatic declamation, as in the classic French theater, different from the delicate inflections of most chamber music. By the nobility of expressive depth, with all traces of sentimentality eliminated, the listener may be certain that something of vital importance is being stated in the music. Obviously, not every tune for a slow movement falls in this category, but those that do create an intensity heretofore known only in vocal music.

Edward Rothstein justly called Beethoven the "progenitor both of the 19th-century music in which most of today's audience makes its home, and the first major representative of the avant-garde."[60] The compositional traits described in this chapter belong partly to one and partly to the other of these directions. Until he became totally deaf, the piano served Beethoven for the expression of his ideas in works in which he could be most free of conventions and practical necessities. Being fully aware of the individual modes of expression in his piano music constitutes an important step in our perception and recognition of Beethoven's mission and of the double impact he made on the evolution of music.

Chapter V

Schubert

I. SCHUBERT'S PIANO TEXTURES

Schubert's piano works are, for the most part, the product of his untested imagination, since Schubert was not a concert pianist and oftentimes did not even own an instrument—a unique situation for the creator of some of the world's greatest piano music! But contrary to the assumption of some nineteenth-century writers, the lack of personal instrumental experience never faulted the idiomatic perfection of his writing. Miraculously, in Schubert's piano music everything works—or almost everything—not just for the ears, but for the fingers. True, the implementation of Schubert's instrumental ideas is not always simple and is especially difficult in the many places where his patterns differ from Beethoven's. The technique necessary for playing Beethoven could be acquired through the thousands of exercises by Beethoven's pupil Czerny, who, through his teaching, also became Beethoven's messenger to later pianists. (Liszt and Leschetitsky, the two most influential teachers of the next generation, were both Czerny's students and were able to bring the direct Beethoven tradition to most of the virtuosos operating at the end of the nineteenth century and the beginning of the twentieth.)

However, no Czerny-like disciple existed to transform Schubert's typical patterns into the small change of didactic pieces, and Schubert himself never taught piano. This means that pianists who wish to perform Schubert's music have to isolate the typically Schubertian figures themselves and learn to cope with their difficulties.

Repeated Tones and Chords

Schubert's repeated notes are different from the quick, repeated single tones, to be played with finger changes, which are the subject of a few Czerny studies and which are also featured in the first three of Beethoven's Thirty-two Variations in C minor. Schubert himself uses these figures for the second theme of the Finale of the E-flat major Trio, op. 100 (D. 929).

But repeated notes and repeated chords appear as a personal, almost an idiosyncratic, pattern of Schubert's piano music in the many instances where they form a continuous accompaniment by way of a *measured tremolo*. The most famous and most unplayable example occurs in the song "Der Erlkönig" (D. 328); here Schubert himself suggested, if necessary, changing the triplets to duplets.[1]* No helpful etudes can be found in the Classical arsenal of the "Three Cs"—Cramer, Clementi, and Czerny. No finger changes are possible for this pattern, which calls for a combined approach of fingertip, wrist, and forearm motions.

Other examples of this type of tremolo occur in the Finale of the G major Sonata, op. 78 (D. 894). In mm. 3 and 7 (Exx. 1a, b) it is divided between the hands. A little later (mm. 14–17, Ex. 1c; m. 50, etc.), the same pattern, actually a motive, is given to the left hand alone, where it is even more difficult to play because of the *pianissimo* marking. In the Finale of the C minor Sonata, op.

Sonata in G major, D. 894, 4th Mvt.

Ex. 1a m. 3   Ex. 1b m. 7   Ex. 1c mm. 14–15

---

*About 1945, Artur Schnabel, who had just received his (and Therese Schnabel's) recording of "Erlkönig," made before the war, but who at the time did not own a phonograph, came to my house to listen to the record. Afterward, another guest, the composer Erich Itor Kahn, said to me: "My hand hurts just from listening," while Schnabel, who had not heard Kahn's remark, stated loudly, "My hand still hurts."

posth. (D. 958), the repeated chord accompaniment is loud and grows into a *fortissimo* (mm. 95–97; Ex. 2); in this instance the difficulty lies in the fullness of the chords, each of which consists of four tones, and in the quicker tempo. In desperation one might play the chords as duplets, following Schubert's emergency solution for the "Erlkönig."

Ex. 2   Sonata in C minor, D. 958, 4th Mvt., mm. 95–97.

Each case offers its own challenges: In the C minor Impromptu, op. 90, no. 1 (D. 899), at mm. 74ff. and 151ff. (Exx. 3a, b), the chord repetitions are relatively slow, but could easily sound thick against the very soft melody. They must therefore be deliberately sustained, in contrast to the pizzicato-like bass notes on the downbeats which precede them. The technical difficulty here consists mostly of jumping smoothly from these bass notes to the soft repeated chords without losing any time in between.

Impromptu in C minor, D. 899, no. 1
Ex. 3a   m. 74   Ex. 3b   m. 152

Where the repeated notes are slower, as in the development of the opening movement of the B-flat Sonata, op. posth. (D. 960), mm. 150–66, first in the left, then in the right hand, they are an imitation of similar notes in string quartets. String players would play them with alternating down- and up-bows, and their articulation on the piano should suggest the same effect. The opening of the C major Fantasy for violin and piano, op. 159 (D. 934), is of a similar nature, and also preserves the character of a measured tremolo.

Quick Jumps

Another typical Schubertian piano texture consists of quick jumps, of the kind just mentioned in connection with the C minor Impromptu. This type of accompaniment was aptly called "three-hand music" by Artur Schnabel, because it duplicates the "oom-pa" executed (with both hands) by the Secondo player in so much of Schubert's original duet music. In the solo music, if the accompaniment to the second subject of the opening movement of the B major Sonata, op. 147 (D. 575; Ex. 4), were to be played by both hands, it would clearly begin with one bass note for the left hand followed by two notes for the right for each half measure. If one wants to evoke this imaginary division of the two strains of the left hand, one will probably have to use the fifth finger twice in succession, beginning with the beat note. In the same sonata, the second subject of the Finale (Exx. 5a, b) combines similar quick jumps with softly repeated chord successions in an imitation of horizontal quartet textures.

Ex. 4 Sonata in B major, D. 575, 1st Mvt., mm. 30–31.

Sonata in B major, D. 575, 4th Mvt.

Ex. 5a mm. 51–54   Ex. 5b mm. 59–61

The texture of Variation 13 of Beethoven's *Eroica* Variations, op. 35, is quite different from these places in Schubert. Beethoven's brilliant passage—difficult as it is—is written without the added complication of soft sonorities and fully set chords.

Melody in Outer Fingers

Schubert was one of the first composers to use the right hand for the simultaneous playing of the lyrical melody and part of the accompaniment underneath. (This practice no doubt developed through transcriptions from orchestral scores.) It is necessary to play the melody with the outer fingers exclusively, a technique possible only with help of the pedal.* Except for the slow movement of the *Hammerklavier* Sonata, op. 106, Beethoven avoided this type of texture, in which a finger legato is either impossible or difficult to achieve. But Schubert employed it for the second subject of the opening movement of his A major Sonata, op. posth. (D.959), and the opening theme of the earlier A major Sonata, op. 120 (D. 664). Subsequently, in Mendelssohn's *Songs without Words* and Schumann's short pieces, such textures became perfectly normal; and Chopin wrote the E major Etude, op. 10, no. 3, and the A-flat major Etude, op. 25, no. 1, to pinpoint the technical problems resulting from this style.

The pianistic challenge here is to the powers of concentration: the ear has to have a perfectly detailed inner image. To achieve that it will always be helpful and—I think—necessary to practice the melody by itself at first, using the most comfortable fingering, without accompaniment or with a minimum accompaniment in the left hand only, until the articulation of the right is firmly in the performer's memory.

Scrambled Scales

In 1956, when Dika Newlin and I played the Rondo in A minor, op. 144 (D. 947; "Lebensstürme"), for four hands, she drew my attention to the fact that Schubert loved to scramble his scales. In the triplet runs at the beginning and the end of the piece (Ex. 6), he inserted chromatic passing tones in normal scales. In the Finale of the A major Sonata, op. posth. (D. 959), an A major scale is mixed with bits from the F-sharp minor melodic scale (Ex. 7); and in Variation 5 of the B-flat major Impromptu, op. 142, no. 3 (D. 935), bits of various diatonic scales and of the chromatic scale are scrambled to such an extent that it is hard work to analyze the passage (Ex. 8). If given a chance, Schubert would at least mix the various forms of the minor scale— harmonic, melodic, natural; see the F minor Impromptu, op. 142, no. 4 (D. 935), mm. 95–120 (Ex. 9). Finding appropriate

---

*One of my students called these melodies "pinkie solos."

Ex. 6   Rondo in A minor ("Lebensstürme"), D. 947, mm. 53–54.

Ex. 7   Sonata in A major, D. 959, 4th Mvt., m. 164.

Ex. 8   Impromptu in B-flat major, D. 935, no. 3, Var. 5, m. 15.

Ex. 9   Impromptu in F minor, D. 935, no. 4, mm. 95–97.

fingerings for these finger-twisters usually necessitates analyzing them theoretically bit by bit.*

---

*Curiously, one finds similar scale mixtures in late Bach works, especially in *WTC*, Bk. II (see the Fugue in A-flat major, mm. 33ff.).[2] In many instances, Bach and Schubert independently reached similar solutions—solutions different from those of the three "classical" composers. For one thing, they both wrote music that is prominently visual, as Albert Schweitzer found out over 75 years ago;[3] and, in their music, earthiness and transcendental communication are very close together, as their dance compositions show. This is all the more remarkable since Schubert was not familiar enough with Bach's music to be directly influenced by it.

II. SCHUBERT, THE COMPOSER OF CHAMBER MUSIC

Schubert, like Brahms after him, stopped writing virtuoso music for solo piano early in his career and turned to chamber music with piano (while Brahms also wrote concertos), realizing that here was a more appropriate vehicle for pianistic brilliance. The reason for the switch was clearly the same for both masters; namely, that some of the most scintillating sonorities are achieved when both hands play in octaves in the highest treble, but for that it is necessary that the bass be provided by other instruments. Typical cases are Schubert's *Trout* Quintet, op. 114 (D. 667), and the Finale of Brahms's G minor Quartet, op. 25. In the Quintet Schubert goes so far in compensating for the high register in the right hand that he adds a double bass to the ensemble at the other end of the sound spectrum. His later trios are based on the same concept, as can be seen in the middle episode of the slow movement of the B-flat major Trio, op. 99 (D. 898), and in the canonic main section of the Minuet of the E-flat major Trio, op. 100 (D. 929). To enhance the glitter of the piano sound, these octave passages should not be played with too much legato; and the unison between the two octaves must be blended so that there is not too much top voice. This technique is quite different from the usual unison playing in solo music (for example, at the end of Chopin's Etude in F major, op. 10, no. 8).

Schubert's sonatas, unlike some of Beethoven's, never became showcases for brilliance and were never considered concertos without orchestra. The *Wanderer* Fantasy, op. 15 (D. 760), was actually Schubert's only solo piece written with virtuosic intentions. Later on, Schubert himself probably realized that since he had had no previous experience in this type of music, either as a pianist or as a composer, he had at times been clumsy in carrying out these intentions. Indeed, the overwhelming effect of the piece owes nothing to the piano writing as such.* Never again did Schubert attempt anything of this kind in his solo music.

---

*Liszt, who apparently understood this fully, coped with the score in two ways: by making a scrupulously accurate edition of the Fantasy with fingerings and only a few pianistic suggestions in small print, and by rewriting it as a piano concerto. Here all awkwardnesses could disappear and all the beautiful tunes, harmonies, rhythms, and sonorities be preserved and effectively projected through Liszt's skillful distribution of the musical material between soloist and orchestra. Unlike so many transcriptions, this arrangement serves only the composer, not the arranger or the performer or both—all of which testifies to Liszt's love and respect for Schubert.

Schubert must be seen as a composer of chamber music as well as, or even more than, a composer of lieder. Unlike Mozart, Beethoven, Schumann, and Brahms, Schubert (like Mendelssohn) very early achieved full mastery of the craft of writing string quartets. The quartets dating from his teens are quite incredible. No wonder that he used quartetlike textures in his piano music, especially in the early sonatas; see the second movement of the A minor Sonata, op. 164 (D. 537; Ex. 10a); the Finale of the E-flat major Sonata, op. 122 (D. 568; Ex. 10b); and the first movement of the B major Sonata, op. 147 (D. 575; Ex. 10c). The last example features three-part not four-part writing, but is at least as intricate as the other examples because of the stretches in

Ex. 10a Sonata in A minor, D. 537, 2nd Mvt., mm. 115–16.

Ex. 10b Sonata in E-flat major, D. 568, 4th Mvt., mm. 55–56.

Ex. 10c Sonata in B major, D. 575, 1st Mvt. mm. 42–43

m. 50

the right hand, stretches which are necessitated by the distance between the two upper parts and by their individual rhythmic patterns. There seems to be no other way to learn these spots than to practice each (quasi-instrumental) part by itself with all available fingers until their cadence and emphasis remain subconsciously in the ear, at which point it is possible to change the fingering to deal with the polyphony.

Just as he does in his quartets, Schubert sometimes decorates a lyrical melody in the next-to-highest voice with light, quick, teasing figurations on the top. Such chirping comments—some of which are played on the violin at the tip of the bow—are found in the Finale of his Piano Sonata in E-flat major, op. 122 (Ex. 11).

Ex. 11   Sonata in E-flat major, D. 568, 4th Mvt., m. 42.

Schubert said in a letter to Kupelwieser of March 31, 1826, that he was writing his Octet in F major, op. 166 (D. 803) and some quartets in preparation for further symphonic works. He may also have considered some of his later piano compositions as such stepping stones; at any rate their pianistic style is more symphonic and consolidated than that of the early sonatas, especially in the three posthumous sonatas. When Beethoven died in March 1827, Schubert realized that he was the only possible successor to that giant of the symphony and the piano sonata, and he consciously took that heavy burden on himself. In the field of piano music, it resulted in the creation of three "super" sonatas, the C minor, A major, and B-flat major, all published as op. posth. (D. 958, 959, 960). From the first measure, the piano writing in the C minor Sonata recalls that of Beethoven. In the other two, there are occasional symphonic elements which have their origin in the orchestral palette of the older master, for instance, the opening of the B-flat major Sonata stems from the slow movement of the *Pastoral* Symphony. However, the string quartet element, so prevalent in earlier Schubert works, is also present in these late compositions. It, too, is Beethovenian in the sense that Beethoven's emphasis in the late years was more and more on quartet writing. But his influence on Schubert seems to have been mostly through piano music and symphonies. Schubert was such a natural composer of quartets that he did not need a model there. Two typical quartetlike passages occur in the B-flat major Sonata: One is the F-sharp minor section in the exposition of the first movement (Ex. 12a), where the melody appears as though played by a viola or cello against a counter-melody by the first violin. The other is the second subject of the Finale, mm. 85–153 (Ex. 12b), a passage which is probably more difficult to play than Schubert realized, because the right hand does double duty, imitating the texture of two violins, while the left hand imitates a cello part in which pizzicato and arco tones alternate.

Sonata in B-flat major, D. 960
Ex. 12a 1st Mvt., mm. 48–49.

Ex. 12b 4th Mvt., mm. 86–87 and mm. 112–13.

The frequent pizzicato imitations in all three sonatas were certainly inspired by the texture of the extraordinary slow movement which Schubert wrote at the same time for his String Quintet in C major, op. 163 (D. 956). Slow melody notes are sustained here against pizzicato accompaniments below and above; the occurrence of this texture in all three late sonatas forms a principal, probably intentional, link between them. It is found in the coda of the slow movement of the C minor Sonata (Ex. 13); and at the very beginning of the A major Sonata (Ex. 14a), where the bass is meant to be pizzicato. These measures should therefore be played with so little pedal that the left-hand chords sound plucked, but not too loudly, so that the sustained chords in the right hand will sound *forte* throughout each measure. The sound is best sustained by the right thumb playing a. In the coda, beginning at m. 331 (Ex. 14b), the same texture is repeated *pianissimo,* and consequently the same articulation is even more obviously required; the sonorities needed here further explain those of the opening. The second movement begins with pizzicato notes on each downbeat (Ex. 14c). Therefore the pedaling should not start before the left hand has come off the bass note; this can be clearly seen during the lead-in to the recapitulation (Ex. 14d). The Trio section of the Scherzo (Ex. 14e) resumes the texture of the first movement coda (Ex. 14b).

Ex. 13   Sonata in C minor, D. 958, 2nd Mvt., m. 94.

In the B-flat major Sonata, the pedaling of the main theme of the slow movement is problematic. Schubert orders *col pedale* (Ex. 15a), which presumably means that the pedal should be held throughout each entire measure. This may have worked on the pianos of his time, since the pedal of the bass notes was feeble enough to permit their pizzicato quality and indeed the entire accompaniment (as in the String Quintet), to sound through. There is no entirely satisfying method of pedaling on a modern grand: If one adopts the same method as in the corresponding movement of the A major Sonata, the harmony sounds less alive than Schubert wanted it—and he prescribed pedal specifically to enliven the harmony. Perhaps the best solution is to depress the pedal at the beginning of each measure, release it immediately after the staccato eighth note following the second beat, and pedal again on the third beat. It is most essential that the long

Sonata in A major, D. 959
Ex. 14a 1st Mvt., mm. 1–3.   Ex. 14b 1st Mvt., mm. 331–32.

Ex. 14c 2nd Mvt., mm. 1–2.   Ex. 14d 2nd Mvt., mm. 147–48.

Ex. 14e 3rd Mvt., mm. 80–81.

chord in the right hand remain audible by itself in mm. 12 and 13 (Ex. 15b), in contrast to the simultaneous g-sharps in four octaves.

It ought to be mentioned here that similar pedaling problems arise, again because of the imitation of string writing, at the ends of the opening movements of the posthumous sonatas. Each of the three sonatas, at this point, has to be pedaled differently. The C minor Sonata presents no uncertainty (Ex. 16): The quarter

Sonata in B-flat major, D. 960, 2nd Mvt.
Ex. 15a mm. 1–2

col pedale

Ex. 15b   mm. 12–13

Ex. 16   Sonata in C minor, D. 958, 1st Mvt., mm. 270–74.

rests, in the two measures preceding the final chord, are meant
for all parts, and this definitely includes the bass, since it is here
that the melody is carried from staccato eighths (m. 270), first to
quarters (m. 271), and then to half notes (mm. 271–72). Only
the last chord is notated as a dotted half note and prolonged.
Clearly, all the rests must remain without pedal.

In the A major Sonata, by contrast, the lowest register is used
only once (one measure before the end)—and very lightly—as
the last note of a descending arpeggio; and for the final chord no
bass voice is notated. However, it seems probable that Schubert
would have liked to retain the low A of m. 356 for the conclusion of the movement (Ex. 17), had he been able to. Today we
are more fortunate and may hold it with the middle pedal, omit-
ting the sustaining pedal except for the final chord.

What happens at the same point in the B-flat major Sonata is
even more complex. The concluding chord of 5 beats reflects the
length of the complete final trill four measures earlier (Ex. 18a).*
That trill, including its ending as accompanied by the right hand,
is slightly different from the earlier ones, all of which lasted for
4½ beats (Ex. 18b). Here the trill is prolonged not only by omit-
ting the staccato dot in the left hand but primarily by holding the
right-hand chord for 5 full beats: in this case, the downbeat chord

---

*Although it must be a coincidence, it is curious that the first movements of the last
two sonatas have the same number of measures!

Ex. 17 Sonata in A major, D. 959, 1st Mvt., mm. 356–57.

Sost. Ped. _____⌐

Sonata in B-flat major, D. 960, 1st Mvt.
Ex. 18a mm. 352–57

Ex. 18b mm. 8–9 (and mm. 223–24)

of m. 353 is written as a quarter note, i.e., it is longer than the left-hand note. While the next two chords (dominant-seventh and tonic) present no interpretive problems, the B-flat major chord of m. 355—the identical tones of the concluding chord, which follows—easily sounds like the end instead of just a preparation for the end. It may therefore be advisable once more to utilize the pizzicato concept and, without pedal, play the left hand a bit shorter than the right, analogous to the downbeat of m. 353.*

III. SCHUBERT, THE SONG COMPOSER

Schubert's song writing influenced both the nature of the themes in his piano music and, indirectly, the structure of his movements.

---

*A parallel situation exists in the first two measures of the F minor Fantasy for piano duet, D. 940. The bass octave F is probably meant to be played by holding the thumb but letting go of the fifth finger.

The Nature of Vocal Themes

Most principal themes in the sonatas must be regarded as though they were song themes. Just as a singer naturally phrases to the end of each breath, the pianist must go to the end of the melody segment even if it does not fall on a downbeat. Every single piano piece of Schubert's presents numerous examples of this rule. At random, let us take the two main themes of the first movement of the posthumous A major Sonata: In m. 6 (Ex. 19a) the pianist is obliged to go through deliberately, tone by tone, to the g-sharp' on the third beat without an intervening stop on the downbeat and with no accent on the last tone (a singer, at the end of a breath, would not emphasize the last tone either). Even more instructive is the second subject, mm. 55–59 (Ex. 19b): in mm. 57 and 58 the melody goes to a long note on the third beat. The first time the note carries an accent, the second time it does not; yet, it is the last note of the phrase that must be the goal right from the beginning of the melody.

Sonata in A major, D. 959, 1st Mvt.
Ex. 19a m. 6   Ex. 19b mm. 55–59

What is it then that the pianist has to observe, if an accent on the final note is ruled out? It is, first of all, the smooth connection between all legato notes, and, second, careful attention to those which fall between the beats. For instance, if the pianist plays the g-sharp' on the second beat in m. 58 lighter than the downbeat (b'), the "breath" of the melody would be interrupted. If any metrical accents are needed, they must be confined to the lower voices (or to some of them, in this instance to the half note e' in the right hand). As a practicing stratagem (to be dropped for the actual performance) a *crescendo* to and a *decrescendo* from the second beat of m. 58 in the melody voice may prove helpful.

Another typical example occurs in the opening of the variation theme of the B-flat major Impromptu, op. 142, no. 3. The first segment goes to the half note on the third beat of m. 2 (Ex. 20),

Ex. 20 Impromptu in B-flat major, D. 935, no. 3, mm. 1–2.

regardless of whether the appoggiatura is played on or before the beat. However, this is impossible to achieve if a metrical melody accent is given on the downbeat, a', of m. 2.

No other composer requests such melodic attention from the performer, who has to lead a melody strongly through to the end of each long breath. The difference between the opening of the A major Sonata, op. 120 (Ex. 21a) and the opening of Beethoven's Sonata in F-sharp major, op. 78 (Ex. 21b), is quite audible. If the Beethoven is played in a flowing, even rhythm, the melodic phrase will carry itself; but in Schubert, it is up to the player to create the long line by giving the top voice his fullest concentration. The ambivalence of moods, so characteristic of Schubert (in contrast to Beethoven), is based on the primacy of the melody; the harmony and rhythm only serve melodic ends, no matter how original and interesting they may be in their own right.*

Ex. 21a Sonata in A major, D. 664, 1st Mvt., mm. 1–4.

Allegro moderato

Ex. 21b Beethoven, Sonata in F-sharp major, op. 78, 1st Mvt, mm. 5–8.

Allegro ma non troppo

Vocal Themes within the Sonata

Some of the sonata melodies were obviously first conceived as song tunes for which Schubert never found suitable texts. (I am not speaking of actual song melodies used by him in the *Wanderer* Fantasy, op. 15, the C major Fantasy for violin and piano, op. 159, or the *Trout* Quintet, op. 114.) To this category belong the

---

*Typically, the sketch for his E minor Symphony, D. 729, contains many places where only the melody is written out, with no indication of harmony or orchestration but complete with "hairpins."

theme of the Finale of the A major Sonata, op. posth. previously
used for the middle movement of the A minor Sonata, op. 164;
that of the Finale of the D major Sonata, op. 53 (D. 850); and the
second theme of the opening movement of the E-flat major
Sonata, op. 122. The spun-out quality of the music is an ingredient absent from nearly all compositions before Schubert.
Among the rare exceptions is the opening movement of the
Beethoven Violin Concerto, op. 61 (in which—not acci-
dentally—the repetitive style of developing the main theme fore-
shadows that of Schubert's development sections). In the presentation of many of these themes, Schubert's song and chamber
styles are fused as the voices alternate; instead of snatching the
motive away from each other, they gently hand it over every
time; see the first movement of the A major Sonata, op. 120 (Ex.
22).

Ex. 22   Sonata in A major, D. 664, 1st Mvt., mm. 9–11.

Unobtrusively, in this manner, a new element, with a totally
new aesthetic viewpoint, was introduced—the element of *length*
for its own sake. Through the use of song melodies as instrumental motives, the duration of each group was automatically extended. In the next two generations this became the rule, not
only in instrumental music. Wagner's operas, Bruckner's symphonies, and Tolstoi's novels exemplify the new aesthetic of
length. It was deliberate and it was programmatic, as it symbolized entering a special world for the listener or reader, no
reservations or instant criticisms being possible. Only by totally
surrendering to the spirit of these works of art could the beholder
hope to receive what their creators had wanted to give, renounc-
ing automatic intellectual comprehension in favor of "letting go."
Schubert was the very first in this endeavor, probably quite unconsciously.

Wagner saw the point of departure for his type of music in

Beethoven's Ninth Symphony. True, this work as well as the Quartet in C-sharp minor, op. 131, and the *Hammerclavier* Sonata, op. 106, are designedly very long, but theirs is a different kind of length, incorporating intricate subdivisions (with the sole exception of the slow movement of the *Hammerclavier* Sonata). Much as Schubert was attuned to Beethoven's styles and forms, he was not particularly influenced by any of these works.[4]

Occasionally, Schubert must have felt that he had gone too far, and he cut out segments of recapitulation without paying much attention to the connections between sections. A case in point is the Finale of the E-flat major Trio, op. 100, the original version of which has recently been published by Bärenreiter in the Neue Schubert Ausgabe. We must presume the existence of other authentic cuts of the same kind. Between mm. 51 and 52 of the Finale of the *Wanderer* Fantasy, op. 15 (Ex. 23), there is a *non sequitur* that would be hard to explain any other way. However, this does not ever give performers the right to make cuts in Schubert's compositions. On the contrary, Schubert himself should not have been making such concessions. Miraculously, his recapitulations and developments, no matter how long, always flow along beautifully, and they are not merciless, like those in most of Fauré's chamber works and in some of Mendelssohn's. Schumann's praise of Schubert's "heavenly length"[5] has not lost any of its validity!

Ex. 23 *Wanderer* Fantasy, D. 760, 4th Mvt., mm. 51–52.

IV. Tempo and Form

In preserving the positive value of length, tempo is a fundamental consideration. Certain simple rules pertain to the selection and maintenance of the tempo. Like all rules, they are not only flexible but hollowed out by exceptions; nevertheless, their principles may come to the pianist's aid.

In Schubert the tempo does not change suddenly when a new

theme appears or a new section begins unless the score is specially marked. In many of his later works Schubert marked, or implied, *istesso tempo*. He made sure that the new section would keep the same speed by setting up metronomelike chords at equal distances on the "near side" of the border. He wrote them into all the episodes in all three of the *Klavierstücke,* op. posth. (D. 946), as well as in the middle sections of the final movements of both piano trios.[6] Schubert himself is said to have insisted on maintaining the same tempo throughout each of his songs, and he cautioned his publisher, Probst, about the *istesso tempo* in the E-flat major Trio, op. 100.[7]

An exception is to be made for the middle sections of scherzo movements. In some cases they ought to be played slightly slower even where they are not so marked; for example, in the E-flat major Sonata, op. 122, and perhaps also in the G major Sonata, op. 78. As in all classical music, the coda sections of first movements are also meant to be slower, and no special tempo marking is needed. This applies to mm. 331ff. of the A major Sonata, op. posth., and mm. 335ff. of the B-flat major Sonata, op. posth. In both instances the coda is preceded by a break. Though a similar break occurs at mm. 249ff. of the C minor Sonata, op. posth., there is no need to slow down for the coda because broken chords in sixteenth notes continue throughout; and in the D major Sonata, op. 53 (D. 850), Schubert himself called for an accelerated tempo at the end.

The strong dialectic element in the sonata movements of Haydn, Mozart, and Beethoven—in which each of the two subjects is separately stated before they confront each other in the development—makes it necessary to keep a strict tempo throughout, as a common battleground for the opposing themes during their fight for unity and sometimes primacy. Each thematic unit is strongly used as a musical substance.

However, the unity concept in all the arts began to change early in the nineteenth century under the influence first of Goethe and Hegel and later of Wagner and Nietzsche.[8] Basing themselves on the ideas of the Greek philosopher Heraclitus—who had seen the world as "becoming" rather than "being," looking at Movement rather than at Substance—artists now emphasized the evolutionary aspect of form. In a sonata, the transitions and the gradual increase toward climaxes, followed each time by a letting-go, became more important than the motivic themes and their divisions into formal sections.

Schubert was the first musician who systematically, though probably subconsciously, embarked on this road. In his work the evolution happens naturally, as a consequence of the spinning forth of a song melody until it generates additional motion, sound, and intensity. This is expressed during the first half of the exposition by an "unnoticeable" (*unmerklich* *) acceleration, which is not so much being engineered as being allowed to happen. The relatively slow tempo markings over the first movements of the G major Sonata, op. 78, and the B-flat major Sonata, op. posth., refer just to their openings.** The first themes in these and in most of the other sonatas (except those of Schubert's youth) are presented in motto fashion, like an engraved inscription on the stone gate through which one enters. Immediately afterward—in the G major Sonata at m. 10, the C minor Sonata at mm. 14–20, the A major Sonata at m. 7, and the B-flat major Sonata at the break in m. 9 (the last three op. posth.)—the opening is being restated in a different way at very gradually increasing velocity. By the time the second subject is reached and the secondary tonality is gained, the tempo has become quick enough to make any further changes unnecessary. In the first movement of the B-flat major Sonata, the segment in F-sharp minor beginning at m. 48 is faster than mm. 9ff (Ex. 24a) and faster even than mm. 36ff (Ex. 24b), but it does not constitute the final step. Though a new thematic substance is acquired at m. 48 (Ex. 24c), the secondary key of F major is not gained until m. 80 (Ex. 24d); and it is only shortly before that measure that the definitive tempo for the rest of the exposition can be reached.

In Schubert, the second theme is generally faster than the first, contrary to the classical tradition, in which the "lyrical" second

---

*Schubert means it, but does not use the term and, in fact, never marks such increases. *Unmerklich* later became one of Mahler's favorite markings, but the practice itself goes back to Schubert.

**Some of Schubert's tempo markings differ in meaning from Beethoven's; for example, *allegro vivace* is slower when Schubert uses the term because it refers to a smaller time unit. Compare *Moment musical* No. 5, (D. 780), the Finale of the B-flat major Trio, the Finale of the A minor Sonata, op. 42, and *Klavierstück* No. 3 with the opening movements of Beethoven's Sonatas, op. 2, no. 2, and op. 31, no. 1, and the Finale of op. 27, no. 1.

Sonata in B-flat major, D. 960, 1st Mvt.
Ex. 24a mm. 9–10   Ex. 24b mm. 36–37

Ex. 24c m. 48   Ex. 24d m. 80

theme (for example, in the *Waldstein* Sonata), if anything, is played slower than the "dramatic" first.[9] Outside of those first movements in which a "motto" introduces the music, I have not found any examples of gradual tempo changes in Schubert's music; here a metronomically identical speed ought to last throughout each movement. I find it quite superfluous, for instance, to change the tempo at all for the middle sections of the slow movements in the last two sonatas—their effect is all the greater if they are presented with the identical beat as before (see above remarks on *istesso tempo*). Where the music comes to a standstill prior to being "taken up" again (the German *Reprise* is better than the English *recapitulation*), as in the *Moonlight* Sonata imitation in the Finale of the last A major Sonata (Ex. 25), it is possible to relax the tempo accordingly, but with utmost caution. The best example of this technique is found in the first movement of the B-flat major Trio, op. 99. Following the development there is a series of false recapitulations, first in G-flat major (mm. 187ff.), then in D-flat major (mm. 198ff.), and finally in the main key, B-flat major (mm. 211ff.): this, too, is definitely a *false* recapitulation, to be played hesitantly and still slightly under the original speed! The tempo is then gradually resumed, with simultaneously increasing dynamic levels, until by m. 222 normal flow is reached at last. This is also what happens

Ex. 25   Sonata in A major, D. 959, 4th Mvt., mm. 200–203.

at the previously described point in the Finale of the A major Sonata, op. posth. Very timidly at first, the rondo theme returns in F-sharp major, *pianissimo* (m. 212). Nine measures later, when it is repeated in the main key, its extreme softness is unchanged. It takes another passage (mm. 229–236) of a new, peculiar setting of the second half of the tune, indicating a struggle, before the music arrives where it was before the "moonlight" episode (m. 237). In performances of these two movements, the fact that there simply is *no* recapitulation of the beginning is frequently unclear because the original tempo and dynamics are resumed too early.*

In the development section of the opening movement of the B major Sonata, op. 147, m. 68 is marked *sempre rit.* (Ex. 26a). But it is not followed by an *a tempo.* The word *sempre* seems to imply that the slowing process began earlier. This is also indicated by the fact that in m. 62 (Ex. 26b), the sixteenth-note upbeats are changed to 32nds, and the rests preceding each upbeat are correspondingly changed from dotted eighths to double-dotted ones. At the original tempo for the movement, *Allegro, ma non troppo,* it would be almost impossible, as well as completely meaningless, to use double-dotted rests and 32nd-note upbeats. Hence, the only sensible explanation is to assume that Schubert wanted

Sonata in B major, D. 575, 1st Mvt.
Ex. 26a   m. 68   Ex. 26b   mm. 61–62

---

*In both examples Schubert's score carries several *a tempo* marks, but they refer exclusively to the *ritardando* marks preceding them and do not concern the overall speed.

Ex. 26c m. 80

[back to tempo]

to preserve the *absolute* speed of the upbeat–downbeat sequence; in other words, that he did not want to lengthen the upbeats along with the *ritardando*. The notation is approximate in any case, for Schubert could not have meant the upbeat to m. 62 to be twice as long as the upbeat to m. 36! The change in the rhythmic notation simply indicates the beginning of a gradual slowing down of the entire music.*

In the late works Schubert became increasingly conscious of organizational needs, as can be seen from the works themselves. In the opening movement of the A major Sonata, op. posth., for example, he unifies the music by means of a motivic device—the rising thirds of the first three measures (Ex. 27a) are used as the bass of the second theme (Ex. 27b)—and by not writing a single completed cadence in the entire movement! It is only at the end of the piece that the music comes down in a conclusive tonic chord. The cyclic constructions used here and in the B-flat major Sonata, op. posth. (which are too well known to need analysis here[10]), also serve the purpose of unification.

At other times Schubert proceeds with the help of sequences that are precisely regulated both metrically and harmonically. The longest such instance in his piano music is found in mm. 309–428 of the Finale of the C minor Sonata, op. posth., as he

*Musicians, even composers, do not always distinguish between the terms *ritardando* (gradual slowing) and *ritenuto* (held back at a steady rate of speed). After the ritard leading to m. 62 (at the key change), Schubert probably meant the tempo to remain at a steady, slower pace, which he indicated by *sempre* (meaning "just as before") *ritardando* (meaning *"ritenuto"*), until the upbeat is retransformed into sixteenth notes at the next key change (back to the original B major) in m. 80 (Ex. 26c). If thus conceived, the first part of the development, in which, symptomatically, the main key is officially left behind and the tempo is changed, emerges as a big parenthesis within the movement. It is fascinating that exactly the same kind of parenthesis, again with key changes marked in the signature, is found at the corresponding place in the Finale, mm. 133–72; and here, too, Schubert probably wanted this section to be slower than the rest of the movement. The only similar parenthesis in a late sonata occurs in the Finale of the C minor Sonata, op. posth., mm. 243–301, where there is an equally "psychedelic" change of key for precisely this episode.

Sonata in A major, D. 959, 1st Mvt.
Ex. 27a mm. 1–3

Ex. 27b mm. 256–58

prepares for the recapitulation. These 120 measures fall into the following divisions:

$$8 + 8 = 16 \ (\text{mm. } 309\text{–}24)$$
$$14 + 14 = 28 \ (\text{mm. } 325\text{–}52)$$
$$15 + 15 = 30 \ (\text{mm. } 353\text{–}82)$$
$$12 + 18 = 30 \ (\text{mm. } 383\text{–}412)$$
$$8 + 4 + 4 = 16 \ (\text{mm. } 413\text{–}26)$$

The first three divisions consist of strict sequences. In the first (mm. 309–24), the music modulates from E minor to D minor (first limb), and from D minor to C minor (second limb). In mm. 325–52 the music remains in the key of C minor for the first tone group and is repeated in F minor during the second. In mm. 353–82 the music begins in B-flat minor and returns to F minor by way of D-flat major at the end of the first part; the second repeats this procedure beginning in F minor, so that it ends in C minor, the key of the second division.

The third division (mm. 353–82) is metrically different from the first two inasmuch as a disguised change of meter takes place here: Three measures now sound like the three beats of a single supermeasure in 3/2 time (similar to the meter change in the Finale of the B-flat major Trio, op. 99, as it enters its middle section). To complicate the situation further, each strain consists not of the normal four, but of five such supermeasures.

The fourth division, adding up to the same 30 measures as the third, consists of two strains unequal in length as well as in musical substance. In the first strain the third sequence is continued throughout four of the five supermeasures (until m. 394). Then the sequential structure is given up, and, in classical tradition, the music begins to gravitate toward the dominant, G (which is reached in m. 413), as a pedal point in C minor. However, it still takes Schubert sixteen more measures before he can begin the recapitulation, for the music is still trembling, as it were. Indeed, at one point it escapes to the remote key of D-flat minor (mm. 421–22) before finally settling down. Only in these last sixteen measures—that is, as late as possible—is the 3/2 meter finally abandoned.

Such colossal planning indicates not only that Schubert, like Beethoven before him, had a natural feeling for shape, but also that at this stage of his accomplishments as a composer he had arrived at a new, thought-out procedure for filling large spaces. He did not subdivide them into flowing, evolutionary passages of thematic development but rather into precise sequences made of thematic material which were repeated as often as necessary, and with definite modulatory directions. This procedure may have been suggested to him by certain techniques in Mozart's piano concertos (for instance, the last part of the development section in the first movement of the C minor Concerto, K. 491), but Schubert used it for infinitely larger purposes. Half a century later, Bruckner's architecture was often quite similar.

In shorter works Schubert uses a much simpler procedure than in the Finale of the C minor Sonata to regain the main key after the middle section. Generally he relies on the dominant minor ninth chord to carry the harmony, a device he uses in all four Impromptus of op. 90. Schubert clearly distinguishes between *decrescendo* and *diminuendo* (=*poco calando*)[11] and, not always so clearly, between *decrescendo* and accent signs.[12]

V. Special Stylistic Features

Schubert's piano music has certain specific qualities, the most obvious feature being its "Viennese" dialect. It appears not only in dances and marches themselves but in a number of other, dancelike and marchlike pieces. For example, compare the second theme of the Impromptu, op. 142, no. 1 (D. 935; Ex. 28), with the Trio section of the G minor March for piano duet, op. 40, no. 2 (D. 819; Ex. 29). Schubert must have known that this quality adds to the charm of the music, but only when it is performed subtly and not underlined. In the Viennese idiom, the second beat in 3/4 is thought of as the feminine ending of the first, especially in waltzes; and—as I learned from Walter Hautzig—appoggiaturas should be clearly enunciated, very short, and late—almost *on* the following beat (see the beginning of the F minor Fantasy for piano duet, op. 103, D. 940).

Ex. 28   Impromptu in F minor, D. 935, no. 1, mm. 45–50.

Ex. 29   March in G minor, D. 819, no. 2, Trio, mm. 1–4.

Another characteristic of Schubert's piano music is melodrama, which is expressed in his late works by tremolos, strettos, and rhapsodic recitatives with brief accompanying chords. For these devices Schubert was probably inspired by Italian composers, especially Rossini and Paganini, whose works he liked, and also by Weber, one of his most celebrated contemporaries. Melodrama is present in the middle section of the slow movement of the A major Sonata, op. posth., and in episodes of the first two of the three *Klavierstücke,* op. posth., of 1828. However, this quality is not the decisive one. For Schubert, who was still young, melodrama simply became one of the appropriate means of expressing feelings and ideas of much greater depth.

The Prater is not very far from St. Stephen's in Vienna, and Schubert is not the only Viennese composer in whose works we find elements from dance music and church music closely woven into the texture of sonata movements. Schubert was especially fond of the traditional church cadence in which the dominant-seventh chord is delayed by a suspension of the key note in the melody voice, and he uses this harmonic device to express solemnity, for instance, in m. 6 of the first movement of the A major Sonata, op. posth. (see Ex. 19a), and during the Trio section of the third movement of the String Quintet in C major, op. 163.

In general, despite his modulations to remote keys, altered chords, major–minor alternations, and delayed cadences, Schubert's harmonic language was conservative. The same is true of his melodies and rhythms; nothing exceeded Mozart's and Beethoven's vocabulary. Schubert's piano music uses higher registers more consistently than even Beethoven's late works, but that trait is simply a result of the many improvements in the instrument.

Schubert used the classical style with the same freedom and inspiration as if he had invented it himself. He has this in common with Palestrina, who, in the sixteenth century, continued to write in the style of the Netherlanders. A composer does not have to be the originator of a style in order to use it superbly. In art, being the first does not necessarily, or even usually, mean being the best. Only in the August sun of Schubert's compositions was the completion of the classical style achieved.

Chapter VI

CHOPIN

Two questions have occupied the minds of Chopin scholars, to the exclusion of other, more—or at least equally—important ones: To what extent is Chopin's music Polish, and to what extent French? To what extent is his music dependent on the instrument of the piano; in what way is it more than just music for the piano?

Obviously, the first question must be answered differently in different countries. The French—as one would expect—see many French characteristics in Chopin, who had a French father and who lived in Paris for the second half of his life; while Polish people, very naturally, point to his Polish roots and affiliations. In other countries, too, similar preferences are found. German eyes, traditionally turned more toward the West than the East, are inclined to look upon Chopin as a French composer; and they regard his Mazurkas and Polonaises as mere ethnic style exercises, comparable to Brahms's Hungarian Dances. On the other hand, in the United States, the Polish folk character of all of Chopin's music, not just his dance music, is regarded as one of its foremost qualities. Most Americans are not even aware that Chopin lived in Paris for so long.

Yet—with few exceptions, mostly concerning the Mazurkas— delving into its regional and ethnical origins does not make us understand Chopin's music any better. Objectively, his situation is not much different from that of the many composers of mixed or foreign origin (like Lully, Offenbach, and Honegger) or of those who, beginning with the Flemish School in the fifteenth century, emigrated from their country of origin during their creative life periods. Their music is not specifically "Flemish" or "Burgundian," etc. Both criteria apply to Chopin. As a child his father provided him with the same knowledge of French civilization—at that time it was largely imbued with Enlightenment and Neoclassicism—that he would have received growing up in France. The rest of his family, as well as his friends, considered themselves totally Polish; so were the writers, singers, and others he admired as an adolescent. Chopin left Warsaw before he was twenty, but not before he had written some of his most important early compositions, including the two concertos and most of the Etudes. At the age of 21, after a relatively long but interrupted stay in Vienna, Chopin made Paris his permanent residence, and he remained there until his death, at 39. The only difference between Chopin and the aforementioned Renaissance composers was that Chopin lived in an epoch of growing nationalism. It is for this reason that he remained deeply attached to the land of his birth and always felt that an essential part of his mission was to become an ambassador of Polish music and Polish spirit in France.

If one were to investigate Chopin's music just from the viewpoint of national origin, one would probably conclude that in the finesse of his intellectual approach Chopin was largely French, but that the character and feeling of his music is predominantly Polish. However, such vague categories cannot be part of a musical analysis: his Waltzes are not Polish waltzes, even his Polonaises are— despite the name—universal dance forms; and, except for the Mazurkas, which are based on folk music, the same is true for the rest of his works. On the other hand, Chopin's music certainly is not French music either. At the time in question, music in France was perhaps at its lowest point in centuries, except for opera. No symphonic, chamber, or solo music of lasting value was written there, except by Berlioz, whose ideals and style, however, were far removed from Chopin's.*

The second question—concerning the importance of the specific pianistic values in his music—is based solely on the negative fact that Chopin wrote no operas, no symphonies, no string quartets, and no choral works. In this he differed from such contemporaries

---

*Besides, according to Delacroix,[1] Chopin's close friend, Chopin detested Berlioz personally. Liszt's importance as a composer only began in earnest after Chopin's death.

as Liszt, Mendelssohn, and Schumann, who had each produced works in at least some of these categories. (Even Rossini wrote piano pieces and sacred music.) We do not know the inner reason why Chopin confined himself to piano music and music with piano (cello music, including a trio; songs; works for piano with orchestra). But certainly, external factors also played a role. For instance, from an early age Chopin had a burning interest in opera and certainly would have liked to produce one. But Poland was a small country, and complete training in subjects like orchestration, vocal writing, and counterpoint was not as readily accessible to a young gifted composer-pianist as it was, for instance, in Vienna. Furthermore, Chopin himself, in his early letters from Paris, mentions that it would take much longer for him to gain a reputation by writing operas than by writing piano music, especially since he had already made such an impression everywhere as a concert pianist.[2] Nevertheless Chopin, too, needed to compose in a big style; hence the Chopin-type Scherzo as well as many features in his Sonatas and other works.

Another important reason for confining himself to piano music lies in Chopin's instinctive creativity in using pianistic sounds and techniques. In his early years, this faculty was so closely allied to his creativity as a composer that no scholar, then or now, has been able to separate instrumentality and substance here; and nobody, not Liszt or even Skryabin, has ever successfully emulated Chopin in this respect. Yet he did not identify his piano music completely with the instrument. For instance, surprisingly, he had absolutely no objection to transcriptions made of his Mazurkas. On the contrary, on June 1, 1848 he wrote about the six vocal transcriptions that the incomparable soprano Pauline Viardot-Garcia, who was also a professional composer, had made: "I also saw the very charming Madame Viardot here again. She was kind enough to sing my Mazurkas at the concert in her theater—and this, without my having asked for it."[3] (But see p. 198 below.)

The theory that Chopin was a composer for piano only is contradicted also by his involvement with the cello. From 1829 to 1846, the fifteen years in which the bulk of his oeuvre was created, he produced a number of idiomatically written works for cello in which he achieved the noblest shadings of tone color and melodiousness. This was at a time when the cello, despite Beethoven, was not generally recognized as a solo instrument. The fact that in his later years Chopin was a close friend of the cellist Auguste Franchomme has nothing to do with this urge: indeed, one finds quite a few passages in his piano works (including early ones) that sound as if they had been transcribed from cello music. Here belong the coda of the A minor Waltz, op. 34, no. 2, mm. 169–89, and four passages in the Mazurkas: op. 24, no. 2, in C major, mm. 70–88 (see Ex. 1); op. 41, no. 1, in C-sharp minor, mm. 127–39 (see Ex. 2); op. 50, no. 1, in G major, mm. 12–16; and op. 50, no. 3, in C-sharp minor, mm. 25–32 (see Ex. 3). The cellist Carter Brey played through these passages as a personal favor to me and made some of them sound better than the greatest pianist could ever render them (the tritones in op. 24, no. 2, for instance). He confirmed that, except for an occasional choice of key that is uncomfortable for string players, Chopin here wrote true cello music, just as one finds in the Cello Sonata in G minor, op. 65.

Ex. 1   Mazurka in C major, op. 24, no. 2, mm. 69–74.

Ex. 2   Mazurka in C-sharp minor, op. 41, no. 1, mm. 130–34.

Ex. 3   Mazurka in C-sharp minor, op. 50, no. 3, mm. 25–26.

Because of these two questions, other, at least equally important approaches to Chopin are often neglected:

1. In what way, objectively speaking, are his pianistic sonorities different from anybody else's? How can his piano texture be analyzed from the viewpoint of sound, independently of technique?

2. Is his music the same for all genres, or is it, like Bach's, different in form, harmonic language, and texture for different species of music? The answer—to be demonstrated later—is that, indeed, very much like Bach (and at least partly influenced by him), Chopin wrote most of his compositions in series, each with its own style.

3. Did his music change over the years, or, as is often said, did it remain to the end identical in style and form? This question has lately become of interest to a number of scholars.

4. The incontestable persistence of elements from the Italian late- and post-Baroque in Chopin's music must be recognized and defined. For whatever reason, his musical personality inclined toward the musical style elements of past generations. His first year in Vienna, where he arrived at age nineteen, opened new perspectives but did not really change his attachment to the more-distant musical tradition. This distinguishes him not only from the Viennese Classicists but also from the Romantic masters of his own time.

Some answers can be found in autographs, letters, and other authentic sources, of which there are fortunately quite a few left. Chopin's autographs are uniquely articulate. Moreover, unlike most other great composers, Chopin frequently spoke of his works in his letters. He was also a most conscientious teacher, so that his personal markings in the scores belonging to his pupils, as well as later testimonies by them, represent valuable source material.[4]

There remains, however, something elusive in Chopin's music. Its essence and its universal appeal are beyond the grasp of scholastic research and analytic theory, a situation of which this study is well aware.

SOUND

Chopin's awareness of the physical origin of piano sound was uniquely perfect, so that his solutions work as well today, for our much stronger instruments, as they did for the weaker piano of his time. The reason is that the laws of acoustics apply regardless of the quantity of sound involved. On the other hand, Chopin's treatment of sound on the piano is largely independent of his technical treatment of the instrument; this is particularly important for the late works.

The following seem to be among his guiding principles:

1. Bass

Chopin's organization of sounds in the low register is modeled on the overtone row. Essentially this means that his textures avoid thickness just above the lowest tone. In a left-hand arpeggio, wherever possible the dominant tone appears only in the second octave and the major (or minor) third in the third octave. The first half-measure of the famous Nocturne in D-flat major, op. 27, no. 2, offers a perfect example (Ex. 4a). Its first seven notes consist of the fundamental tone D-flat and its first four overtones, the last of which appears twice. In the beginning Chopin spans a direct bridge from the lowest to the highest note; he subsequently fills in the middle, from the dominant tone, A-flat, upward. Last comes the D-flat of the middle, the first overtone, whose relative weight is used to establish a metrical feeling for the second half of the measure. There is much wisdom in this arrangement, which is ob-

Nocturne in D-flat major, op. 27, no. 2, mm. 1–3.
Ex. 4a   as written

Ex. 4b   in sarabande-like rhythm

viously an instinctive not a calculated procedure, for it is never rigidly applied. Chopin is always able to find analogous solutions for varying situations. However, its effect also depends on sensitive handling of sound balances by the performer, who must be aware of Chopin's principle. In Nature, fundamental tones are much louder than their overtones, which get successively weaker. This proportion must have been the basis of Chopin's concept, and the pianist-performer must respect and combine it with the necessary concern for rhythmic and metric clarity and flow. In our example, this leads to leaning very slightly on the a-flat of the second beat, resulting in a subtle sarabande-like (eighth-note, quarter-note) rhythm (Ex. 4b). As stated, the seventh note will then become another, softer first beat, opening the next pattern without a break, for this is not a second 3/8, but the second half of a true 6/8 meter. A better setting of a 6/8 meter in natural harmony cannot be imagined.*

Chopin's arrangement of the ascending arpeggio of the F minor Ballade, op. 52 (Ex. 5), seems to contradict this arrangement and at first looks un-Chopinesque and awkward. But one soon realizes that the chord structures are grouped around the various E-flats as root tones coordinating everything. The first E-flat, in accordance with Chopin's overtone awareness, occupies the lowest octave by itself. The following e-flat reigns over three chords (second to

Ex. 5 Ballade No. 4 in F minor, op. 52, mm. 117–18.

---

*André Gide[5] suggests bringing out the top notes, f', comparing this place with the repeated f-sharps" in the trio section of the B minor Scherzo. The f-sharps" are, however, simple quotations of Schubert's bell effects in the trio of the Minuet of his G major Sonata, op. 78, which is in the same key of B major (see below, p. 256, Exx. 2a,b). The two places have no parallels that I can see. Gide's advice to emphasize the major third, f", is wrong, because the constant repetition of this tone emphasizes it enough.

fourth eighth notes): its repetition in the higher octave (e-flat′) simply represents a first overtone. But then, in the fifth eighth note the same tone becomes the root for the final three chords of the group. They are similarly constructed, with e-flat″ as the first overtone, sounded at the sixth eighth note.

The left-hand parts of the Waltzes are full of instances of Chopin's use of overtone distances and sound proportions. This is easily seen in some of the recapitulations, where Chopin wants to establish a vigorous and full-sounding return after the end of the middle section. In m. 78 of the "Minute" Waltz, op. 64, no. 1 (Ex. 6), he changes only the first tone, which is now played an octave

Ex. 6 Waltz in D-flat major, op. 64, no. 1, mm. 74–78.

lower than before. The chords on the second and third beats remain unchanged but they sound different, for both the a-flat and the f′ are now heard as overtones of the low D-flat. Therefore they produce a fuller sound than in m. 5, where, squeezed between the bass and the treble, they merely exert a rhythmic function. The low B in m. 98 of the B minor Waltz, op. 69, no. 2, has a similar effect, except that in the minor mode the top note, d′, is not a direct overtone. Much greater subtlety reigns in the arrangement of bass chords in the A-flat major "Grande Valse," op. 42, with its most carefully elaborated texture. The "refrain"—the sentence repeated at the end of each section—begins with a low E-flat in mm. 41, 73 (see Ex. 7a), 105, and 165. Two measures later (in mm. 43 and 75) the E-flat is replaced by e-flat, while in the second half of the refrain the order is reversed (see mm. 49 and 53). This has to do with the direction of the bass melody as well as with the vertical arrangement, but in the coda of the Waltz Chopin's concern for sound can be clearly perceived as a goal in itself, for in mm. 213–14 (Ex. 7b), the same refrain is introduced "*leggiero*": not only is the downbeat bass e-flat and not E-flat, but the top note of the chord on the two other beats is b-flat′ and not (as before) g′!

Above E-flat, in the earlier passages, the note g′ had formed the fourth overtone of a major third plus two octaves. Now the b-flat′ finds itself an octave and a half higher than the bass e-flat; in other words, it has become a second overtone (octave plus a fifth).

Chopin's overtone-like bass structure was of special importance for the brilliant, fast passages in his Etudes and Concertos. The trills and fast tone repeats in these virtuoso works needed the strong, natural support which these configurations created. In the Etudes one often finds these passages after the end of the first section, when the music modulates or moves on thematically, as in the C major Etude, op. 10, no. 7 (Ex. 8). In the left hand, the broken A major chord, as dominant of D minor, in m. 17, and especially the ensuing D minor chord of m. 18, conform exactly to the distribution of natural overtones as explained above. The capricious rhythm of these broken chords, together with the "delicate" tone repeats (g″ is sounded twelve times in m. 17!) constitutes a perfect sound configuration, as does, for the same reasons, the pedaled-through ending of the F major Etude, op. 25, no. 3 (Ex. 9). The *cambiata* arrangement of the ascending scale variant in m. 69 is supported by the lowest F from mm. 66 and 67, with its proper overtones, and this gives the passage a marvelous spotlight, quite different from the arrangement of the same tone sequence in m. 78 of the earlier F major Etude, op. 10, no. 8 (Ex. 10). Since Chopin, in

Ex. 8   Etude in C major, op. 10, no. 7, mm. 17–22.

Ex. 9   Etude in F major, op. 25, no. 3, mm. 66–70.

Ex. 10   Etude in F major, op. 10, no. 8, m. 78.

his prolific inventiveness, usually does not use the same figuration twice, one may presume that he rewrote the passage because the earlier arrangement did not please him any longer, as it was not properly supported by the bass. In the G-sharp minor Etude, op. 25, no. 6, too much agitation would have slipped into the left-hand figures if he had used the very low bass tones as support, but even here Chopin descends to the bottom as often as he conveniently can (see Ex. 11).

Ex. 11 Etude in G-sharp minor, op. 25, no. 6, mm. 7–8.

2. Top Voice

André Gide,[6] speaking of the A-flat major Prelude, warns against exaggerated emphasis of the top voice. With a certain amount of justification he says that Chopin is not a Romantic. He obviously means that he does not consider Chopin a *late* Romantic. Gide is right. There are very few passages where the pianist has to "mark" the melody by using the kind of powerful, "pulling" tone described by Mikuli; for Chopin normally avoids any obvious form of emphatic expressivity. Yet occasionally he can be emotionally very direct, as in the opening of the slow movement of the B minor Sonata, op. 58 (Ex. 12), with its initial upward-surging major sixth (see p. 143, above). Otherwise, as Gide says, a Chopin melody floats in a stream mainly carried by the lower voices. Poetically it sometimes happens that a melody is recognizable in

Ex. 12 Sonata No. 3 in B minor, op. 58, 3rd Mvt., m. 1.

retrospect only. This is the case when it only gradually emerges from its background—an effect that Chopin possibly derived from Bach. The soft repeats on g″ at the very opening of the F minor Ballade, eventually leading to the introductory melody, fulfil the same function and have a similar sonorous structure as the initial g-sharp of the solo violin in the second movement of Bach's E major Violin Concerto.

Chopin frequently compared his melodies with Bellini's and felt that his tunes were indeed derived from Italian opera. This is psychologically true, for it was surely Italian vocal style that enabled Chopin to find an alternative to the empty mechanical tunes used by his colleagues in their virtuoso music (especially Hummel and Kalkbrenner). But they remain piano music nevertheless. Just put texts to a lyrical Chopin melody and try to sing it! Without the equilibrating function of the diverse piano registers, these tunes (as their bad arrangements for ballet orchestra prove) are without fragrance and often even sound vulgar (but see p. 189 above). Chopin's actual songs for voice and piano are supported by a completely different, unoperatic texture; and their sound has no resemblance whatever to Italian opera.

A totally unexplained phenomenon is Chopin's involvement with the sound of the tone c″. It cannot be a coincidence (though it may have been an unconscious act) that Chopin uses that particular tone as an evocation, to introduce a piece of music or to effect a transition between one section and the next. This is best described by telling how I discovered this, many years ago. When I first learned the A-flat major Polonaise, about 1924, I came upon the transitory passage, mm. 137–42, in B-flat minor, in which the dominant tone, F, plays a major role, both as a pedal point in the bass and as a center of pitch for the melody. Immediately following, in mm. 143–51, the same passage is prolonged by an exact transposition to F minor, with C playing the same role as F played before. This time, all of a sudden, Chopin sets sharp accent marks (very deliberate and visible in his autograph) every time c″ appears in the melody (see Ex. 13), regardless of the position of that tone in the measure. In m. 143 there is one accent on the downbeat and another on the tenth sixteenth note; in the following measure there is one on the seventh sixteenth note, and in m. 145 it is on the second sixteenth. This pitch has a special ring as an absolute tone, independent of its melodic-harmonic functions as part of a group of notes. Somehow, the accented tone, which recurs at ever-shorter intervals, seems to call us back from a dream and into reality. The nature of the accent that Chopin prescribes becomes less mysterious when it is compared with other examples. Because the tone C is so frequently repeated, it has no need of accents, particularly at the very beginning of a piece or of a new section, in any key in which C is either the fifth or the third tone of the scale, that is, in F (major or minor) or in A-flat major.

Ex. 13 Polonaise in A-flat major, op. 53, mm. 143–45.

In the F major Ballade, op. 38, as in all the Ballades, the opening is gradual (see p. 230, below). The softly repeated tone c″ makes both the performer and the listeners focus slowly but surely on the traditional tune that rises from it. In the A-flat major Ballade, op. 47, c″ plays its role twice: first to introduce—unaccompanied except by its upper octave—the countertheme (m. 52 to downbeat of m. 54; Ex. 14a) and then to effect a stunning, Schubertian modulation from C major (as dominant) back to A-flat (mm. 115–16), this time as the top note in a C major chord (Ex. 14b). A similar situation is found in the Mazurka in A-flat major, op. 50, no..2, mm. 36–40.

Ballade No. 3 in A-flat major, op. 47.
Ex. 14a mm. 52–53   Ex. 14b mm. 115–16

The late (1843) Nocturne in F minor, op. 55, no. 1 (Ex. 15), perhaps best illuminates the hallucinating character of the dominant tone *c″*. As an unaccompanied upbeat, it opens the piece, and for five measures the melody keeps centering around it, somewhat in the same fashion as in the A-flat major Polonaise (see above); finally a descent to the keynote over mm. 6–8 resolves the situation. See also the F minor Fantaisie, op. 49 (Ex. 16). Less distinct, but also, in my opinion, part of the same group of examples, are the arabesques around this same tone in the F minor Etude, op. 25, no. 2, especially between the first section and its repeat, mm. 18–19.

Ex. 15   Nocturne in F minor, op. 55, no. 1, mm. 1–4.

Ex. 16   Fantaisie in F minor, op. 49, mm. 76–77.

In conclusion, one must regard Chopin as a composer who—more than any other great composer except Mozart and perhaps Ravel—was almost oversensitive to sound. A primary task for pianists who play his music is to approach this sensitivity as much as possible.

BAROQUE AND PRE-CLASSICAL ELEMENTS

By 1810, when Chopin was born, Beethoven had already published more than seventy works, including the *Emperor* Concerto; Mozart had been dead for almost twenty years; and Haydn, too, had died. Clementi (born 1752) remained the only living composer of note whose childhood reached back to pre-Classical times. By the time Chopin began to compose for the piano at the age of seven, the piano as instrument, too, had undergone considerable changes in action and sound since its early use during the second half of the eighteenth century.

Under these circumstances it is strange that Chopin, alone among his contemporaries, preserved traditional style characteristics of pre-Classical music. This cannot be explained by the fact that Poland was outside the mainstream of musical activity. Much of Chopin's music sounds as if Haydn, Mozart, and Beethoven had never existed. On the other hand, Chopin was by no means unaware of these masters.[7] He was particularly devoted to Mozart, and in accordance with his request, Mozart's Requiem was sung at his funeral. Nor was Beethoven without importance for Chopin. One can feel in his C-sharp minor music—such as the Fantaisie-Impromptu and Etude No. 4—that Chopin was impressed by Beethoven's *Moonlight* Sonata (see also p. 111, above). We know that on one occasion Chopin privately played the Beethoven Variations in A-flat major, from the Sonata, op. 26, and that he did so in a rather casual manner, according to his pupil W. von Lenz. On the way home Lenz had the nerve to interrogate him about his attitude. Chopin replied that he had only been "indicating": it was up to the audience "to do the rest [parachever]"!*

The atavistic streak in Chopin's nature is beyond explanation.[9] Perhaps, as an expatriate, he was holding on to educational values from home; also, though extreme traditionalism was hardly in his line, he may have liked to lean on traditional values as a counterbalance to his Romantic whims, such as leapfrogging melodic lines and spontaneous free rhythms.

Chopin's old-fashioned habits show up in his notation. In the third and fourth decades of the nineteenth century, he was one of

---

*Chopin had a special affinity for Schubert's music.[8] He came to Vienna only a few months after Schubert's death, at a time when everybody was speaking about Schubert and his works. The young, brilliant, and attractive pianist Josefine Blahetka, whose father was one of Chopin's supporters, had known Schubert well. One of Chopin's friends, the great operatic tenor Adolphe Nourrit (1802–1839), had introduced Schubert's songs to France. After Nourrit's suicide, Chopin played Schubert's song "Die Sterne" on the organ at the memorial service. There are certain reminiscences in Chopin's music: the close of Ballade No. 4 may have been fashioned after that of Schubert's E-flat major Impromptu and the coda of Ballade No. 2—which, according to Schumann, was added later—after Schubert's "Erlkönig." But whether there existed a substantial influence in general—whether, in particular, Chopin's idea to write short pieces was inspired by those composed by Schubert—has to my knowledge not yet been investigated.

the few composers who still wrote whole notes in the middle of
the bar (as in the B minor Mazurka, op. 33, no. 4, shown in Ex.
17). His rhythmic notation of two uneven (longer and shorter)
triplet eighths consists of a dotted eighth plus a sixteenth (see
above, p. 5). True, one finds the same notation in the clarinet
part of Beethoven's Fifth Symphony, second movement, m. 19.
But that symphony was written at least two years before Chopin
was born. Only Schubert, on rare occasions,* still used it in the
1820s. Chopin persevered in this notation to the end; see particularly his Polonaise-Fantaisie, op. 61, mm. 242ff. Although Chopin
does not write appoggiaturas in small print, he frequently uses
mordent signs or grace-note notation for similar purposes. Sometimes he also writes out the three notes of a mordent in large print,
and occasionally he combines both kinds of notation. In the F
minor Mazurka, op. 7, no. 3, the mordent on the downbeat of m.
10 is written out (Ex. 18) but that on the second beat of the secondary theme (m. 29) is notated with a mordent sign. Two measures later the same pattern appears under a trill sign; probably all
three instances are to be played alike, and the only reason for writing out the mordent the first time is that, falling on a downbeat, it

Ex. 17   Mazurka in B minor, op. 33, no. 4, m. 9.

Ex. 18   Mazurka in F minor, op. 7, no. 3, mm. 9–10.

---

*In the second movement of the B-flat major Sonata, D. 960, m. 57, Schubert uses this
notation for the fifth and sixth notes in the upper part of the left hand, but *not* in the closing
theme of the finale of this sonata, mm. 185ff.; compare the rondo theme of the fourth
movement of the C minor Sonata, D. 958.

has greater thematic significance. In the famous D major Mazurka, op. 33, no. 2, the notation is reversed: the light, quick mordent on the downbeat of m. 2 is written as a grace note while the mordent on the second beat of the following measure appears as a triplet in large notes. Here it seems likely that a difference of performance was intended. Probably the written-out mordent should be played in time, like a regular triplet—that is, not accelerated—while the grace-note mordent ought to be realized as an embellishment, *molto leggiero.*

We are on safer ground in other areas of Chopin's use and notation of embellishments, thanks to the notes taken by students or entered by Chopin in their scores. Thus we learn that normally *all embellishments were to be played on the beat, not before the beat,* and that *trills had to begin on the auxiliary note*[10] and were to be absolutely even, rather than extremely fast. These rules were the same as in Italian *coloratura,* a style that Chopin consciously emulated, aiming at grace and beauty rather than at acrobatics. These are the same rules, on the whole, as those set down for the keyboard by Bach's second son, Carl Philipp Emmanuel, more than 50 years before Chopin's birth. Although Hummel—a composer whose works Chopin played in his Warsaw years—declared in his *Pianoforte School* of 1828[11] that from now on trills had to begin on the principal note, that meant nothing to the younger composer.

Baroque, or at least pre-Classic, elements are also found in the substance of the music. Certain lateral structures, otherwise obsolete in Chopin's time, recur in his scores. The opening tutti themes of both piano concertos, especially of the E minor Concerto, are based on a chromatic chaconne-style bass, which descends from the key note to the dominant note in the lower octave (Ex. 19). Listening to these openings for the first time, one might easily attribute them to, say, Tartini or Cherubini. Chopin used the same bass in the first episode of the E minor Waltz, op. posth., mm. 25–40 (see Ex. 20a), which was composed in the same year (1830) as the E minor Concerto. As a contrast, in the opening theme of the Waltz (mm. 9–24), the bass rises diatonically from the leading tone (Ex. 20b). The opening of the Allegro de Concert, op. 46, similarly suggests Baroque openings. Since this work was originally written as a sketch for a third piano concerto, one must regard the passage as a quasi-reduction from a nonexistent

Ex. 19   Concerto No. 1 in E minor, 1st Mvt., mm. 1–8.

Waltz in E minor, op. posth.
Ex. 20a   mm. 25–32

Ex. 20b   mm. 9–12

orchestra score. Apparently Chopin thought in terms of old-style ritornellos whenever he was introducing a major work (not only a concerto); hence the first eight measures of the B minor Sonata, op. 58, which imitate the broad detached chords of a late-Baroque string orchestra (see below, p. 245). In this context the E minor Waltz also appears as more than just another waltz. If we acknowledge these steps into the musical past as a characteristic of Chopin's music, we may assume that other unexplained features of his compositions may also have historic roots. His *rubato,* as described by

his contemporaries, is identical with C. P. E. Bach's as well as with
Mozart's, as described by himself and his father (see above, p. 90).
Like Mozart, Chopin avoids the use of the term itself, probably in
order to prevent rhythmic eccentricities.

Chopin, like the Baroque masters, preferred to compose his
works not singly but in series, writing different pieces in varying
moods and keys. Unlike Beethoven in the *Hammerklavier* Sonata
or the *Diabelli* Variations, Chopin never attempted to exhaust the
essence of a certain genre in one huge comprehensive opus; one
does not find "the ballade to end all ballades," for example. In this
respect he was less modern than Bach himself, who, by the end of
his life, had written such a "summa" several times—in the *Goldberg Variations,* the *Musical Offering,* and the *Art of Fugue.* Finally,
Chopin's attachment to Baroque values in music possibly explains
his curious attitude regarding some of the music by those who
surrounded him. On several occasions Chopin declared his lack of
understanding and sympathy for Schumann's music, which is con-
spicuously absent from the list of pieces he gave his students to
learn—a list that included the music of Schubert, Mendelssohn,
Moscheles, and other contemporaries. On other occasions Chopin
voiced some resistance to the music of Beethoven (see below).

What distinguishes Schumann and Beethoven—who, to this
day, are regarded in France as the two most Teutonic masters—
from the rest is the relative lack of Baroque ingredients in their
music (but see p. 148, above). Chopin is said to have hated the
opening of the Finale of Beethoven's Fifth Symphony. Of course!
For someone listening with Baroque-trained ears, strong beats, as
Quantz and others explicitly stated, must be dissonant in order
later to be resolved downward. Beethoven's blast of triumphantly
alternating tonic and dominant harmonizations of a melody that
consists exclusively of harmony tones basking in the sunlight of
victory, without a clouding dissonant, must have sounded atro-
cious to Chopin. If, for fun, one were to add a few mordents, sus-
pensions, and turns to the melody tones, Beethoven's music would
be ruined, but Chopin might resurface as a listener!

The notation of some of the cadenza- or *fioritura*-like quick passages makes it difficult to determine how Chopin wanted to fit
them into the continuing accompaniment rhythm in the left hand.
The F-sharp major Nocturne, op. 15, no. 2, has good examples in

m. 11 and in a parallel place in m. 51, where the *coloratura* is more elaborate. These measures contrast with the simple polyrhythmic notation in the beginning of the middle episode (mm. 25–32). Here the left hand has four eighth notes to the bar while in the right hand each half measure is subdivided into five sixteenths, so that the second and fourth eighth notes of the left hand fall exactly halfway between the third and fourth and the eighth and ninth sixteenths in the right (Ex. 21a). In some editions, the same method is applied to m. 11 (Ex. 21b), but that may not be the cor-

Nocturne in F-sharp major, op. 15, no. 2.
Ex. 21a mm. 25–27

Ex. 21b m. 11

rect realization of Chopin's intentions. The passage is less regular than that. Chopin expressed himself partly through his unexpected slurs at the beginning (one slur for the first fifteen notes) and the end (the last nine notes divided between one slur for three notes and another for the remaining six, leaving the chromatic up and down of the six center notes without a slur); and partly by the score alignment of the two hands, as far as it can be reconstructed in the absence of a manuscript. The 30 notes of the right hand in this measure are not exactly matched by those in the left. Mathematically, one note in the left hand corresponds to seven and a half in the right. In reality, the last nine notes emerge as three melodic triplets, the a-sharp″ coinciding with the last note in the left hand.

This leaves two and a half beats (taking the eighth note as the beat for our purpose). Of these, the first fifteen notes, as indicated by Chopin's slur, form the first half of the measure (the inbetween tone in the left hand is best played together with the eighth small note in the right hand, which is a harmony note). That leaves half a beat for the six unslurred notes. The next three notes, under Chopin's slur, occupy the same time, and are therefore half as fast as the first six. Summing up, there are nine notes under the first beat; six under the second (much slower, that is); nine notes—subdivided into six subbeats—under the third beat, the first half being at double speed; and again six notes under the last beat. One could state this by saying that there are basically six notes to the beat, except that the first beat is a *little* faster, and the first half of the third beat is *much* faster. However, there is nothing rigorous about this distribution. It definitely must not be heard as such; it is flexible and approximate and may also be modified to some extent so that certain bass notes do not come *with* the right-hand note, but immediately before or immediately after.

This analysis of Chopin's slurs helps to determine in which direction the *rubato* ought to go, but it is apparently not clear to everyone. The Paderewski edition reports Chopin's slurs (which are the same in both original editions) in the critical notes, but in the text it replaces them with the editor's own, unsubstantiated ideas.*

The second passage, m. 51 (Ex. 22), is more elaborate, but ends with the same nine notes, which ought to be slurred the same way as before. They form the fourth and last beat. The first two beats are filled with seven descending chromatic broken sixths (the last

Ex. 22 Nocturne in F-sharp major, op. 15, no. 2, m. 51.

---

*This happens frequently.[12] I find it necessary, in all doubtful cases, to read the critical notes of the Paderewski edition if I want to know what Chopin himself notated. Editors sometimes go so far as to replace Chopin's c-sharp by d-flat; they must think that the composer was not capable of analyzing his own harmonies correctly!

not complete), and this time the ensuing chromatic center is almost a straight chromatic scale. Its first note, d′, harmonically still belongs to the descending sixths. The end, in which the last two scale notes are repeated, naturally leads into the nine-tone concluding melody.

The famous passage in m. 52 of the D-flat major Nocturne, op. 27, no. 2, follows the same laws (Ex. 23). Its 48 notes could be evenly subdivided among the twelve sixteenths of the left hand. But the Paderewski edition correctly states in its critical notes that this was not Chopin's intention. Applying the same principles as before, only the first half is evenly subdivided into six groups of four notes, while the second half starts with only three notes to the bass beat, so that the c″ coincides with the f′ below. Then the right hand accelerates as soon as the ascending scale begins, so that its nine notes are played in the time of two bass notes; the passage then ends regularly, as each of the last three bass sixteenths fit with four notes in the right hand.

Ex. 23 Nocturne in D-flat major, op. 27, no. 2, m. 52.

ARTICULATION

Chopin grew up with pianos rather than harpsichords, so that, unlike Haydn and Mozart, right from the beginning he was used to seeing and handling the markings typical of piano music: accents, crescendos, diminuendos, *legato* and *staccato* signs—that is, the complete arsenal of a pianist who would be working with recent music by Clementi, Beethoven, Weber, or Hummel. But on one essential point Chopin's scores are different: they feature a declamation in which emphasis is produced without loudness. This particularity must have been as much in Chopin's nature as it was in Mozart's. Both composers shrank from sudden or abrupt noises. Many of Chopin's students have described how he tried to avoid banging or even great loudness as such, whether at home or during public concerts, and how herein lay the principal difference between his playing and Liszt's at that time.* (Forty years later, when as a teacher Liszt posed as the authentic interpreter of Chopin, he "changed his tune" and now became equally careful in avoiding all unnecessary display of noise.)

There clearly exists a law of cultural evolution according to which articulation tends to develop, with time, from emphasis by length to emphasis by accent, for a similar development took place in the field of verse prosody. According to *The New Columbia Encyclopedia:*

> In ancient Greek poetry the pattern was in the quantity of the syllables, i.e., the duration of the time required to express a syllable . . . in modern languages stress has been substituted for quantity. . . . Modern poets, such as Gerard Manley Hopkins, have recognized both the time and stress measures of verse. . . .[13]

In music, this principle sometimes works in reverse, the emphasis being conveyed by shorter instead of longer duration. Probably the most important aspect of Chopin's melodic articulation is his way of emphasizing a downbeat: Chopin does not plant a melody accent on it—especially if the melody ascends to it from the upbeat—instead he shortens it. Sometimes the pedal sustains portions of the sound, sometimes not, but under no circumstances is the downbeat meant to be accented. We have observed a similar type of articulation in Mozart (see above, p. 104). In Chopin's music this type of articulation has a much wider field of application and can be observed in every type of piece and every type of melody. Most congenial to the species is the nonemphasis of short downbeats in the Mazurkas: see op. 7, no. 1, in B-flat major, first theme (Ex. 24); and op. 30, no. 3, in D-flat major, (Ex. 25). But one also finds the same situation in the Waltzes (Grande Valse Brillante in E-flat major, op. 18; Ex. 26); the Polonaises (Polonaise-Fantaisie, op. 61, where this articulation becomes an essential ingredient of the main theme; see Ex. 27); the Nocturnes (see the

---

*If one can believe Lenz, Chopin did not necessarily object when other pianists played loudly, particularly not in the case of his pupil Adolf Gutmann, a questionable character who became one of Chopin's intimates and for whom Chopin wrote the C-sharp minor Scherzo. It is probable that some of the loudest, fastest passages in this piece were specifically meant to display Gutmann's big tone and style. Since his own keyboard sonorities were exactly the opposite, we can infer that Chopin did not always have himself in mind as performer when he wrote piano music.

Ex. 24   Mazurka in B-flat major, op. 7, no. 1, mm. 1–4.

Ex. 25   Mazurka in D-flat major, op. 30, no. 3, mm. 9–11.

Ex. 26   Waltz in E-flat major, op. 18, mm. 117–21.

Ex. 27   Polonaise-Fantaisie, op. 61, mm. 24–27.

first two measures of the B major Nocturne, op. 9, no. 3; Ex. 28);
and the Sonatas (in Ex. 29, from the second movement of the B-
flat minor Sonata, op. 35, the third beat of m. 1 is accented, the
downbeat of m. 2 very definitely not, but it is marked *staccato*).
There may be an indirect relationship with ballet—which, just at
Chopin's time, began to come into its own in Paris—since a light,
unaccented, short downbeat here helps lighten the dancers' feet.

Moreover, there must have been some connection with string articulation, at a moment when a school of great violinists, following Paganini, began to develop in France (Beriot, Vieuxtemps, and
the Pole Wieniawski, among others).[14] One can still hear this style
on recordings by Fritz Kreisler of his own music. At the end of a
phrase, with an elegant stroke of the bow, he glides up to the next
downbeat, where the tone magically disappears with Houdini-like
speed and lightness—an astonishingly effective device!

Ex. 28   Nocturne in B major, op. 9, no. 3, mm. 1–2.

Ex. 29   Sonata No. 2 in B-flat minor, op. 35, 2nd Mvt., mm. 1–2.

Therefore, even when there is an accent mark, it only means
that the tone in question ought to sound important, not necessarily that the emphasis has to be achieved by playing it louder.
Chopin here appeals to the performer's imagination for finding the
most appropriate means of emphasis. Some of Chopin's marks are
meant more literally and pianistically than conceptually. Thus one
finds slurs that merely indicate that several tones should be played
with no interruption of sound, but that does not mean that they
have to be parts of the same musical phrase. Frequently, in the
Waltzes and the Mazurkas, all the left-hand downbeats that can be
reached by the fingers are written as dotted half notes, while those
that cannot are notated in quarter notes and pedaled to the end of
the bar. No difference in length or importance is meant to be heard
between the two.

After a century of negligence in pedaling Chopin, at last it has been brought to the attention of performers, by Maurice Hinson[15] and by others, that the pedals, just as Chopin wrote them, are part of the articulation. By his notation he became the first modern composer for the pedal. Beethoven confined his pedal marks to lengthy damper eliminations. He never bothered to prescribe pedal for an average phrase; Chopin was the first to do so and the first, especially, to mark the lifting of the pedal under all circumstances. In the Waltzes and the Mazurkas some of the pedalings that begin on the downbeat go only as far as the end of the second beat, while some go to the end of the measure, but in every case Chopin specifies what he wants. He is so particular about it that he frequently changes the pedaling—as we can see in his manuscripts—even when nothing else in the music is being changed.

What Chopin tries to achieve, it seems, is less than an overall color effect, and certainly not a clarification of harmony progressions. His pedals are rather a form of orchestration, comparable to the special pedals previously available to performers on the fortepiano (see above, pp. 81–82). Periods of constant pedal alternate with periods in which a minimum of pedal is employed. This is a point that deserves more attention than it usually gets: pianists today are trained to observe Chopin's pedals exactly but unfortunately they are not prevented from freely adding their own wherever Chopin's score has no pedal marks. The reason is that they have trouble playing a perfect *legato* with the fingers only. But if it is true, as Irma Wolpe once phrased it, that Chopin's principle of pedaling is "alternate overpedaling and underpedaling," we must try our utmost to realize a transparent *legato* by touch only, as part of the tone color scheme that Chopin had in mind. If despite our efforts the *legato* remains imperfect, this is still the lesser evil, compared to an unindividualized gravy of pedaling.

EVOLUTION OF STYLE

The change in Chopin's style that occurred during the last part of his life resembles Schubert's evolution inasmuch as it reflects a general change of values rather than a musical change. In Chopin's case it hardly appears in the fields of harmony and formal design, where scholars have been searching for it. It rather has to do with a changed attitude, after about 1845, toward the act of composing. Gone are the days when inspiration was accepted by Chopin as an inseparable unit of hearing and playing, of inner ear and piano fingers! Composing now is dissociated from performing at the piano. Also—as Liszt,[16] in the case of the Polonaise-Fantaisie, was the first to observe—Chopin's textures no longer automatically fit onto hand and fingers; at times the writing becomes almost awkward in the intense compositional effort toward "poetic precision." * Nor does the inspiration always remain immediate.

Among the several instances in which the principal melody is preceded by an improvisatory search are the Third Impromptu, op. 51, and the Polonaise-Fantaisie, op. 61 (see pp. 238 and 227). Both pieces to some extent reenact the miracle of melodic inspiration as Chopin experienced it. In the Impromptu, the first two measures indicate that there is as yet no melodic substance. The first theme is indeed nothing but a search for new ideas, based on a neutral passage resembling the First Impromptu. Almost deliberately, the opening of the Third Impromptu fails to develop until, suddenly, in m. 32, an extremely strong and visionary motive appears that has the power instantly, and retroactively, to transform everything into a firm, if dreamy, texture (see Ex. 30). It obviously is what we have been waiting for all along. In the Polonaise-Fantaisie the process is similar but takes less time. After a search, Chopin discovers a phrase ending (Ex. 31) that has a meaning, though it is as yet undeveloped. The composer repeats it as if reenacting the moment of inspiration. He toys with it, then stops, and surprisingly gets into a polonaise rhythm in the left hand with such energy that the end melody of the previous phrase quite naturally takes its place in this new context. What, to me, proves the

Ex. 30   Impromptu No. 3 in G-flat major, op. 51, m. 32.

---

*A term created by Kurt Appelbaum.

Ex. 31 Polonaise-Fantaisie, op. 61, mm. 13–15.

plausibility of this analysis is that these two melodies—of the Impromptu and the Polonaise-Fantaisie—distinctly resemble each other.

It follows that the great and principal difference of the later works lies in their lack of immediacy of music making, compared to the earlier compositions. Nothing is permitted to come so naturally now that it can go unchecked into the definitive text. The act of composing becomes part of the composition. Although it happens in a quite different way than in Beethoven, this is indeed a common trait of these two composers,* though certainly Chopin here was in no way influenced by Beethoven.

Chopin's textures progressively became more linear. This seems to be a normal development. We can observe the same phenomenon in Bach's late works, in Mozart's F major Sonata, K. 533, and in the late Beethoven Fugues. Chopin's melody lines, which had always been transparent in all voices, at times became totally polyphonic. Clashes between independent melody lines could produce unusual dissonances and audacious harmonies as "fringe benefits" of clashes, as exemplified in mm. 59 and 60 of the Second Impromptu (see p. 239 and Ex. 61). In general, unlike Liszt, Chopin did not experiment with new chord combinations or modulations as such. Only in his early music, and even then only rarely, did he go outside the tonal region. For example, near the end of the first movement of the E minor Concerto, in a passage in the tonic (Ex. 32a), Chopin suddenly inserts a G minor chord, which is repeated twice more in sequence. In his early years he also liked a confrontation of fixed bass notes and chromatically moving upper voices, either ascending or descending (see, for instance, Exx. 32b

---

*See the opening of Beethoven's D minor Sonata, op. 31, no. 2; his C major Quartet, op. 59, no. 3; his C minor Sonata, op. 111; and especially his Ninth Symphony, among many other examples where we share in the (gradual or sudden) establishment of a sonata theme.

Concerto in E minor, op. 11, 1st Mvt.
Ex. 32a   mm. 628–29

Ex. 32b   mm. 211–16

Ex. 32c   mm. 322–24

and c). Later, suffering from depression and finally, total despair, he frequently used chromatically descending lines in inner voices to express his deep frustration. It suffices here to cite the E minor Prelude from op. 28 and the late Mazurka in F minor, op. 68, no. 4, mm. 1–4 and 11–14.*

WALTZES AND MAZURKAS

These two dance forms share the time signature of 3/4 and a tempo that varies, for the most part, between Allegro and Andante. A listener can usually determine at once whether the piece in question is a waltz or a mazurka. A waltz, no matter how slow, is essentially a one-beat dance; while a mazurka, no matter how fast, always has three beats. This is correct, for instance, for the "Lento" of the A minor Waltz, op. 34, no. 2, as well as for the "Vivace" of the F-sharp minor Mazurka, op. 59, no. 3 (Ex. 33). In the latter one can visualize an agile conductor emphasizing every beat, and in the former, a melancholy maestro with low pulse rate stretching a single beat through an entire measure.

Ex. 33   Mazurka in F-sharp minor, op. 59, no. 3, mm. 1–4.

On occasion, however, Chopin momentarily slips from one dance form into the other. In the A minor Waltz, for instance, the first episode, beginning on m. 37, is more mazurka than waltz. Near the end of the main section of the C-sharp minor Mazurka, op. 41, no. 1 (Ex. 34), the left hand has an ordinary waltz beat. What this means is that Chopin, for purposes of rhythmic-metric contrast, inserts a different dance beat into an otherwise normal dance—just as in the F-sharp minor Polonaise, op. 44, mm. 127ff.,

---

*Posthumously published, it exists in several versions of different length, but its essential features are the same.

he inserts a mazurka. In no case is the dance as a whole affected by this brief encounter.

Ex. 34 Mazurka in C-sharp minor, op. 41, no. 1, mm. 17–20.

Waltzes

In 1789, at exactly the same time as Parisian commoners began to rebel against the aristocracy and the Church, the rough "Jump-Dance" of the Austrian Alps, in which the men stamped their heavy mountain boots, occasionally throwing the women over their shoulders, began to replace the elegant minuet as a dance proper. Thereafter the minuet survived only as a symphony or sonata movement. Gradually, as the new dance penetrated the ballrooms of Vienna, it began to lose some of its angularity and took the name "Waltz." * Its principal perfector, Franz Schubert, probably improvised most of his hundreds of waltzes, writing down only some of them afterward. These were pieces to which one was supposed to dance; not before 1819, when Weber, with a single stroke of genius, composed *Invitation to the Dance,* was there anything one could call a concert waltz. Subsequently, Weber was imitated by everyone, including Schubert (*Valses Nobles,* op. 77, 1827).

In 1829, when Chopin came to Vienna, Schubert had just died. Johann Strauss, Sr., and Joseph Lanner were at the height of their popularity. Chopin was clearly upset by their success and voiced his contempt for this type of entertainment. At the end of December 1830 he wrote to his family: "Among Vienna's numerous amusements the garden concerts are famous in which Lanner and Strauss play waltzes while the public is eating dinner. After each waltz the musicians receive a thunderous bravo." In the next paragraph, he mentioned that he was going to send his Warsaw people a waltz he had just composed, as well as some mazurkas: "but they are not for dancing."[17] One month later, on January 26, 1831, he

---

*The German root of this word indicates a smoothly turning motion.

wrote to his teacher Elsner to explain why he had no success in getting some of Elsner's compositions published:

One calls waltzes here *works,* and Lanner and Strauss—who lead the orchestra from their desks for the performance of these dances—are given the title of *Kapellmeister* [conductor]. This does not mean that everybody here agrees with such a classification; on the contrary, there are many who laugh about it. Nevertheless the fact remains that waltzes are practically the only type of music now being published.[18]

The date of Chopin's G-flat major Waltz, published as op. 70, no. 1, is uncertain, but from surviving sketches it seems likely that Chopin wrote it originally during, or close to, his Vienna days. This makes good sense. The waltz is indeed markedly different in style from all his other waltzes, being in an exaggerated Viennese musical "dialect" throughout. It has to be understood as a brilliant, graceful, and inventive parody on the Viennese waltz style that he so despised. The main theme and especially the first episode are free transcriptions of the yodeling of Austrian peasants, which the *Harvard Dictionary* defines as "a style of folk singing . . . characterized by rapid shifts between full voice and falsetto combined with rapid alternation between two pitches or the arpeggiation of several." In sharp contrast, the middle part, which is only a third as fast (the metronome changes from 88 for the whole measure to 96 for the quarter note), offers an exaggerated specimen of the sentimental slow "German dance." One is reminded of Mozart's *Musical Joke,* K. 522; the only difference is that Mozart indulges in such burlesque vulgarities as shrill dissonances and parallel fifths while Chopin always writes beautiful music even in a parody. It must have been the same kind of fun for him as when he mimicked the voices of his personal friends, which he did brilliantly and loved to do (see p. 244 below). Chopin did not publish this waltz himself, but he probably would have done so eventually, since the work, even if one does not know its implications, is so enjoyable as music.

The rest of Chopin's Waltzes fall into two general categories—concert waltzes and short piano pieces. Chopin started out with four big concert waltzes, op. 18 (E-flat major); op. 34, no. 1 (A-flat major); op. 34, no. 3 (F major); and the best and most sophisticated of them all, op. 42 (A-flat major). In form and style these are elaborations of Weber's *Invitation,* translated into Chopin's personal idiom. Being subdivided into an introduction, numerous waltzes complete in themselves, and a recapitulation-coda, Weber's and Chopin's concert waltzes became the models for Johann Strauss, Jr., and his contemporaries.

All the other Chopin waltzes, beginning with the A minor Waltz, op. 34, no. 2, are similar, in their much smaller form, to the Mazurkas, but their different rhythmic pulse makes them feel quite different. There is very little ornamentation and a much greater concern for flowing melody; these Waltzes are much more (and much less) than just "mazurkas in waltz rhythm." Two of these later Waltzes, to some extent, pick up the character of the earlier concert waltzes: the posthumous E minor Waltz and the— unique—"Minute" Waltz, op. 64, no. 1, compress the style of the concert waltz into the proportions of the small-size waltz.

Mazurkas

Chopin's most personal and most genuinely Polish art form was the mazurka. Much more than the polonaise, the mazurka was and is *the* national Polish dance. In recent years numerous studies have been devoted to the various types of popular mazurka before and during Chopin's lifetime, and more than one scholar has tried to identify the differing patterns of the various mazurka types in Chopin.[19] For Chopin uses all sorts of speeds, accentuations, and modes of expression throughout his more than fifty Mazurkas. However, his varieties are not identical with the traditional mazurka types. Chopin creates something new out of the patterns found in all traditional mazurkas. His own Mazurkas renovate these old forms without, however, continuing to keep them separate.

Chopin himself often calls his Mazurkas "mazur" when they are written at the average moderate tempo, for of the three traditional species, the *mazur* was neither brilliantly fast, like the *oberek,* nor romantically slow, like the *kujaviak.* In both types, phrases periodically end on the second beat with an accent: every fourth measure in the *kujaviak* and every second measure in the *oberek.* Chopin borrowed many other patterns as well. This whole field is largely guesswork, because we cannot be sure how any of the three types of popular mazurkas was played. Certainly the written versions that have come down to us have no more resemblance to actual performance practice than has a sheet of popular music today.

Traditional instrumental tone colors can also be essential for certain types of traditional mazurkas, especially the drone pipe, or *Dudelsack,* which is found in many of Chopin's Mazurkas. One obvious example of the drone bass occurs in the E major Mazurka, op. 6, no. 3 (Ex. 35). The original manuscript of the A minor Mazurka, op. 7, no. 2 (which no longer exists), is said to have contained the word *duda* between the staves of the first measure in Chopin's own hand. One also finds it beginning in m. 42, as F-sharp and C-sharp sound in the left hand on each downbeat. The drone bass is easily overlooked here, since the two tones occur in different voices in the notation. One may learn from this example to read Chopin's scores vertically as well as horizontally, even in the polyphonic passages that abound in the late Mazurkas.

Ex. 35   Mazurka in E major, op. 6, no. 3, mm. 1–6.

As mentioned before, Chopin once wrote that his Mazurkas were not for dancing. In another letter, however, he reported that he had been dancing mazurkas all evening.* The situation therefore is not the same as we reported earlier on waltz dancing: Chopin disliked and looked down on the dancing as well as on the dance music for waltzes.

Before examining some mazurka patterns used by Chopin, it is necessary to ask whether there exists a "normal" mazurka rhythm common to the fast and the slow, the more vertically and the more horizontally built, the elegiac and the energetic mazurkas, in the same way as one can find common traits in most Bach dance types (see p. 21, above). This is quite doubtful. The only common denominator for the Chopin mazurkas seems to be Chopin's general

---

*This passage indirectly reveals Chopin's idea of what Art is. Today, following Adorno and others, most of us are convinced that the purpose—which may be a utilitarian one—for which a work of art was devised is immaterial for the artistic value of the work; that, in other words, a beautiful chair can be a more important work of art than a mediocre sculpture. In Chopin's time, however, it was indeed normal to think of works of art absolutely. For Chopin, a mazurka or a waltz for dancing were utilitarian productions. He saw his own Waltzes and Mazurkas as growing on totally different soil.

emphasis on the first beat. Although the usual dictionary defini-
tions deal primarily with accents on the third and sometimes the
second beat, these accents, though important (see below), are secondary. In Chopin's practice, the downbeat must be firmly secured; only then can the other beats be emphasized.[20]

In a majority of Chopin's Mazurkas, the stressed downbeat is realized by means of an energetic dotted rhythm, as in the Mazurkas
in B-flat major, op. 7, no. 1 (Ex. 24, above); D-flat major, op. 30,
no. 3 (see Ex. 25, above); B major, op. 63, no. 1 (Ex. 38, below);
and E minor, op. 41, no. 2 (Ex. 36). It is immaterial that most of
these have no upbeat: the presence of upbeats is not necessary for
the definition of the mazurka rhythm. Although the F major
Mazurka, op. 68, no. 3 (Ex. 37), is based on an actual folk mazurka
theme, it belongs to the same upbeat-less type. The *rubato* prolongation of the first beat is achieved by lengthening the eighth note
itself, not the sixteenth rest that follows. Needless to say, this is
such a fine nuance that, applied correctly, it can barely be noticed
by the listener. One might think of it as a down-bow, after which
the up-bow on the ensuing sixteenth note quite naturally comes a
trifle late.

Ex. 36   Mazurka in A minor, op. 7, no. 2, mm. 33–36.

Ex. 37   Mazurka in F major, op. 68, no. 3, mm. 1–2.

A dotted rhythm does not necessarily have to appear in the first
measure; see the B major Mazurka, op. 63, no. 1 (Ex. 38). The
same rhythmic pattern can be created by dotted rhythms on the

second and third beats, as in the E minor Mazurka, op. 41, no. 2 (Ex. 39).

Ex. 38 Mazurka in B major, op. 63, no. 1, mm. 1–3.

Ex. 39 Mazurka in E minor, op. 41, no. 2, mm. 1–2.

In a different procedure, which involves an abbreviation of the second or the third beat, the downbeat remains as important as in the earlier examples but functions primarily as a springboard, as in the beginning of the C major Mazurka, op. 33, no. 3 (Ex. 40a).[21] Wilhelm von Lenz reports that Meyerbeer came into Chopin's studio unannounced ("he was a king") while Lenz was playing this piece for Chopin. "'That's in 2/4,' said Meyerbeer. Only once have I ever seen Chopin lose his temper, and it was at that moment—and what a wonderful sight he was! A faint red suffused his pale cheeks. 'It's in 3/4,' he said in a loud voice." The argument went on and on. Chopin, in extreme fury, played the piece himself three times, counting in a loud voice and stamping his feet to the beat. Meyerbeer finally left, unconvinced. Lenz adds in conclusion .that Chopin "was right, all the same: for though the third beat loses some of its value, submerged as it is in the flow of the melody, still it does not cease to exist." Essentially, this means that the piece is in 2/4, not 4/4; that the flow of the melody continues, not halting on a fermata; and that the third beat loses some, but not all, of its value. This leads to the conclusion that it was again the *first* beat that was, though indirectly, stressed in Lenz's and Chopin's performances by way of abbreviating the two other beats, somewhat like the rhythm shown in Ex. 40b.

Mazurka in C major, op. 33, no. 3, mm. 1-2.
Ex. 40a   as written   Ex. 40b   in $\frac{7}{8}$

Another example of the abbreviation of the second and third beats occurs in the autograph, preserved at the Library of Congress, of the B minor Mazurka, op. 33, no. 4. It contains a strange vertical arrangement during the B-flat major episode, in mm. 50, 52, etc., as well as in mm. 114, 116, etc. In all these places the half note in the left hand *on* the second beat is written directly underneath the sixteenth note in the right hand that *precedes* the second beat (Ex. 41a) and not underneath the dotted eighth on the second beat itself (Ex. 41b)! Musically, it is inconceivable that Chopin could have wanted the left hand to anticipate the second beat. On the contrary, he must have wanted to delay the entrance of the right hand so that the upbeat sixteenth is played *on* the beat and the dotted eighth following sounds like a prolongation, for, in order to preserve the pattern, the accent in the right hand must remain on the long note and not occur on the sixteenth-note upbeat. If the second beat is thus prolonged by one sixteenth, an unusually complex metric-rhythmic pattern emerges.

Mazurka in B minor, op. 33, no. 4, mm. 49-50.
Ex. 41a   autograph   Ex. 41b   printed version

These comments apply generally to this dance form in Chopin's hands. Artistically, what matters is the individual differentiation of each Mazurka. At least in the later Mazurkas that makes for many treasures, each unique in itself. And so the point is reached where the scholar may safely let go of research and analysis and just listen.

POLONAISES

   Bach and Chopin shared an uncommon sensitivity for the rhythmic particularities of each dance form. It is therefore no surprise that their essential understanding of polonaise rhythms was the same. They heard it—correctly, in terms of its history—as a slow, noble, and dignified "walking dance" in which the first and second beats were rhythmically more strongly connected than were the second and third beats; in fact, Mattheson spoke here of an iambic rhythm similar to that of the sarabande.[22] The comparison, though not quite accurate, illuminates an often neglected aspect of polonaise rhythm. It is exemplified by the two best-known Bach Polonaises, from the Orchestral Suite in B minor, BWV 1067, and from the French Suite in E major, BWV 817 (Ex. 42a). The latter is often taken too fast, because people do not recognize its typical polonaise character; it should be played at about the same speed as Chopin's Polonaise in A-flat major, op. 53 (Ex. 42b). An even more famous precedent of Chopin's polonaise rhythm is Scarlatti's Sonata in E major (Longo no. 23), especially mm. 19–21 (Ex. 43). Although it is not called "polonaise," it obviously was conceived

Ex. 42a Bach, Polonaise from French Suite in E major, BWV 817, mm. 1–4.

Ex. 42b Polonaise in A-flat major, op. 53, mm. 17–18.

Ex. 43 Scarlatti, Sonata in E major, Longo no. 23, mm. 19–21.

as such. The subdivision of the second beat is not important. What matters is the subdivision of the first beat into one eighth and two sixteenths. This unit ends with the second beat; the following eighth note belongs with the next two eighth notes; together they form the second half of the measure. All three of these notes are meant to be played separate from and lighter than the first half. In other words, the measure is divided into two portions of equal length, the second of which begins on the count of "two *and*." This principle applies in many cases, for example, in the main theme of the F-sharp minor Polonaise, op. 44 (Ex. 44a), and especially in the episode in the same work beginning in m. 83 (Ex. 44b). Here it means that the two groups of 32nd notes belong to different groups. This idea also explains the rhythmic structure of the E-flat minor Polonaise, op. 26, no. 2, as well as that of the

Polonaise in F-sharp minor, op. 44.
Ex. 44a mm. 9–10

Ex. 44b mm. 83–84

"Military Polonaise," op. 40, no. 1, in A major. In performance, the first three notes of the "Military Polonaise" ought to sound like the beginning of Beethoven's *Fidelio* Overture inasmuch as the second beat provides a feminine ending to the first; if the second beat is heavy, the piece loses its momentum.

Only occasionally does Chopin use a different rhythmic structure. In the A-flat major Polonaise, op. 53, the bass is built on a rhythm that goes directly to the third beat, as Chopin indicates by his pedal mark (see Ex. 42b), while the melody line conforms to the traditional rhythm. Note that the second beat as a feminine ending is further emphasized by being followed by a rest. Even more exceptional are two episodes in the E-flat minor Polonaise, op. 26, no. 2, in which there is an unusual isolation of the downbeat in mm. 21 and 69 (Exx. 45a, b). The first "phrase," as it were, consists of a single tone! One is reminded of Bach's A major Fugue, *WTC,* Bk. I (Ex. 46). Was Chopin perhaps experimenting here with a deliberate reversal of the polonaise pattern by isolating the first beat so that the second beat became connected with the third? Or did there exist a Polish folk dance model?

Polonaise in E-flat minor, op. 26, no. 2.
Ex. 45a   mm. 21–22

Ex. 45b   mm. 69–70

Ex. 46 Bach, Fugue in A major, *WTC,* Bk. I, mm. 1–2.

In character, Chopin's Polonaises are unexpectedly dramatic. In most cases, there is also a tendency toward brilliance. The violent ending of the otherwise subdued C minor Polonaise, op. 40, no. 2, written in Nohant during a deep depression, is symptomatic of Chopin's conception of the polonaise as a concert composition in dramatic style, comparable to the famous polonaise in Moussorgsky's *Boris Godunov*.

The Polonaise-Fantaisie, op. 61, in A-flat major, one of the last full-length works Chopin completed, opens with a description of the birth of a polonaise rhythm out of improvising (see above, p. 213). From the first measure, the first two beats are rhythmically connected, without as yet suggesting a polonaise rhythm. At m. 10, sixteenth-note triplets are added, establishing more flow to the motion. Then, as if by sudden inspiration, this leads to the significant motive in eighth-note triplets (m. 14, see Ex. 36), Chopin, as it were, surprises himself. He develops this new thought further until, between mm. 21 and 22, he discovers that it can become a polonaise melody. Despite accents on the third beat and the next downbeat (mm. 22–23), the rhythmic grouping remains the same; that is, the first two beats form a single rhythmic unit.

If for Chopin the Polonaise was perhaps less "Polish" than the Mazurka, it was still an important member of his family of musical genres, as is proved by the quantity of Polonaises he wrote in his very early days, as well as by the great variety of moods expressed in this form. One may also include Chopin's *Bolero*, op. 19, written in 1833, in this category. However, its rhythm is less contracted into two halves than is the proper polonaise rhythm. It rather resembles that of Beethoven's C major Polonaise, op. 89; Mozart's Fandango, from the Third Act of *Le Nozze di Figaro;* and perhaps Ravel's *Bolero*.

NOCTURNES

It is of no use to speculate why Chopin chose the name "Nocturne" for his sustained, lyrical piano compositions. Their role in his *oeuvre* corresponds to that of an Adagio in the ballet repertoire. Chopin admired John Field, who had first successfully employed this title, and he was pleased when he learned that Field had spoken highly of him (apparently he did not know that this was the exception rather than the rule);[23] but in terms of artistic aim and scope, Chopin's Nocturnes are utterly different. But neither for Field nor for Chopin does the title suggest "nocturnal" soirées in the salons of Paris, filled with lovely aristocratic ladies, where one might picture the composer playing soft music by candlelight; there is not a trace of this in the music itself. We must therefore consider the name "Nocturne" a convenient heading, indicating a type of semi-short piece that was different from the Impromptus and the Bagatelles.

How was it different? The Chopin Nocturne, as an art form, can only be defined in strictly musical terms. Essentially it is an "Aria without Words." For, like Mendelssohn's Songs without Words, these nocturnes are fine voice music. But in contrast to Mendelssohn, they are operatic in character. Usually they are presented in two-part form, like the Nocturne in G minor, op. 15, no. 3, or in A–B–A form (with or without variants at the return of A). This illustrates how different Mendelssohn and Chopin, though contemporaries, were in their approach to composing. As Chopin himself declared, his melodic style was formed under Bellini's influence, and his melodies are in *bel canto* aria style; while one of Mendelssohn's outstanding gifts was his gift of inventing simple, folklike German *Lied* tunes. However, Chopin's originality is such that nowhere does his *bel canto* music sound like a Lisztian opera transcription. This has mainly to do with the *fiorituras* and cadenzas inserted at many junctures. Though they are based on vocal *coloratura,* instead of *portamentos* and shadings of intonation that do not exist on the piano, they feature a chromaticism beyond what is possible for the human voice: the tones are colored throughout by chromatic alterations. This substitution of instrumental embellishments for vocal ones constitutes one of Chopin's most remarkable accomplishments. Chopin rarely proceeds by direct chromatic scale segments; rather he mixes diatonic and chromatic intervals in zigzag lines in a manner never attempted before and never successfully imitated since (see Exx. 22 and 23, above).

The left hand moves in widely spanned arpeggios—more so here than anywhere else in Chopin—in order to support the meanderings of the aria tune. In its regulated rhythmic energy the left hand seems to be pumping blood into the imagined singer's veins.

Though they are entirely different from Schubert's *Lied* accompaniments, these left-hand textures serve similar purposes.

Within this frame, Chopin's infinite variety of deep emotions, dreams of beauty, contemplations of nature, fears and laments, utterances of energy and even of brilliance recalls Bach's in the *Well-Tempered Clavier*.

BALLADES

Of the series of non-dance forms, the ballades are probably the most important. Though they were composed at different times, with years between them, they form a definite unit, displaying common traits. Their principal shared feature is their time signature of six beats to the measure: the first is in 6/4, the other three in 6/8. Only the Introduction and Coda of the First Ballade are written in common time. Chopin may have considered this a lapse, for there are no further such incidents in the three later ballades.

Why six beats? Although to my knowledge Chopin never explained it, six-beat time has accurately been described as the "narrative" meter—one that suggests a quietly told but coherent, intense, and important tale to which we listen at the narrator's feet with glee, horror, or whatever other emotion the story may produce. Narrative means nondramatic. Even the most bloodcurdling tales are only reported; they are not staged. Chopin was the first composer to use the poetic name "Ballade" for instrumental pieces. He declared that his Ballades were based on those by his great Polish contemporary Adam Mickiewicz, whose poetry Chopin admired mostly for patriotic reasons.[24]

Perhaps because singers are customarily classified as "dramatic" and "lyric" tenors, sopranos, etc., many musicians have come to overlook the fact that the *epos,* or narrative poem, has occupied a leading role in Western literature since Homer's time and has always been considered as important as drama and lyric poetry.[25] Chopin's Ballades are archetypal epic compositions, that is, neither lyrical nor dramatic. The opening of the First Ballade grips us like a shouted "listen!" to get our attention for a report on important events, but we are not participating in the events directly, as we would in a drama.

The openings of all four Ballades prove their narrative character. Instead of bluntly stating a theme, as Chopin does in his Concertos and Sonatas, he starts, as Plato—who was being rediscovered just then—does in his Dialogues, with almost nothing, and he brings his listeners to full attention so gradually that they are not even aware how intently they are listening.* This is obviously so in the Second and Fourth Ballades. In the Third Ballade, the long initial e-flat, from which the tale begins to flow in opposite directions, fulfils the same function, provided it is played with this in mind. In the G minor Ballade the opening is handled with more complexity (Ex. 47). At the end of the introductory measures, the famous $\frac{9}{6}$ chord over D (m. 7), after a hold, begins to cadence and reaches G minor—an event that had been anticipated for a long time—so easily that we discover only in retrospect that the tale had already started, half a measure earlier!**

Ex. 47 Ballade No. 1 in G minor, op. 23, mm. 5–9.

In all ballade-poems there is some connection with folk song and legend. Chopin's musical Ballades are no exception. Most noticeable in this respect is the first part of the Second Ballade, whose modal melodies seem to have come from a source similar to that of "Greensleeves." The B-flat interlude of the Fourth Ballade, mm. 80 ff., is in the same category.†

In form, the four Ballades are each different, but they are all

---

*Arthur Schnabel once remarked: "You only begin really to listen when you are no longer aware that you are listening."

**Many pianists fail to hold the f-sharp′ in the right hand in m. 8 so that they may use the fourth finger for the last note, a′. But Chopin's fingering 5–5 for the last two top notes definitely calls for a glide from b-flat′ to a′, which is only possible if the f-sharp′ is held. The glide produces a particular super-*legato* not otherwise achievable.

†There exist other such moments in Chopin's works, especially in the Nocturnes; see, for instance, the E-flat major episode (mm. 41 ff.) in the G minor Nocturne, op. 37, no. 1. The B major episodes in the Fantaisie, op. 49, and Polonaise-Fantaisie, op. 61, also display such a special mood, like a whiff of aural incense. For a moment, listening becomes a mystical experience here.

built on the confrontation of contrasting themes. This is clearest in
the Third Ballade; after the first section, there is a complete break
and a switch of tonalities from A-flat major to F major. Before the
opening theme returns triumphantly at the end, there is a moment
where both themes fight for dominance as they alternate in the
final development (mm. 183–200). This section opens with four
accented calls to duty on the tone b, interrupting everything, almost as though sounded by the strongest brass instruments (Ex.
48). Although they are part of the second subject, they prepare for
the return of the opening theme in m. 189. In the Second Ballade
the two conflicting themes are given to the contrasting tonalities of
A minor and F major, so that the piece becomes bitonal—see mm.
17–18 and 33–37; thus it is logical that, after having opened in F
major, the Ballade ends in A minor.*[26] In the First Ballade, the
entrance of the romantic second theme in E-flat major is lovingly
and most engagingly prepared for by using empty fifths and
fourths in the left hand, suggesting traditional hunting horn calls
(Ex. 49). When Wagner wrote the opening of Act 2, Scene 1,
of *Tristan und Isolde* (Brangäne: "Noch sind sie nah: noch tönts

Ex. 48 Ballade No. 3 in A-flat major, op. 47, mm. 183–85.

Ex. 49 Ballade No. 1 in G minor, op. 23, mm. 64–68.

---

*But Schumann reported that when he heard Chopin play this piece prior to publication
it ended in F major.

daher"), he may have been inspired by this passage in Chopin, for in both places, quite similarly, the hunting sounds gradually melt into sounds of nature. The Fourth Ballade is more unified thematically than its predecessors, its contrasting themes being confined to episodes after each of which the theme returns ever-more animated, see mm. 58 and 152 (Exx. 50a, b, c).

Ballade No. 4 in F minor, op. 52.
Ex. 50a mm. 7–8

Ex. 50b mm. 56–58

Ex. 50c m. 152

Today, the popularity of the Ballades, in concert halls and music schools, is largely due to the brilliance of their piano textures. In the First and Second, the virtuosic element is still somewhat external, as it sometimes is in Liszt. It becomes more thematic in the Third Ballade (see above). In the late Fourth Ballade the pianistic highlights are no longer separable from the musical substance, form, and feeling—as in the greatest sonatas of Chopin's predecessors Beethoven and Schubert. Even more than his Sonatas, Chopin's last Ballade constitutes his greatest success in integrating form, substance, and texture.

SCHERZOS

Chopin's four Scherzos prove most clearly that Chopin, like Bach, composed differently for different species. Being prevented by circumstances from writing symphonies (see p. 189, above), Chopin here discovered a field in which it was possible for him to write symphonically for the piano without abandoning his idiomatic piano style. It goes without saying that he had to follow Beethoven's model, for it was Beethoven who—in his Septet, and later in the early Quartets and Symphonies—had created the scherzo as a *Sturm und Drang* replacement for the traditional minuet. Even in Chopin's time, Beethoven still remained practically the only composer who had used it.*

What Chopin copied was the large scherzo form of the later Beethoven symphonies, in which a totally contrasting trio section is played twice, between three appearances of the main section, the last of which is usually followed by a coda. Chopin, like Beethoven, repeats each section without variants, note for note— quite an unusual procedure for someone who otherwise followed the Baroque practice of inventing additional small decorations, melodic variants, or chromatic harmonies at each return of the theme. Full chords, octaves, and solid left-hand accompaniments all help to emphasize the symphonic meter, in which each measure forms a beat, and four measures form a single supermeasure. Chopin was more consistent than Beethoven in sticking to this metric arrangement. To the student of these Scherzos it is therefore a considerable help to count measures in terms of four and four, and at every fourth measure to insert a double bar. Here are a few examples in which otherwise the structural connections might easily get lost: In the First Scherzo, mm. 77–88, two four-bar

---

*Schubert's C major Symphony, unearthed by Schumann and first performed by Mendelssohn in 1839, could not have been known by Chopin when he started writing scherzos in 1831.

supermeasures form a *super*supermeasure, as new periods start in
mm. 85 (Ex. 51) and 93. In the Second Scherzo (Ex. 52), the
downbeat in m. 9, at the beginning of a supermeasure, could easily
be misunderstood as an end; and one might not recognize that the
bass in m. 20 is an anticipated downbeat and that the next supermeasure starts on a rest (m. 25). Other notable instances of supermeasures occur in the Third Scherzo, mm. 33–41 (Ex. 53), 63–
71, and 525–41; and in the Fourth Scherzo (Ex. 54), where there is a
most curious transition. This metric organization is so deliberate
that it feels artificial: again the downbeat in m. 385 is anticipated in
the previous measure.

Ex. 51 Scherzo No. 1 in B minor, op. 20, mm. 77–86.

Ex. 52 Scherzo No. 2 in B-flat minor, op. 31, mm. 9–25.

Ex. 53 Scherzo No. 3 in C-sharp minor, op. 39, mm. 29–37.

Ex. 54 Scherzo No. 4 in E major, op. 54, mm. 377–95.

Chopin's four-bar supermeasures also explain the character of the trio theme in the Third Scherzo (Ex. 55). In truly symphonic style Chopin holds the melody note f′ in m. 159 with the help of a long pedal, meanwhile inserting glittering arpeggio figurations downward in mm. 159–62. This connects the f to the same note in m. 164. The same procedure, regarding the melody note e-flat′ in mm. 167 and 172, holds the following phrase together, and so forth. One is reminded of the long A in the second measure of Johann Strauss's "Blue Danube," which is very audibly held throughout the ensuing short interjections in the upper register in just about the same manner (Ex. 56). One hardly ever hears the connection between these two melody notes, five measures apart, partly because most pianists, unnecessarily, arrive late on the second beat of m. 159 and partly because they do not emphasize the first beat enough.

One of the few exceptions to the rigidity of Chopin's metrical

Ex. 55 Scherzo No. 3 in C-sharp minor, op. 39, mm. 155–71.

Ex. 56 Strauss, "The Beautiful Blue Danube"
Waltz, op. 314, mm. 1–3 (autograph).

periods occurs in the trio section of the Second Scherzo, mm.
293–302. As Beethoven did in the Ninth Symphony, in order to
produce the effect of a spontaneous transition, Chopin uses a
"ritmo di tre battute," a division into three-measure periods. Finally, here—as in the Sonatas—he sometimes intellectualizes the
motivic connections to the point where they almost become paper
music. The motive of the introduction (Ex. 57a) is a derivative of a
casual transition pattern that appears later (Ex. 57b). In the First
Scherzo, Chopin extricates the bass line of the first nine mea-

sures—G–A-sharp–B—to use it as an unaccompanied left-hand melody (Ex. 58).*

Scherzo No. 3 in C-sharp minor, op. 39.
Ex. 57a mm. 1–4

Presto con fuoco

Ex. 57b mm. 39–40

Ex. 58 Scherzo No. 1 in B minor, op. 20, mm. 44–54.

The most beautiful parts in the Scherzos occur where the composer did not feel restricted by formal and textural demands. This can happen either toward the end of middle sections—which are sometimes stretched by complete repeats of each of their parts—or at the end of the return of the main section, directly preceding the coda. Here Chopin, every so often, freely inserts magic potions. In the First Scherzo, mm. 594ff. (Ex. 59) are as demonic as Mahler's Second Symphony or Ravel's "Scarbo." In the Third Scherzo the

---

*It is uncertain whether the octave bass notes B in mm. 51–52 and 53–54 are tied. Musically it seems likely that they were meant to be. At any rate the *staccato* dots on these notes in mm. 52 and 54 do not argue against a tie. Their traditional meaning is that there must be an audible rest before the note is repeated on the second beat. Regardless of whether these notes are tied, there must not be a tie between mm. 55 and 56.

moment comes earlier and consists of a big increase in grandiose suspense on top of a giant dominant pedal point in the bass (Ex. 60); and in the Fourth Scherzo the four thematic notes B–C-sharp–G-sharp–E (the last in the bass) are heard like the bells of the Great Gate of Kiev. Except in the First Scherzo, a positive spirit triumphs at the end.

Ex. 59 Scherzo No. 1 in B minor, op. 20, mm. 593–96.

Ex. 60 Scherzo No. 3 in C-sharp minor, op. 39, mm. 541–46.

IMPROMPTUS

According to Lenz, Chopin's most intelligent pupil, Chopin had a predilection for the First and especially for the Third Impromptu.[27] The music of all four Impromptus, as has been remarked, is rather closely related. Their resemblance in form and melodic traits could mean that they were perhaps meant to be successive stages of one and the same work. It is less clear why Chopin chose to call them "Impromptus." In no way do they resemble Schubert's Impromptus, which were already quite popular when Chopin came to Vienna (although it cannot be proved that he knew them then). Perhaps the (subjectively) unfinished character of this music, as Chopin reused similar material several times, accounts for a title that suggests that these were off-the-cuff pieces.

Nevertheless, their differences are profound. The Fantaisie-Impromptu, the earliest of the four, deals with certain influences of Beethoven's harmonic style. It not only recalls the finale of the *Moonlight* Sonata, but, even more directly, the development section of the first movement of Beethoven's Cello Sonata in A major, op. 69, especially m. 132.*

The A-flat major Impromptu is lovely and unproblematic but apparently did not entirely fulfil Chopin's concept, since two years later he wrote the remarkable Impromptu in F-sharp major, which is full of risky experimentations with pianistic effects, rhythms, and modulations. No single work presents clearer evidence of Chopin's harmonic genius. A theorist could write an essay just on mm. 59–60 (Ex. 61), during which, in order to be able to recapitulate the theme in the key of the leading tone, F, the music has to go through no-man's-land for a brief moment.**[28] The triumphant return to the original key of F-sharp later on makes a similar impact in its directness.

Ex. 61 Impromptu No. 2 in F-sharp major, op. 36, mm. 59–60.

The last Impromptu, Chopin's own favorite (see above, p. 238), brought the composer the fulfilment he must have been seeking from the start. As mentioned before, in the three years since the Second Impromptu, Chopin's approach to composing had changed (see pp. 212–13). Although the material is nearly identical, it no longer appears to be the work of a pianist-composer. The sustained lament of the middle section, for instance, is music in the big style of, say, Verdi's Requiem. The simple chords at the end of the main section (Ex. 62) are genuine hymn sounds. The inspired tune in subdominant harmonies that introduces this section represents a new kind of music making altogether (see above, Ex. 30).

---

*The cellist John Sessions pointed out to me that Chopin's cello writing was more idiomatic in this passage than Beethoven's own!

**The modulation is supported by the chromatic descent on the second and third beats in mm. 59–61: e'–d'; e-flat'–d-flat'; d'–c'.

Ex. 62 Impromptu No. 3 in G-flat major, op. 51, mm. 35–36.

Though the Impromptus take up the least amount of space in Chopin's *oeuvre,* musically they are equivalent to his greatest works.

PRELUDES

Unlike the Etudes, with which they are sometimes compared because of the specific technical problems featured in some of them, the Preludes constitute a genuine series. Although for special reasons Chopin wrote down a few of them singly, they ought to be performed as a unit and not, as happens to some of them, be sliced off for use in piano beginners' primers. They are essentially a series, since their aim was admittedly a partial imitation of the most famous keyboard series of all, Bach's *Well-Tempered Clavier.* In the Scherzos Chopin took one movement out of a symphony for his own purposes; here, correspondingly, he separated the Prelude from its Fugue, using Bach's device of composing in every key, but arranging the order by key relation, as Bach himself had done in the Inventions and the Symphonies. It mattered not at all to Chopin that, without a fugue, the Prelude was no longer "preluding" anything. Little did he foresee how frequently other people, including even Schumann, would be baffled by his title. To this day the Preludes are the least understood of Chopin's piano works.[29]

What must have attracted Chopin so much in Bach's Preludes was their monothematic nature. In this respect, 23 of the 24 Preludes are very similar to Bach's in structure. The C-sharp minor Prelude, with its contrasting middle section, sits there like a veritable *Kuckucksei* (cuckoo's egg), also because it is much bigger in size than the others. Its inclusion is justified, however, by the Bachian principle that no rule can exist without exception (see above, pp. 9ff.).

One understands why the Preludes have been favorite Chopin pieces of many later composers such as Busoni. The best qualities of Chopin's coordinated originality are combined in this work, which stands on the borderline between early and late Chopin style, lyrical and brilliant textures. No tone is ever wasted or replaceable, yet the effect of the music remains spontaneous and full-voiced. The only other composer ever to have attempted such deliberate conciseness for a single large work was again Bach, in his *Magnificat,* in which each movement is considerably shorter than the usual length.

The melancholy of Chopin's depression comes out in the chromatic descent of lower and middle voices, as in the E minor Concerto (see Ex. 32a) and the C minor Prelude, mm. 5–6; but also in poignant and unusual dissonances, such as the diminished octave in the left hand of mm. 5 and 10 of the A minor Prelude (Ex. 63). In the B minor Prelude, the expressive natural seventh on the last beat of m. 22 (Ex. 64a) is melodically anticipated in the right hand of the A minor Prelude (Ex. 64b). And I see a deliberate

Ex. 63 Prelude in A minor, op. 28, no. 2, m. 5.

Ex. 64a Prelude in B minor, op. 28, no. 6, mm. 21–23.

Ex. 64b Prelude in A minor, op. 28, no. 2, mm. 8–9.

harmonic correspondence between this natural seventh and the famous "Gershwin" natural seventh, E-flat, in the last full measure
of the F major Prelude.

The E-flat minor Prelude shows that differing tempo choices
may be momentary decisions taken by the composer, as well as by
a responsible performer, in order to project various emotional aspects of one and the same piece. Apparently Chopin changed the
Allegro of the manuscript to *Largo* when he corrected the proofs
of the first edition. Both, of course, are possible, and therein is a
further resemblance to the Bach Preludes, for here, too, various
tempi may be taken without affecting the accuracy of interpretation. Other instances of radical tempo changes exist in Chopin:
See, for instance, the E major Etude, op. 10, no. 3, which, in the
course of successive autographs, finally came down from *Vivace* to
Lento ma non troppo. The texture, but nothing else, of the E-flat
minor Prelude shows similarity with the otherwise quite different
Finale of the B-flat minor Sonata. The Preludes in F-sharp minor,
B-flat minor, and D minor are known for their etude-like virtuosity, but Chopin uses all these passages only to express extreme
passion, as indicated by the markings *Molto agitato, Presto con fuoco,*
and *Allegro appassionato.* The spatial limitations of the monothematic form further enhance the emotional intensity; sometimes
its violence becomes almost unbearable. Not even Beethoven ever
explodes within such a small space.

Though the Preludes were not influenced by Schubert, they,
more than any other works by Chopin, recall Schubert's music;
for nearly all of them are in mixed moods. The A major Prelude,
for instance, is not as idyllic as one usually hears it. Consonance
and dissonance, key fidelity and sudden modulation, major and
minor chords coexist here, very much as in Schubert.

ETUDES

Chopin's music is as beautiful in the Etudes as in all his other
works. Chopin himself always liked to play one or a small group
of them for friends. Nevertheless they remain etudes, that is, they
were written as pieces in aid of specific technical and instrumental
difficulties. Their style and melodic-rhythmic substance, their har-

monies, their bewitching sonorities, sublime as they are, remain
secondary to their pianistic purpose. Any performance of the
Etudes as a series—such as all twelve of op. 10, for example—can
therefore only bring out the performer's acumen, but it does a dis-
service to the music. For the Etudes, musically speaking, do not
form a series, as do the Mazurkas, Waltzes, Polonaises, Nocturnes,
and Scherzos. Their purpose is primarily technical, and their
beauty, according to Chopin's intention, only makes the pianist's
technical practicing more agreeable.

In this respect Chopin's Etudes are different from those of Liszt,
Debussy, or Rachmaninoff, and rather recall those by Czerny and
Clementi. At best they are on the borderline between both types of
piano studies. My experience as a listener at recitals in which all or
half of the Chopin Etudes were played confirms this statement.
There are so many reiterations of the same modulations, developments, and sequences in these works that, heard *in toto,* they are
monotonous. It is impossible to imagine that Chopin would have
agreed to such performances! The music lover is finally resigned to
just listening to the pianist; the performance has become an end in
itself.

The Etudes are also not a series in the sense in which the Bach
Partitas form a series. The term implies that each unit within the
whole presents a different aspect of the genre, so that only by
studying the complete series can we receive the total picture. But
each of these Etudes stands by itself, and Chopin's concept of the
etude form as a whole emerges clearly from almost every single
Etude. Furthermore, their practical purpose unfortunately ex-
cludes improvisatory free rhythms, which are so characteristic
of Chopin's purpose-free music. Practically all the music of the
Etudes is strictly measured. This factor adds to the monotonous
effect when many are played in succession.

Taken singly, the Etudes turn out to be carefully crafted. Some
use lovely folk-like tunes, and all of them are particularly concerned with a beautiful distribution of sound. The phrasing, however, dominated by concerns of practical exercise, consists of
identical patterns, presented with alternating accents and with
alternating *staccato* and *legato,* soft and loud, etc. As etudes, these
pieces are not only of unique pedagogical help but also of unique

beauty, even though they are not comparable to Schubert's Impromptus or Brahms's Capriccios, simply because their author did not *mean* for them to belong to these categories.

All this has to do with objectivity and restraint—prominent traits in Chopin's character. When Chopin had a job to do, he did it as unobtrusively and professionally as possible, with no thought of overstepping the boundaries traced by the task itself.

INDIVIDUAL COMPOSITIONS

Like Bach, Chopin composed some of his most interesting works outside of a series. Some of them must be regarded as experiments in composing, for instance, *Berceuse,* op. 57. It is constructed over an ostinato bass having the effect of a key note pedal point under alternating tonic and dominant harmonies. The pedal point as such is already lulling, but its effect is strengthened by the mellow bass rhythm that makes one listen with total relaxation to the *fiorituras* in the treble. As in a chaconne, these are at the same time too long and too short for any normal four-measure tune. Characteristically, in the autograph—which was deliberately changed in the Paderewski edition!—an uninterrupted slur goes from the beginning to the end of m. 13. Chopin's genius proves itself once more in the sudden changes of the ostinato pattern shortly before the end; they are almost as radical as Ravel's in his *Bolero,* though their purposes are contradictory. Chopin wants to give a finishing touch to the lullaby effect, while Ravel pushes for a frenzied exit and climax.

Tarantella, op. 43, embodies another experiment, for—as Chopin himself intimated in a letter—it was meant to be a recognizable imitation of Rossini's famous *La Danza.*[30] At times it comes close to being a free transcription, justified by its charm, provided it is played with the appropriate sense of lightness and humor. (It is to be remembered that, for the entertainment of his friends, Chopin often gave voice impressions of people he knew.[31] One might almost call the *Tarantella* a Rossini "Impression.")

A much more important composition is the *Barcarolle,* op. 60. Though it is also based on an imitative design, incorporating Venetian gondola songs and other Italian folklore, the piece is full of

inspired absolute music. Twice it becomes very serious, in the free
fantasy used as transition (mm. 71ff.) and in the tense section preceding the coda (mm. 103ff., Ex. 65). The pedal point on F-sharp
corresponds to the pedal point on C-sharp in the two and a half
measures of the introduction. Similarly felicitous motivic and formal correspondences are found elsewhere in this masterpiece.

Ex. 65 Barcarolle in F-sharp major, op. 60, m. 103.

Chopin's two most important individual compositions are his
Second Sonata, op. 35, in B-flat minor, and his Third, op. 58, in B
minor. However, in no way do they constitute the beginning of a
series, for their only common ground is negative, in that neither
has any trace of a regular—or even an irregular—sonata form
structure. It is impossible to speak of sonata form when the opening theme never returns.* It is not easy to discover why Chopin
abandoned both opening themes on the first page. The most likely
explanation is that he was thinking in terms of concerto form, so
that the opening was only an introductory ritornello, the true solo
texture beginning right afterwards. This sets up a dialogue of tone
colors between *tutti* and *solo* sections, much as Bach had done in
the *Italian Concerto*.

Chopin tends to replace the missing recapitulation by abstract
manipulations with motives (described in detail by Alan Walker
for the B minor Sonata[32]) and weird, abstract modulations—
music for the eyes rather than for the ears. In the development of
the B minor Sonata, especially in mm. 110–17 (Ex. 66), he runs
uphill, sideways, downhill, back and forth, from key to key, moving so fast that one cannot even grasp the various tonalities; he

*Young Haydn, at his most extreme, in the G major Sonata, Hob. XVI 6, avoids going
that far by recalling the beginning at the moment of starting the development section.

Ex. 66 Sonata No. 3 in B minor, op. 58, 1st Mvt., mm. 110–13.

leaves them before you have a chance to accept them in your ear, and rushes on to the next.

But this does not mean that the Sonatas are not beautiful and original in form as well as in substance. Chopin's idea, more than two years after writing the Funeral March, of following it with a stormy and nearly atonal unison presto is equal to the greatest formal invention by the Classical masters. It meets the challenge of writing a finale better than do most last movements in Classical sonatas. In the B minor Sonata, a great structural moment is the anticipation of the slow movement by the B major middle section of the Scherzo, which is in a similar mood as well as in the same key. B major must not be understood here as C-flat major, the flat submediant of the main key (E-flat major) of the Scherzo, but indeed as B major, the tonic major of the main key. This makes the direct connection between the Scherzo and the Largo fully convincing. The proportions between the various sections of the Largo are equally just and structurally right. Many other such pillars were erected by Chopin to uphold each of these sonatas quite firmly. Though this proves once and for all that a multi-movement piece named "Sonata" may be extremely viable without adhering to sonata form, it does not contradict the fact that these works are individual compositions with nothing positive in common to justify classifying them as part of a series.

CONCLUSION

Chopin's music is at present undergoing the same reevaluation that Schubert's music experienced in the last generation. More and more musicians and music lovers realize that "Chopin's music has great strength" (Maria Curcio), and that it is by no means "effeminate"[33] or simply lovely, scintillating, entertaining, and full of charm and sentiment.

Chopin's strength flows from his character. All the romantic biographies, films, and TV portraits, as well as the legion of over-refined, overdramatized pianistic approaches, have led to a total misunderstanding of his personality. Chopin seemed self-absorbed, decadent, almost pathologically depressed. He was pictured as individualistic to such an extent that, in order to do justice to his scores, there arose a number of pianists, mostly Polish, who practically abandoned all other music and devoted themselves full time to becoming little Chopins, with highly unsatisfactory results.

In reality, Chopin was proud to follow in the footsteps of his greatest predecessors and was so little self-absorbed that he emerges—from his letters and from reports of friends, family, and pupils—as perhaps the most objective, unprejudiced, and generally open person of all. For example, he was immensely excited to learn that a new planet, Neptune, had just been discovered—an important event that had no connection with music, with Poland, or with his own person.[34]

Chopin did not like to play for big audiences, less and less so as he grew older. However, if he was asked to give a concert, he did so without fuss. Quite obviously he knew his worth, yet he did not have a particularly high opinion of himself. The first time he came to Vienna, he was amused and surprised to find his works already on the shelves of the Vienna Library.[35] On the other hand, when, shortly after Chopin's arrival in Paris, Kalkbrenner suggested that Chopin study with him, all those close to Chopin were indignant. But Chopin himself found the idea perfectly reasonable and declared that he could learn a great deal from Kalkbrenner.[36] He loved people and Nature, he studied strangers and talked to children out of sheer interest. He was definitely not a snob (as Liszt tended to be) and was not easily taken in by fame or aristocracy but always remained open-minded about everything and everyone.

Contrary to what people used to believe, it was not his nature that later caused Chopin to become terribly unhappy and depressed, so that finally his health, too, began to fail. He had every reason, physically and emotionally, to feel as he did (but that subject is outside the scope of this book). Even then, as long as he could, he remained a marvelous piano teacher, truly interested in the progress of each of his students. His students were not trained just to perform his music. He taught them his pieces—and why not?—but many others as well. Patiently and systematically he taught technique, phrasing, and dealing with rhythms. There are few geniuses of his caliber, in any field of art, who could match this kind of selfless dedication.

Fortunately, leading musicians and scholars are finally recognizing the true character of Chopin the man. An objective and yet sensitive approach by pianists and researchers alike has led to Chopin's music being appreciated in an entirely new way. This has come about partly through a more objective type of analysis (ever since the publication of Alan Walker's Chopin anthology) and partly through more profound studies of primary sources. These include comparison of autographs and first editions, exploration of the musical information left behind by his pupils, examination of the instruments he used, and most of all the increased interest in Chopin's music by performers whose scope is universal rather than specialized.

Chapter VII

BRAHMS

After listening to the overture to *Die Meistersinger,* Nietzsche compared this music to the

German soul, which is young and at the same time overaged; overripe and at the same time abundantly filled with the Future. . . . This type of music best expresses what I think of the Germans; they have their existence Before Yesterday and After Tomorrow—*they do not yet have a Today* [italics added].[1]

What Nietzsche says about Wagner's music—at exactly the time that he turned from a vociferous Wagnerian into a rabid anti-Wagnerian—applies even more profoundly to Brahms, who was then considered, both by his own followers and by the Wagnerians, to be Wagner's opposite number.

On the one hand, Brahms was a true conservative. More than any other great composer, he was steeped in music history. He trained himself, by studying books and manuscripts, to become a full-fledged musicologist. Later, he did considerable editing. He also befriended some of the most important music historians of his time—Spitta, Nottebohm, and Chrysander, among others. He once told Spitta that if he had Spitta's brains, he might chuck composing and devote himself full-time to musical research.[2]

On the other hand, unlike his conservative friends, including Clara Schumann, but also unlike Wagner, Brahms felt the imminence of a total upheaval of music in his bones* and anticipated

---

*So did Liszt, according to his first biographer, Lina Ramann. He went so far as to predict quarter-tone music as the only unexplored branch of music for the near future.[3]

many of the important features of twentieth-century music in his later works. Schoenberg, who sometimes described himself as a "learned Brahmsian" (see p. 262, below), analyzed in great detail the elements he felt were common to Brahms's and to his own music.[4] But he did not exhaust the subject of Brahms's progressiveness; besides, a comparison of Brahms and Schoenberg is not the only one from which Brahms emerges as a musician ahead of his time.

In his piano music, an essential part of which is chamber music with piano, Brahms, just like Schubert, consciously wrote as a pianist for pianists. His technical experiments, some of which were isolated in his *51 Studies,* permeate most of the late Intermezzos. More important are his innovations in the field of piano sound. Obviously it bothered him that in Bach's and Beethoven's piano music, harmony was usually provided by blocked chords on strong beats wherever the texture was homophonic. In his solo music, and even more in his chamber sonatas as well as in his trios, quartets, and quintet, Brahms deliberately dissolved the texture in ways we shall investigate. The direction he took was influenced by the development of the piano into an instrument of overwhelming fullness of sound, by such piano makers as Bechstein, Steinway, and Bösendorfer. Brahms was the first master to adjust to the scope of the new instrument in his concertos and chamber works; and so it is no wonder that today listeners marvel at the sonorities of this music. The use of rhythm and meter as well as certain melodic and harmonic practices applied by Brahms need closer definition.

Brahms's importance to the history of piano music is based on such a complex set of assessments that it might seem relative to the peripeteia of cultural history. But through all this shines a quality of greatness which assures Brahms an absolute place among the masters.

BRAHMS AND THE PAST

Brahms, perhaps more than other composers, needed the support and inspiration of many kinds of music for his own composing. Not only was he the first great composer to study folk music seriously, but also throughout his life he kept learning from the masterworks of the best composers of the past. His endeavors went back as far as the late Renaissance and extended to all genres, including French and Italian operatic music. Appreciative and humble by nature, Brahms admired other composers for what was special in their works without comparing himself to them. Many times he stated his conviction that his music was not going to live more than 50 years after his death, for he felt so firmly anchored in the past.

Brahms knew well how to learn from others. He rationalized his thirst for knowledge of the compositional skill displayed by his predecessors by making the perfectly amazing statement that he—whom posterity considers one of the most skillful craftsmen of all time—had to learn everything as an autodidact, since there was no school of composing in Germany at which he would have received adequate training! Speaking with his personal friend Richard Heuberger, he pointed to Haydn as perhaps the last great craftsman among the German masters. "Neither Schumann nor Wagner nor I was decently taught, in contrast to the pupils of Cherubini,* Halévy, and Auber in France; I am thinking of composers like Ambroise Thomas, Léo Delibes, and Georges Bizet."[5] This evaluation is surprising, but it is quite true! His appraisal of the French school did not imply putting these musicians on a level with the best of their German contemporaries (except for Bizet, of whose *Carmen* Brahms was extremely fond). All he said was that they were better trained so that for them the *métier* was much less a problem than it had been for him. (One might add Gounod, Massenet, and especially Saint-Saëns to Brahms's list of well-schooled composers.)

Studying so many scores of all kinds and from all ages, Brahms reached the point where he perfectly understood how to learn exactly what he needed. Each master taught him something special. Separate analytical studies could be undertaken to set down exactly what he learned from Bach, from Handel, from Haydn, from Mozart, from Beethoven, from Mendelssohn and Schubert, of course from Schumann; and, let us not forget, from the innumerable minor, yet good composers, many of whom we hardly know today. Even Wagner's music occasionally helped him, for—unlike his followers, the so-called Brahmsians—Brahms himself had

---

*Like Beethoven, Brahms considered Cherubini "one of the greatest."

great, unqualified admiration for Wagner as a composer. In 1894, long after Wagner's death, he remarked: "Wagner is much closer to Mozart than people imagine." The surely intentional resemblance of the main theme of the A major Violin Sonata, op. 100, to Wagner's "Meister" song is unimportant, but not the chromatic, *Tristan*-like, four-note motive hidden inside two of the Intermezzos of op. 119: in mm. 27ff. of no. 1 and mm. 27–28 of no. 2.*

When he studied the music of others, the obvious did not attract Brahms, nor did he normally concentrate on their best-known pieces (although his C major Sonata, op. 1, begins like Beethoven's *Hammerklavier* Sonata). He preferred hidden gems like Beethoven's song "La Marmotte" or the Presto in G minor that had been Schumann's original Finale for the G minor Sonata, op. 22. He discovered the importance of Schubert's unpublished "Drei Klavierstücke," op. posth. (D. 946), and edited them for publication; arranged an unknown Gavotte by Gluck for piano; and picked for his Haydn and Handel variations characteristic themes that were far from popular.

Brahms studied older composers' ways of notation and often discussed notational problems in his correspondence, for instance, whether the second note of a two-note slur should be played as though it were shorter than the first,** but what fascinated him

---

*This chromatic four-note motive was already prominent in the slow movement of Mozart's E-flat major Quartet, K. 428, as Brahms undoubtedly knew!

**In a letter of May 20, 1879,[6] Joseph Joachim quotes a violin example that resembles the figurations of the solo violin in the third movement of Brahms's Violin Concerto, op. 77, mm. 49ff. He uses it to demonstrate that if slurs connect each group of six of twelve sixteenths, to a fiddler this notation connotes only bowing, not phrasing:

A violinist will create two phrases only if the last sixteenth note under the slur is replaced by a 32nd note and a 32nd rest. Brahms answered, on May 30:

> By the way, I believe that a slur over several notes does not shorten any of them. What it indicates is *legato,* and one draws the slur depending on grouping, [metrical] period, or whim. Only in the case of a two–note slur is there a diminution.

With regard to bigger groups of notes, this [shortening

of the last note] would appear as a liberty and nuance of interpretation. Admittedly, though, most of the time such liberty is called for.[7]

more than anything else was audacious experimenting by established Classical masters. He is the only musician who ever systematically collected the parallel fifths and octaves in the masterworks. Perhaps he wanted to draw courage to use them himself. In the B minor Capriccio, op. 76, no. 2, m. 88, he had written nice, humorous parallel fifths, but he may have had "cold feet," for he took them out of his private copy, which Mandyczewski found and used for the collected works after Brahms's death (just as he used a similar autograph notation in the A minor Intermezzo, no. 7, to justify eliminating a single 3/2 bar in the first ending of the second section). In my view Mandyczewski was wrong, for I believe that in the end Brahms would have decided to retain these mild audacities.

Bach's harmonic planning was more important to Brahms than his fugue writing, and Brahms's use of secondary dominants and sequences of seventh chords on all degrees of the scale reflects a thorough study of Bach's hymn harmonizations (an activity already recommended by Schumann in his slogans for young players). As for Mozart, Brahms became his direct successor in the loving use of the clarinet, especially at the end of his life.* Furthermore, when he told Heuberger that "Beethoven handled dissonances less well than did Bach and Mozart,"[8] Brahms must have thought of the places in Mozart's music where the tonality is extended almost to the breaking point (Pedrillo's "Romance," for instance) or regains the main theme of a slow movement only after going through a series of extreme dissonances (see above, p. 87). Indeed, Brahms's own treatment of tonality and dissonances is at times clearly influenced by Mozart (see below, p. 270).

From Haydn, Brahms received solid confirmation of his own tendency to favor asymmetric metrical periods—a tendency in both composers that had its root in folk music. The classic example, of course, is the St. Anthony Chorale ascribed to Haydn. It had been quite unknown, and it is a tribute to his scholastic endeavors that Brahms found and used it, in two versions, in his

---

Brahms's statement that slurring does not imply shortening of the last note corresponds with Classical performance practice (see above, p. 106). The last sentence reads as though Brahms had second thoughts when thinking of the music of his own time.

*Even some parts of the solo piano pieces from this period—for instance, the Intermezzi, op. 118, nos. 2 (middle section) and 6—almost sound like clarinet music transcribed.

Variations, op. 56. Its first half consists of two five-bar periods, the second of three four-bar periods, and the coda of one seven-bar period. Both halves are repeated: 10 + 10 + 19 + 19 = 58 measures, a most unusual length, but one that exactly fits the melodic substance.

Schubert's music, to which Brahms was extremely attached, first of all encouraged him to write many lengthy, spun-out melodies without a preconceived time frame. The early sonatas are full of them, the most beautiful being the coda, in D-flat major, of the slow movement of the F minor Sonata, op. 5. The music does not sound like Schubert, but its scope, one imagines, could not have been devised if Brahms had not known and understood Schubert's time concept (see above, p. 176).

Without any doubt, it was one particular Schubert piece, the *Divertissement à la Hongroise,* D. 818, which was responsible for Brahms's numerous uses of the rhythms and harmonies of Hungarian popular music.* Strange as it must have seemed to the chauvinistic German critics of the time**—for whom only a German was qualified to play Beethoven or Bach, and for whom Hungarian music was considered secondary and reserved for the Hungarians—Brahms had both an immense craving for Hungarian music and a unique ability (except for Schubert) to write it. In addition to the pieces which are openly Hungarian, such as the Variations on a Hungarian Theme, op. 21b, the *alla zingharese* Finale of the G minor Piano Quartet, op. 25 (which contains some near-quotations from the Schubert *Divertissement*), the Hungarian Dances for piano, four hands, and a number of songs, Hungarian elements pervade many of his other pieces. They are usually immediately recognizable, for instance, in the last movement of the B-flat major Piano Concerto, op. 83, beginning eight measures before letter *H* in the Simrock edition[10] (Ex. 1). See also Variation 3 in the slow movement of his C major Trio, op. 87. These passages are meant to be played much more freely in time than the rest, and not too loudly, so that the etched, sharp Magyar rhythms and chords are heard with their typical metallic sound. It is quite

---

*The piece was also loved by Chopin[9] and by Liszt—whose Hungarian Rhapsodies reflect a very different kind of Hungarian music. I wish I had been there when Liszt played it with, of all people, Anton Bruckner!

**And the breed is not extinct yet!

Ex. 1 Concerto in B-flat major, op. 83, 4th Mvt., mm. 325–28 (mm. 8–5 before *H* in Simrock edition).

possible that Brahms's early friendship with Joachim and Remenyi helped develop the inborn Hungarian side of his talent.

Brahms took from the German masters what made them revolutionary rather than what made them Classical. Knowing that Bach or Mozart had used a certain type of dissonance or polyrhythm gave Brahms a feeling of legitimacy, so that he felt less like a composer who goes out on a limb.

It never occurred to Brahms to take credit for inspirations deriving from other composers' music, in the way Handel, nearly always, and Wagner, some of the time, composed their music. The famous anecdote about his C minor Piano Quartet, op. 60, is surely authentic. When somebody pointed out to Brahms that the theme of its Finale was almost identical with the opening of Mendelssohn's Piano Trio in the same key, op. 66, his response was: "Any fool can see that!" Indeed, Brahms was so scrupulously honest that in many cases—as I have discovered over the years— where the dependency was less obvious he managed discreetly to sneak musical "credit lines" into his scores.[11] The middle episode, in B major, of his B minor Rhapsody, op. 79, no. 1, is inspired by the trio of the third movement of Schubert's G major Sonata, op. 78. Since he was certainly aware of this, Brahms made sure that his texture, with an ostinato f-sharp" on top, would be recognizably similar (Exx. 2a, b). The Finale of his Piano Quintet in F minor, op. 34, owes a lot to that of Schubert's Gran Duo for Piano Duet, D. 812; therefore, in the Introduction, instead of anticipating the quintet theme to come, Brahms quotes the Schubert theme (Exx. 3a, b). The *Allegretto vivace* in the slightly Beethovenian second movement of his String Quartet in A minor, op. 51, no. 2, bears this tempo mark—surely to recall Beethoven's occasional use of it, especially for the Scherzo of his op. 31, no. 3. The entire Violin

Ex. 2a Schubert, Sonata in G major, D. 894, 3rd Mvt., Trio, mm. 1–2.

Ex. 2b Rhapsody in B minor, op. 79, no. 1, mm. 94–96.

Ex. 3a Schubert, Gran Duo, D. 812, 4th Mvt., mm. 4–8.

Ex. 3b Piano Quintet in F minor, op. 34, 4th Mvt., mm. 36–46.

Sonata in G major, op. 78, is built on a single motive consisting of a dotted rhythm on one note in which the dot is replaced by a rest (Ex. 4). Although Brahms had used this rhythm in the Scherzo of his B major Trio, op. 8, it is manifestly related to Schumann's piece "Chopin," from *Carnaval,* op. 9. Brahms beautifully expresses his appreciation at the very end of the entire Sonata—which, by the

Ex. 4 Violin Sonata in G major, op. 78, 1st Mvt., mm. 1–2.

way, is also biographically connected with the Schumann family [12]—by quoting the beginning of Schumann's *Davidsbündler,* op.
6. That all these acknowledgments are more or less hidden is in
accordance with Brahms's general practice, inherited from Schumann (especially in *Carnaval*). Even where Brahms quotes himself, as in the basso ostinato of the epilogue to his *Neue Liebeslieder,*
op. 65, which is taken from the *Alto Rhapsody,* op. 53 (Exx. 5a, b),
he does so in such privacy that the spontaneity of the music is not
disturbed. The Schumannesque inclination toward in-jokes quite
naturally finds its strongest outlet in Brahms's *Schumann Variations,* op. 9. The use of various compositions of Schumann in these
variations is well known and documented. [13]

The origin of the Finale of the E minor Cello Sonata, op. 38, is
so obvious that Brahms did not have to explain it. Everybody
knows at once that it is a mixture of paraphrase and elaboration of
Bach's two-piano Fugue, no. 13, of *The Art of Fugue,* BWV 1080.

All this points to cerebral attitudes. In many ways Brahms was a
German professor: who else would compose a Rhapsody in sonata
form (the G minor Rhapsody, op. 79, no. 2), complete with a first

Ex. 5a *Neue Liebeslieder,* op. 65, "Zum Schluss," secondo piano, mm. 1–2.

Ex. 5b *Alto Rhapsody,* op. 53, beginning of last section.

repeat and coda? That the title "Rhapsody" was selected only after
the piece was finished does not make any difference. Some of
Brahms's contrapuntal games are simply a playful, abstract amuse-
ment—musical anagrams, as it were. See, for instance, the Violin
Sonata in D minor, op. 108, first movement, mm. 56–60. Nevertheless, his use of older music and his musicological zeal emanate
entirely from his artistic creativity, not from a dry scholarly mind.

Two generations later, so did Thomas Mann's research of the Bible, of Goethe's life, of modern music.

Simplicity attracted Brahms more than complexity. We see that in his choice of folk songs for transcription and in his love of waltzes, Hungarian dances, and nursery rhymes. What he was looking for in the older composers was their vitality, expressed in originality of forms, textures, dissonant harmonies, and irregular rhythms.

Despite the importance of Baroque and Classical music for Brahms's styles and textures, the actual types and forms in his music for piano and with piano are strictly those of the nineteenth century. Brahms wrote no preludes and fugues, no dance suites, no toccatas, no eighteenth-century-style sheer decorative variations—and no chaconnes either, for the left-hand version of Bach's D minor Chaconne is strictly a transcription. The fugue that ends the Handel Variations, op. 24, is not modeled on Handel or Bach but on Beethoven's *Hammerklavier* Sonata, op. 106, which was then less than half a century old. In Brahms's Finale similar elementary fugue procedures, such as augmentation and inversion, are displayed in a showy, extrovert manner; but unlike Beethoven, Brahms uses an organ style in the manner of Liszt's Bach transcriptions, full of pomp and circumstance. While Brahms kept his sense of proportion—regarding both form and sound—unfortunately the same cannot be said of the numerous Reger fugues that attempt to follow the Brahms model. A more faithful rendering of Brahms's spirit is found in the fugue that concludes Barber's Piano Sonata.

The center of Classical style is sonata form. Early in life, Brahms had stopped writing for solo piano in sonata form. On the exceptional occasions when he cast a piece in this form, e.g., the G minor Rhapsody, he may have thought that the wild and uninhibited expression of a rhapsodic piece would counterbalance the academic limitations of sonata form, as they appeared to him. The chamber sonatas and the bigger ensembles, as well as the piano concertos, are more conservative in form, but here too one feels that Brahms used the later Beethoven, Schubert, and Schumann as his role models, rather than Mozart and Haydn. The forms grow larger primarily because the melodies grow larger than they were in early Classical times.

Because of his lack of adherence to sonata form, Brahms also became more liberal toward tempo changes within the same movement. Most of all he used *accelerandos* more frequently than had his predecessors. Some of them are marked in the score, like the *animando* at the end of the slow movement of the G minor Piano Quartet, op. 25, and the *poco a poco Tempo primo* before the recapitulation in the first movement of the G major Violin Sonata, op. 78. Others are left to the discretion of the players, as in the second theme of the opening movement of the F minor Sonata, op. 5, where the *più mosso* did not have to be marked. According to Diran Alexanian, whom I heard explaining this to a student, Brahms himself made a huge *accelerando* in the coda of the opening movement of the E minor Cello Sonata, op. 38, in mm. 13–6 from the end. In a related situation, after each *ritardando* the proper tempo resumes at once at full speed, sometimes, especially in the Waltzes, even an instant before the *a tempo* marking.

In his later piano music, just as Chopin did, Brahms mostly wrote short pieces in tripartite form. Most of them are Bagatelles and Impromptus under the new name of "Intermezzo," derived from Schumann's music. The sprightlier ones among them go as Capriccios, a Mendelssohnian name, possibly originally inspired by the Finale of Bach's C minor Partita. The three Rhapsodies are slightly bigger in scope, and the last one, in E-flat major, op. 119, no. 4, is written in the big, sweeping style of a sonata rondo in an approximate imitation of that form. Here, too, the influence of older music shows only in textural melodic detail, and not at all in the shape of the piece as a whole. Most of these pieces are heard as single items. Only rarely does one feel that several pieces belong together—op. 76, nos. 7 and 8, for instance, and op. 118, nos. 1 and 2 (see below). The first, and still quite early, collection of Four Ballades, op. 10—a most original series—is an exception. It coheres almost like a sonata, as movements of various length, form, and character complement each other to achieve total unity on a larger scale. Also, as with Beethoven's Bagatelles, the very last group of short pieces, op. 119, for various reasons (see below) belongs together so strongly that one may suppose that Brahms wanted it performed as a unit.

·It is strange, in looking over this aspect of his music, to see that Brahms, who was so utterly different from Chopin in every way, in his best works created a unity of Baroque and Romantic style, just as Chopin had done, but so differently in substance that the idea would not normally occur to a listener.

BRAHMS AND THE FUTURE

The music of Brahms, at least in his later years, had little in common with other music being written in Germany at the time. Although he was deeply anchored in the past and thus infused his Romantic music with elements based in the Classical tradition, Brahms was truly a modern artist, and much of his music—especially many works from his late period—properly belongs to the twentieth century. However, until the different branches of twentieth-century music were firmly established, no one recognized this important feature of his music. On the contrary, in the opinion of friend and foe alike, Wagner had an exclusive hold on the "Music of the Future."* Wagner's music—like Nietzsche's philosophy—was indeed ahead of its time and, in that sense, progressive. But once the spirit of the times (*Zeitgeist*) began to catch up with Wagner's ideology, his music ceased to be futuristic.

Not so with Liszt and Brahms. It is all right to name them together, just as one couples Haydn and Mozart, who were separated in age by about the same number of years. As different as Liszt and Brahms were in their ideas and convictions, they both were ready for something radically new to happen to music so it would survive into the next century. Liszt, as we have learned only recently, was fully aware of the crisis that had befallen composition. He frequently said that the various tonal systems, including chromaticism, were coming to an end; and in his late piano works he tried experimentally to break out of what to him was becoming a vicious circle. Brahms, who was much less intellectually ambitious than Liszt, instinctively utilized his intimate knowledge of older music to extract from it those compositional features that had not been used up before and therefore could now become fruitful for revitalizing music. His was the more effective position in the long run, for brand-new ideas are often ephemeral, while

---

*Die Musik der Zukunft was the title of an essay written by Wagner in 1850 under the influence of Ludwig Feuerbach's *Grundsätze einer Philosophie der Zukunft* (1843). Wagner's enemies shortened the term to *Zukunftsmusik,* in which form it has reached posterity.

lasting progress is achieved whenever something which exists already but is considered secondary suddenly gains prime importance—in this case, a breaking away from traditional tonality through emancipation of each of the musical elements. This does not mean, however, that Brahms's works are transitional, as were most of those of C. P. E. Bach, a century earlier. Brahms's place is not *between* the times. Wherever Brahms sticks to tradition, he does it wholeheartedly and without any idea of trying to improve on the old masters. In the few cases where he composes in sonata form, he uses the form as he found it and does not try to find new twists in the old scheme. But where Brahms decides to go forward, he never contents himself with half a step. His experiments in the fields of melody, harmony, rhythm, and meter—the four elements, one might say—belong wholly to modern music.

The onset of twentieth-century music made it possible for us to see these modern features in Brahms, especially Schoenberg's system of composing. If Schoenberg had done nothing more than sharpen our ears for Bach's, Mozart's, and Brahms's melodic-harmonic audacities, he would richly deserve his fame! Among Brahms's circle of friends, Clara Schumann—whose judgment was the most important to Brahms—criticized him nearly every time he digressed from the expected course of music. Elisabeth von Herzogenberg had an inkling that there were things in Brahms's music which she could not grasp but which were valuable. She occasionally observed that "strange things" were happening there, but she was also disturbed by harsh dissonances. Unfortunately this marvelous musician and unique connoisseur of Brahms's style died on January 7, 1892, before his late works for clarinet, for piano, and for voice were written; she might have understood where these dissonances were leading him.

It is paradoxical that the first composers to be deeply influenced by what was modern in Brahms were two of the obvious Wagnerians, Mahler and Schoenberg. In their early works, both of them had used and even exaggerated Wagner's massive orchestrations and theatrical climaxes; and Schoenberg had also built his approach to twelve-tone procedure on chromaticism, another Wagnerian tool. He may have been aware that Brahms, in a different way, had also contributed to the discovery of the twelve-tone system (see below, p. 269 and Ex. 18).

Mahler had a warm personal relationship with Brahms, which derived from Brahms's enthusiasm about Mahler's conducting of *Don Giovanni*. Mahler certainly learned from Brahms how to make melody lines stretch above and below a melodic center.* Schoenberg took this up and developed it further. Many of Brahms's other ideas were fully explained in Schoenberg's essay "Brahms the Progressive"; with one exception (Schumann on Berlioz's *Symphonie Fantastique*), this is the most explicit essay ever written by one great composer about another! Another line led from Brahms to Reger and later to Hindemith. Reger understood the workings of Brahms's textures, in which fullness is balanced by linear polyphony. Hindemith in turn learned from Reger, and also directly from Brahms.

Brahms, way beyond his expectations, is so alive and popular today not only because of the substance of his inspiration but also largely because his seemingly smooth late-Romantic style, on the surface akin to his friend Max Bruch's, is secretly spiced with many features of twentieth-century music. To grasp this phenomenon more clearly, it is necessary to look at each of the musical elements in turn.

1. Melody

At a time when the urge for Romantic expression became so strong that composers and their teachers began to neglect the ground rules of composition, Brahms stepped in to restore the original values and functions of all the musical elements, but especially of melody. His melodic strength forms the center of his creativity. From Bach and other Baroque masters he had learned to listen to melodic intervals independently of harmony and rhythm, so that his melodic planning became a forceful and innovative basis of composing. This does not mean that Brahms was another Mozart, Schubert, or Johann Strauss in creating catchy tunes. It is well known that he envied Strauss for that gift, which he knew he lacked. It does mean that through his textures—particularly the

---

*See, for instance, the horn melody of the Introduction to Mahler's Third Symphony, 8 mm. before number 5. The note A remains at the center throughout, despite the fact that the melody extends from the major third above to the octave below. This is the kind of melody that Brahms used in the Introduction to his C minor Symphony, op. 68, mm. 5–6.

more polyphonic ones—he reestablished the vitality of melodic rises and falls as the core of musical events.

Brahms presented melody lines not in isolation, as in fugal art, but in a lively two-part structure formed by top and bottom. This is by no means as common as one might think. Most nineteenth-century composers never thought of a bass *tone* as part of a meaningful bass *line,* but only as the bottom note of a chord. Sometimes this is true even of Schumann, Brahms's immediate model. On the other hand, the great masters of the late Baroque and Classicism were inclined to write either in four parts (Haydn and Schubert, for example) or in three parts, following Bach's example. Three-part writing came so naturally to Bach that in his two-part and four-part music the sensitive listener will often notice places where one voice was deliberately dropped or deliberately added; it is not by accident that the majority of the Fugues of the *Well-Tempered Clavier*—26 out of 48—are cast in three-part writing.

But Brahms was a natural two-part writer. When young composers showed him their scores, he is reported to have been in the habit of putting his hand over the inner voices and declaring: "Top voice and bass are what matters—all the rest is stuffing." In his own works, the melody frequently becomes understandable only when one simultaneously studies the bass line. At the beginning of his G minor Rhapsody, op. 79, no. 2 (Ex. 6), the top voice ascends for two measures—the second measure being an exact sequence of the first—and then leaps up for only one beat, after which it descends at once. Though this tune is pretty, in itself it does not constitute a very convincing gesture for an opening in the heroic vein. However, it makes perfect sense as soon as one studies the bass line that comes with it. The bass steadily ascends throughout these first four measures: by a fourth in the first measure, by a sixth in

Ex. 6 Rhapsody in G minor, op. 79, no. 2, top and bottom lines, mm. 1–4.

the second, and by a tenth in the third—a straight and logical increase of melodic tension that compensates for and completes the inconsistent ups and downs of the top voice. This creates a perfect equilibrium, for in this type of music the top voice has the simple function of establishing a singable melody in an evenly flowing rhythm. Similarly, in the G minor Ballade, op. 118, no. 3, during the first four measures of the second subsection (Ex. 7), the top voice, in folk music style, repeats the first measure in the second one and the third measure in the fourth one. This deliberately weak melodic order is beautifully enlivened by an ascending fourth in the bass of the third measure. Conversely, the bass, taken by itself, is equally incomplete. Its function—as Michael Campbell put it in a conversation—is to qualify the treble melody.

Ex. 7 Ballade in G minor, op. 118, no. 3, top and bottom lines, mm. 11–14.

The Brahmsian melody is different from other melodies by being essentially a combination of scale and arpeggio intervals balanced so that no overall direction of the melodic line appears as a prominent factor (as in the "fencing" tunes of Richard Strauss). Very often the melody seems to hover over a single central tone, like a bee over a blossoming flower. Its delimitations are normally open, so that they appear to be without a beginning and an end— very different from Beethoven or from Schubert.[14]

Brahms's melodies express his nature: North German, introverted, unassuming, somewhat defensive, craving beauty and harmony, severely Lutheran at heart, and overcome by the futility of human endeavor. In many ways Brahms resembles his great compatriot Theodor Storm (1817–1888), sixteen years his senior, whose poems and short stories express a similar view of life. However they do not approach the universal spirit that led Brahms to become a master of the music of earlier times and of foreign peoples.

Typical Brahms melodies occur in some Scherzo movements that hover between tears and smiles. The third movement of the D minor Violin Sonata, op. 108, immediately achieves its poignant effect by centering on the keynote and its minor third, connecting them sometimes by direct leap and sometimes diatonically. Although this type of melody is related to German folklore it is at the same time an integral part of Brahms's individual style, in its precise, logical construction. See also the theme of the A minor Intermezzo, op. 116, no. 2, where the first eight measures could be an actual folk song, but the echo in the ninth measure lends the Brahms touch. The resemblance to German folk songs is sometimes more pronounced when a melody that has been centering in one place momentarily leaps up or down for just one or two tones. The melody of the famous Intermezzo in A major, op. 118, no. 2, would be confined to the minor sixth between g-sharp and e were it not for the sudden leap to a″ in m. 2 (Ex. 8). The hidden tune in E minor of the Intermezzo, op. 116, no. 5, after remaining in the immediate vicinity of the dominant tone, suddenly goes down to the keynote at the end of the first phrase, in m. 2 (Ex. 9).

Ex. 8 Intermezzo in A major, op. 118, no. 2, mm. 1–4.

Ex. 9 Intermezzo in E minor, op. 116, no. 5, mm. 1–2.

Brahms's originality in melody was strengthened by his awareness of its problems. It is interesting to discover that he invented his own version of the four-tone subject of Mozart's "Jupiter" Fugue. Mozart uses the first, second, fourth, and third tone of a major scale, circumscribing the third tone in *cambiata* fashion (Ex. 10a). Beethoven, in the late quartets, sharpened it considerably by using, in the A minor Quartet, op. 132, a circumscribed fifth in a harmonic minor scale (Exx. 10b, c); and, in the *Great Fugue,* op. 133, a circumscribed minor sixth between the raised key note and the sixth tone of a major scale (B-flat–B-natural–A-flat–G). This motto (see Ex. 10d) is heard in a minor key because its direction goes toward C minor, the minor superdominant. Brahms returns to Mozart's C–D–F–E, but he raises all but the D by a semitone (Ex. 10e), so that the four tones—like Beethoven's four tones in op. 132—constitute part of a harmonic scale. The ways in which the three masters shaped their four-note motto is deeply connected with their nature as individuals. Mozart conveys an eternal truth; Beethoven, an eternal search for truth; and Brahms, a personal sorrow in the face of eternity.

Ex. 10a Mozart, *Jupiter* Symphony. K. 551, 4th Mvt., mm. 1–4.

Beethoven, String Quartet in A minor, op. 132, 1st Mvt.
Ex. 10b   mm. 1–2

Ex. 10c mm. 13–16

Ex. 10d Beethoven. *Great Fugue*, op. 133, mm. 26–29.

Ex. 10e Capriccio in F-sharp minor, op. 76, no. 1, mm. 14–15

Another four-tone melody arrangement is so typical of Brahms's way of listening to scales and arpeggios that it almost works as a theme song for him. It consists of the dominant tone followed by the keynote above and the next two upper scale tones (Ex. 11). Brahms uses it in the major and in the minor, inverted and in

Ex. 11

RETROGRADE   INVERSION (see Ex. 5b)

retrograde. He probably was never aware of the frequency with
which his themes are built on this four-tone sequence, which
ideally fulfils his aim of building motives on the simplest possible scale and chord intervals, that is, with seconds, thirds, and
fourths.* The same motive appears in the B major trio section of
the B minor Rhapsody, op. 79, no. 1 (see Ex. 2b), clearly inspired
by Schubert's use of it (see Ex. 2a), but Schubert was not the only
earlier composer to use this tone combination: It is also prominent
in Chopin's Third Scherzo, in C-sharp minor, op. 39; and it forms
the end of the exposition of the opening movement of Beethoven's
D major Sonata, op. 10, no. 3. However, nowhere is it as frequent
as in Brahms, so that one must accept it as a characteristic constellation of his melodic language: It opens the Waltzes, op. 39; it
forms the second subject of the first movement of the D minor
Concerto, op. 15 (Ex. 12); and (in the minor mode) it appears in
the opening theme of the Piano Quintet in F minor, op. 34 (Ex.
13). An old German *Minnelied,* also in minor, which starts with
the same four notes, serves as the basis for the slow movement of
Brahms's C major Sonata, op. 1 (see also his very late arrangement
of the same song, in *Deutsche Volkslieder,* vol. 7, no. 49). The
retrograde version appears in the character of a community or fra-
ternity song in the D-flat major section of the Finale of the F minor
Sonata, op. 5 (Ex. 14, top voice). Perhaps the most outspoken,

Ex. 12 Concerto in D minor, op. 15, 1st Mvt.,
"poco più moderato" section, mm. 1–2.

p legato

Ex. 13 Piano Quintet in F minor, op. 34,
1st Mvt., mm. 1–3.

Allegro non troppo

mf

Ex. 14 Sonata in F minor, op. 5,
5th Mvt., mm. 140–41.

pp legato sempre

*Leon Fleisher first drew my attention to this phenomenon, and for a while we had a
game going in which we competed in discovering new examples of this constellation.

near-vulgar setting is found in the trio section of the Scherzo of the F-sharp minor Sonata, op. 2, Brahms's earliest full-length work; and an inversion of the four-note pattern appears in the conclusion of the *Alto Rhapsody,* op. 53 (see Ex. 5b).

Quite early in his life, Brahms began to indulge in melodic experiments, from the time of his *Variations on a Theme by Robert Schumann,* op. 9. Still in the spirit of Schumann's *Carnaval,* in which the letters *A, S, C, H* are hidden in each movement, in the G minor Quartet, op. 25, Brahms reuses the fourth to eighth tones of the opening—g–f–c–e-flat–d (Ex. 15a)—as the ninth to thirteenth tones of the slow (third) movement (Ex. 15b).

Piano Quartet in G minor, op. 25.
Ex. 15a 1st Mvt., mm. 1–2

Ex. 15b 3rd Mvt., mm. 1–4

In his later works Brahms relied on traditional contrapuntal practices. He regularly used inversions as a pattern, mostly for decorative purposes. In the slow movement of the C major Trio, op. 87, for instance, mm. 24–27 are an inversion of the four preceding measures (Ex. 16), and the same thing happens again in each of the ensuing variations. There is no particular meaning to this detail; it is merely one of the ways in which Brahms escaped the exaggerated homophony of the music of his contemporaries. In the first movement of the D minor Violin Sonata, the violin completes the melody of the piano by imitating it as a canon in the inversion (Ex. 17). The most flagrant use of an inversion occurs in mm. 46–52 of the Finale of the Clarinet Trio in A minor, op. 115, where the entire second subject is stated by the cello and then inverted, at the distance of one beat, in the continued cello part while the clarinet repeats the theme in its original form.

Ex. 16 Piano Trio in C major, op. 87, 2nd Mvt., mm. 24–30.

Ex. 17 Violin Sonata in D minor, op. 108, 1st Mvt., mm. 56–59.

In an early work, the Finale of Brahms's Piano Quintet, op. 34, the first violin, complemented by the second, opens a new episode with no less than an eleven-tone row in which only a-flat is missing (Ex. 18). Except for one tritone between the violins, the row uses only ascending and descending semitones, ascending minor thirds, and descending fourths, and it generally moves in a descending line. A lesser emancipation of the melodic line and its intervals occurs in two Intermezzos from op. 119, Brahms's last group of works for piano solo. The writing here is of more importance than that in the quintet, for it now becomes a prime factor of construction. The second and third Intermezzos employ an identical three-tone motive consisting of the third scale tone (minor or major) with its upper third and upper fourth: G–B–C in no. 2, in E (G-sharp–B–C-sharp in the middle section), and E–G–A in no. 3, in C major. The motive is thrown around in every kind of rhythm, and in no. 3, a piece in scherzo character, it produces cheerful permutations of its three tones.

Ex. 18 Piano Quintet in F minor, op. 34, 4th Mvt., mm. 95–100.

In these late pieces of op. 119 Brahms started something new. Isolating the musical elements (no. 1 isolates harmony, and no. 4 plays with meter changes, see below), he injected new vitality into old musical devices. Nobody would have expected melody to play such a role. It was assumed generally throughout the nineteenth century that harmony was the progressive, melody the conservative, element. This started in the 1830s with the rivalry between Rossini and Meyerbeer in Paris. Heine wrote, in May 1837:

Characteristic of Rossini's music is . . . the prime importance of melody—which is always the immediate expression of a private emotion. In Meyerbeer however we find a predominance of harmony: in the stream of the harmonic masses the melodies sound no longer; they drown, just as individual feelings of a single person must succumb to the mass emotion of an entire population.[15]

Wagner started from here, but later on—particularly in *Tristan und Isolde*—he also expressed individual emotions through harmony instead of melody, by leaning on the strong medium of chromaticism as a musical equivalent to the subconscious human mind.

While harmonic thinking prevents dissonances from becoming too harsh for further harmonic progression, melodic thinking has no limits in this direction, as Bach and Mozart already knew. Although Brahms was impressed by Mozart's audacity (see p. 253 above), he does not go as far. His intervals are tame and usually consonant, and they are also close together: one rarely finds melodic sevenths in a Brahms score. Nevertheless, it was *his* melodic thinking, not Wagner's, that enabled the German and Austrian composers of the period 1910–1930 to express themselves in harsh melodic clashes. And occasionally, in extreme musical emotion, Brahms uses them himself; see the Finale of the Piano Quartet in C minor, op. 60, mm. 328–32. There is one respect in which Brahms resembles Wagner more than he does Schumann; namely, in his use of melodies which are not sharply subdivided into phrases corresponding to the length of a singer's breath. No singer could breathe with Brahms's spun-out melodic-rhythmic top voice progressions, such as the B major theme in the G minor Ballade, op. 118, no. 3 (Ex. 19). It is thinkable that Brahms intended to transfer Wagner's utopian concept of "unendliche Melodie" (unending melody; 1860) to instrumental music.[16]

Ex. 19 Ballade in G minor. op. 118. no. 3. mm. 41–48.

pp una corda

2. Harmony

Brahms's remarkable achievement is that, perhaps for the first time since Bach, harmonic planning is not influenced by the autonomous directions of the melodic lines, but remains independent, just as the melody lines in Brahms's music exist free of harmonic considerations.

One may start with the observation that, compared to Wagner and Liszt, Brahms sounds not only traditional but in many ways old-fashioned. This was said hundreds of times during his lifetime, and many more times since then; it is quite true, even in comparison with Mozart and Beethoven. Brahms's scores never contain attempts to jump to remote tonalities without modulation, as Mozart does in the G minor Symphony, first movement, mm. 101–104 (G minor to F-sharp minor) or in his Piano Concerto in B-flat major, first movement, mm. 184–91 (F major to B minor). In these examples the harmonic change is accomplished by diminished-seventh chords, which go by so fast that the ear still feels the full impact of the abrupt key change. Beethoven is even cruder in Variation 22 of the *Diabelli* Variations, op. 120, as he juxtaposes, between mm. 8 and 11, the keys of G major, A-flat major, and E major without any attempt at modulation at all. See also the first movement of Beethoven's A-flat major Sonata, op. 110, mm. 38–40.

Nowhere does Brahms even use chromatic descents of diminished-seventh chords, as Mozart does in the first movement of the F major Sonata, K. 494 (Ex. 20), or in the Piano Quintet in E-flat major, K. 452, second movement, mm. 106–108. Even Bach occasionally uses them; see mm. 34ff. of the Gigue of the First Partita, in B-flat major.

However this does not by any means indicate that Brahms's harmonic language lacked daring. Here is where the Wagnerians

Ex. 20 Mozart. Sonata in F major. K. 494. 1st Mvt.. mm. 215–16.

made their big mistake; they had no ear for Brahms's subtle introduction of his progressive ideas by stretching the use of conventional chords and chord progressions. Of the 49 chords, including
inversions, which form the triads and seventh chords of each
major and minor key, most nineteenth-century composers, including Beethoven, normally used only the 21 derived from the
tonic, dominant, and subdominant, with occasional use of the first
inversion of the seventh chord on the second degree and the root
position of the triad on the sixth degree. Brahms—deliberately,
skillfully, and beautifully—uses all 49; and that also means that he
returns to the eighteenth-century use of sequences of all the seventh chords.* This was natural to him, and it was not an exercise
in old-fashioned or folklore-exotic ways of writing. Therefore one
accepts these chords as a fitting and essential ingredient in his
scores.

   A typical model of this procedure appears in the C major
Capriccio, op. 76, no. 8. Strictly in F major, without using any
outside tones, Brahms stages a sequential descent in one seventh
chord after another. The roots fall by fifths, first from the key note
to the fourth degree, then to the seventh and the third, and finally
to the sixth and the second, after which a dominant-seventh at the
beginning of m. 44 completes the regular progression through all
seven roots of the F major scale (Exx. 21a, b). The melodic interest
is kept up by means of the first note of each group of four notes in
the right hand, in which a harmony tone from the preceding chord
is maintained as an appoggiatura (Ex. 21c). This creates one 3/1
supermeasure on top of the already complex hemiola situation between the two hands; the left hand counts one *and* two *and* three in

Capriccio in C major, op. 76, no. 8, mm. 42–44.
Ex. 21a   as written

* Erich Itor Kahn first drew my attention to this, many years ago.

Ex. 21b harmonic progression

$$\text{I}^6_5 \quad \text{IV}^2 \quad \text{VII}^6_5 \quad \text{III}^2 \quad \text{VI}^6_5 \quad \text{II}^2 \quad \text{V}^6_5$$

Ex. 21c appoggiatura effect

whole notes. Additionally, Brahms also creates some metric tension by using his customary hemiola notation: while the right
hand is in 6/4 (corresponding to the time signature), the left hand
has its stems in 3/2 (according to the actual harmonic rhythm), see
Ex. 21a. See also the last ten measures of the B minor Intermezzo,
op. 119, no. 1.

   The lavish use of all the chords belonging to a key makes it easy
for Brahms, as it once did for Bach, to think in terms of an entire
"tonal region" (Schoenberg's term), including neighboring keys to
define the tonality that is the center of the music at any given moment. In his later years Brahms became a virtuoso in such indirect
defining of tonality: in the Intermezzo in A minor, op. 118, no. 1,
he accomplished the astounding feat of making the tonality quite
clear without ever using an A minor chord in root position on a
full beat except for the first ending in m. 30 (Ex. 22).[17]

   When Brahms moves through remote keys, he usually selects
the same cautious, step-by-step technique of modulation. Only
rarely does he undertake to modulate abruptly, as in the F minor
Intermezzo, op. 118, no. 4, mm. 25–28 (A-flat major to B major),

Ex. 22 Intermezzo in A minor, op. 118, no. 1, m. 30.

and in such cases the result tends to sound awkward and artificial.

The beginnings of the two Rhapsodies of op. 79 testify to Brahms's original yet coherent structural use of remote keys. They sound so natural that only the expert will notice that Brahms has replaced routine harmony progressions by a daring chord and bass structure. In the exposition of the G minor Rhapsody, op. 79, no. 2, the first thirteen measures, into which Brahms compresses the first theme and a bridge passage, contain not one G minor chord, not even on a weak beat! The chords of the respective downbeats of the eight measures of the theme are E-flat major, F major, C major, G major (two measures), A major, E major, and B major! And yet, there is a strong G minor feeling in the first four measures, engendered most of all by the bass progression D–G with which the piece begins. It makes the E-flat major chord over G appear as a recognizable replacement of a tonic G minor chord. Measure 2 is nothing but a harmonized melodic scale in the Bach tradition (see above, p. 16), and what follows amounts to an emphatic plagal cadence in the tonic major (Picardy Third)—a favorite closing device of Brahms, who ends both his First and Second Violin Sonatas that way. He thus moves quite far from the tonal center without using any but traditional means. His solution here for the harmonic problems is entirely independent of his handling of the melody lines in the bass and treble (see above, p. 263).

The initial harmonic construction in the B minor Rhapsody, op. 79, no. 1, is similar. Again, the theme and the bridge passages are not separate from each other. The dominant minor is reached in m. 16, but unlike the situation in the other Rhapsody, though the tonic minor chord is sounded on a number of off-beats, it is heard as the fourth degree of the dominant, F-sharp major (Ex. 23a). The most daring and most significant measure is m. 9, where the root (G-sharp) and third (B-sharp) of the superdominant (G-sharp major) of the next key (F-sharp minor) are enharmonically introduced as A-flat and C, as part of an F minor chord. (The F minor tonality here is derived from a double key ascent in minor thirds from the main key of B minor. The first four measures are harmonically governed by the dominant of B minor; the next four by that of D minor, after which F minor is the next sequential step.) The enharmonic change in m. 10 sounds quite smooth since the bass, from the beginning of m. 9 to the downbeat of m. 11, de-

scends in a regular progression of (major and minor) thirds: C–A-
flat–F–C-sharp (= D-flat) –A–F-sharp–D (Ex. 23b). The enharmonic procedure can be seen clearly in Ex. 23c.

Rhapsody in B minor, op. 79, no. 1.
Ex. 23a mm. 1–4

Ex. 23b mm. 9–11

Ex. 23c mm. 9–10

The same descending thirds, this time from the top, form the
core of Brahms's most dissonant piano piece, the B minor Intermezzo, op. 119, no. 1. While the Second and Third Intermezzos of
op. 119 experiment with a tone row (see above, p. 269), this piece,
as Brahms himself wrote to Clara Schumann in May 1893,

is crawling with dissonances. . . . The small piece is exceptionally melancholy,
and "to play very slowly" is not saying enough. Each measure, each note must
sound like a *ritardando,* as if one wanted to suck melancholy out of each one, with
sensuousness and gratification from these dissonances![18]

This letter shows—as do all his remarks concerning his musical
emotions*—that Brahms remained a full-blooded Romantic all
his life. His late progressive experiments were always emotionally

---

*See his letter to Clara Schumann of December 23, 1892, in which he compares Schu-
mann's Variations for Two Pianos with "a lovely, mild day of spring . . . when one never
tires of enjoying the quiet air, which is neither cold nor warm. . . ."[19]

motivated. The B minor Intermezzo, one measure before the end, culminates in a chord in which all seven tones of the harmonic scale are sounded simultaneously, by way of a descent in thirds over an interval of a thirteenth (Ex. 24).

Ex. 24 Intermezzo in B minor, op. 119, no. 1, mm. 65–66.

The B minor Rhapsody is interesting not only for its harmonic progressions as such (pp. 274–75) but also for their functions in the structure of the piece. What is accomplished by its fascinating accumulation of different tonalities within a few measures indeed amounts to a variation of the expected modulation from tonic (B minor) to dominant (F-sharp minor). Technically, Brahms could have done this in the regular way, by using a root progression B–D–G-sharp (not A-flat!)–C-sharp–F-sharp. The remote chords are therefore substitutions fulfilling the function of the regular harmony. In the terminology of Schoenberg's book *Structural Functions of Harmony,* the chords of a remote region temporarily replace those of the regions to which the tonic and dominant belong. No other composer of Brahms's generation possessed such awareness of the "shaping forces" (to use Ernst Toch's book title[20]) of the musical elements—an awareness that, to a large extent, accounts for the totally changed approach to composing in our day.

Let us examine two more examples of this technique: In the opening movement of the Second Piano Concerto, preceding the second subject in the solo exposition (mm. 118–28), the dominant of the secondary key of F major is already reached in a C major chord on the downbeat, so that Brahms could have proceeded directly with the theme. Instead, he inserts ten measures, mostly played by the orchestra alone, during which he visits D-flat major twice and the dominant of F minor in between. Finally, by enharmonic change, he jumps to the key of D during the seventh measure, continuing from there through G minor (the second-degree chord in F major), only to land on the very same C major chord

from which he started! Structurally, therefore, these meanderings
are a waste, especially when compared to the somewhat similar
progression in the fourth movement of Schubert's Trout Quintet,
op. 114, Variation 5 and the return of the theme. The chord sequence here does not, as in the Brahms example, lead back to the
beginning; there is a definite purpose to Schubert's juggling of tonalities, namely, to modulate from B-flat major, by way of B-flat
minor and D-flat major, back to the remote original key of D
major. The chords here are not substitutions for other chords but
directly serve a purpose. What may be seen as a bit of Romantic
byplay in Brahms is severe Classical form in Schubert—though
the harmonic doings in the two passages may sound similar at first
listening.

The final example, from Variation 1 of the second book of
Paganini Variations, op. 35, shows a sophisticated instance of simultaneously varying both the melody and the harmony in such a
way that the original harmonic sequence remains recognizable to
the ear. The original harmonies proceed very simply by falling
fifths in the bass (A–D–G–C) to the final cadence. In Variation 1
the substitutions begin with the last chord of the first half, as
Brahms puts a major mediant, G-sharp major, in the place of a
dominant chord. The second half proceeds regularly up to the D
minor in m. 9. But from there one substitution follows the other
(compare Exs. 25a and b). We hear C minor instead of C major,

Paganini Variations, op. 35, book II.
Ex. 25a Theme, mm. 9–16, harmonies.

Ex. 25b Var. 1, mm. 9–16, harmonies and harmonic rhythm.

and this substitution, as Brahms (according to Schoenberg[21]) told his pupils, "opens the gates to the flat keys": B-flat minor (instead of a diminished chord on B as the second degree of A minor), A-flat minor, F-sharp minor (enharmonic for G-flat), and back to A (Picardy Third); and only from here does Brahms return home—quite a tour de force!

Finally, in speaking of harmony, we must mention pedal points, simply because Clara Schumann, for whom Brahms wrote practically all his piano music,* loved pedal points, according to their correspondence. Harmonically there is nothing very distinctive about Brahms's passages built on an ostinato tone in the bass or elsewhere. His use of the ostinato is distinctly influenced by Bach. This is true for two of the best-known examples: the first movement of the D minor Violin Sonata, op. 108, in which a dominant ostinato fills the entire development and a corresponding keynote ostinato fills the coda; and the beautiful, mysterious pedal point on low G, dominant of C minor, in Brahms's last piano piece, the E-flat major Rhapsody, op. 119, no. 4, mm. 168–87. On July 2, 1893, he wrote to Clara: "In a dozen measures I imagine I can see you smile a bit (which ones?)." She answered, on July 13, 1893: "I think I'll be able to find the dozen measures which you mention." In August 1893 he replied: "The pedal point in the E-flat piece is of course the passage where I have been counting on your happy face. I know your old weakness for pedal points!"[22] (See Ex. 26, m. 168.)

Ex. 26 Rhapsody in E-flat major, op. 119, no. 4, mm. 168–72.

3. Rhythm and Meter

We start from the premise that rhythm, comparatively speaking, is a picture, and meter is its frame.

---

*Including his last pieces, op. 119. After her death, Brahms stopped writing for piano.

Meter. We will explain Brahms's approach to metrical problems with two examples. In his song "Sapphische Ode," op. 94, no. 4, of 1884 (see Ex. 27, which shows the entire vocal part of the first verse), the "picture" consists of the four lines of the poem. Each line has a duration of exactly six beats, the half note being the beat. The first line is preceded by two beats of instrumental introduction. The second line follows the first immediately; then comes one beat of rest before the third line, which is immediately followed by the concluding line. There are two verses, each followed by five instrumental measures. In short, the verse consists of 2 + 6 + 6 + 1 + 6 + 6 + 5 = 32 beats. (Normally, 32 beats are the result of four times eight measures.) The time signatures for these 32 beats keep changing. The first eight measures are in 2/2, followed by one measure in 3/2, one in 2/2, another measure in 3/2, and four measures in 2/2. The 2/2 measures add up to a total of 26 beats, the 3/2 measures to six beats, for a total of 32 beats.

Ex. 27 "Sapphische Ode," op. 94, no. 4, 1st Verse.

In planning his metrical scheme with such refinement, Brahms wanted to translate the exact prosody of the poem into music without its getting monotonous. He used the same care and skill that August von Platen (1796–1835) had taken in his famous sonnets and odes, which are full of refined rhyme schemes and verse-length variety. To create the necessary rhythmic flexibility in identical verses, Brahms proceeded in two ways. First, he changed the rhythmic patterns from line to line while keeping some of the same rhythmic motives. The first three lines begin with four even quarter notes. But only twice (after the second and third openings) do the lines continue with the same rhythm of quarter note and two eighths. Second, he let the third line start in the middle of a measure—dividing the four even quarter notes between two successive measures—while lines 1, 2, and 4 each *begin* a measure.

Thus both the rhythmic picture and its metrical frame vary a bit from line to line.

This example from Brahms's vocal music illuminates the case of his Rhapsody in E-flat major, op. 119, no. 4, which is more complex. The four pieces of op. 119 (as shown above, p. 269) are those in which Brahms experiments with musical elements. The Rhapsody, the last piece, is concerned with meter. The first 60 measures consist of five-measure phrases. This length is not unusual, but while earlier pieces, such as the Haydn Variations and the Variations on an Original Theme, op. 21a, had a folkloristic basis, the metrical arrangement here is primarily an abstract, deliberate construction. Several times Brahms varies the rhythmic picture within the five-measure frame in order to avoid placing the point of greatest gravity at the same spot in every phrase. Nevertheless, the five measures (= five beats, since the half note is the beat, the time signature being 2/2) are consistently subdivided into 3 + 2, never into 2 + 3 measures. After the fourth five-measure period, from m. 21 onward (see Ex. 28a), the ear is forced to take into account the fact that the harmonic progressions now converge toward the fourth beat. In the first four periods the situation is not as obvious, and Schnabel, for instance, heard mm. 3–5 as two 3/4 measures instead of three beats in 2/2 (Ex. 28b), for he did not realize the preponderance of the dominant in the beginning of mm. 4 and 9, expressed by the upward leaps in the bass. (Neither did I when I reported it;[23] see Ex. 28c.) Only in this reading does the tune, despite its artificiality, reveal a little of the folklore character of Brahms's earlier five-measure tunes.

From these examples it is easy to analyze other instances of metrical irregularities in Brahms's piano music. In the C-sharp minor Intermezzo, op. 117, no. 3, the main section is presented in five-measure phrases, but here each phrase is subdivided 2 + 3, as can be heard and also seen: the only long slur in the first phrase connects mm. 3 and 4 (Ex. 29).

Rhythm. Brahms has a reputation for writing "syncopated" music, especially in the accompanying parts of his songs and chamber pieces. But what looks like syncopation rarely sounds that way, for these patterns are primarily devices to spread the tones of the accompanying chords and thus avoid the tone clusters one finds in Beethoven's and Schumann's chamber music. Brahms's recipe is

Rhapsody in E-flat major, op. 119, no. 4.
Ex. 28a melody, mm. 1–40

Ex. 28b Schnabel's interpretation, mm. 1–20

Ex. 28c

Ex. 29 Intermezzo in C-sharp minor, op. 117, no, 3, mm. 1–5.

molto piano e s. v. sempre

simple and effective, from the viewpoint of the number of tones heard during one beat. This is easy to figure out: a quarter note beat subdivided into eighth-note triplets produces three notes; into sixteenths, four notes. By giving triplets to the left hand and simultaneously sixteenths to the right, as Brahms frequently does, notes are played at six different times, benefitting the solo part by fluffing the texture (Ex. 30). Schumann, in his late years, had invented this mode of accompaniment in his *Phantasiestücke,* op. 73, for clarinet and piano (1849). It took Brahms some time to develop this "syncopated" accompanying style. It first came to full use in his First Violin Sonata, in G major, op. 78 (1880). Another device used by Schumann united both melody and triplet accompaniment within the same voice. Brahms employed this as early as the Fourth Ballade, op. 10 (Ex. 31a). The notation here amounts to a *rubato* prescription, for if the melody is played in straight eighth notes, the triplets would disappear (Ex. 31b). If it is played strictly on the first and third triplet note (Ex. 31c), it could not sound even, as its notation on extra stems demands, but would limp at the rate of 2 : 1.

Ex. 30

Ballade in B major, op. 10, no. 4, m. 55.
Ex. 31a   as written

Alternate solutions for the tenor voice
Ex. 31b   Ex. 31c

The Brahms hemiola, which is almost always hidden behind a nonfitting time signature, serves a similar purpose of relieving the measure of gravity. As we hear six successive quarter notes simultaneously divided by three and by two, we are unable to invest any of the five beats following the downbeat with a specific heaviness.

Something like a typical Brahms melody rhythm exists every time one meets his gently dotted notes moving up and down in narrow intervals of seconds or thirds (see above, pp. 264–65). The center tone is featured on the dotted quarters, and its oscillations occur on the ensuing eighth notes. In piano music, the middle part of the G minor Ballade, op. 118, no. 3 (Ex. 19, above), and the Intermezzo in A minor, op. 76, no. 7 (Ex. 32),* well illustrate this type of tune; see also the second subject of the *Academic Festival Overture* and of the first movement of the A minor Quartet, op. 51, no. 2.

Ex. 32 Intermezzo in A minor, op. 76, no. 7, mm. 1–4.

These melodies seem to represent Brahms's personality in his later years, with his ever-increasing qualities of moderation and modesty—attributes that are twins in more than an etymological sense.

4. Pianistic Concerns

Just like Beethoven and Chopin, Brahms was a concert pianist. He also played music by others in public, more than they did. His repertoire and his performing vitality were rare even for his times. For a recital on April 7, 1867, in Vienna, at the hall of the Gesellschaft der Musikfreunde, Brahms listed the following program in his own hand:[24]

1. Rob. Schumann—Fantasie op. 17
2. a) Dom. Scarlatti—2 Capriccios [sonatas?].
   b) J. S. Bach—Toccata, F major [originally for organ]
3. Songs
4. Joh. Brahms. Variationen u. Fuge über ein Thema von Handel, op. 24
5. a) Franz Schubert. Adagio (comp. in 1817)—unpublished

---

*For fun, it could be called "Après une Lecture de 'For Elise.'"

b) the same, Allegro (comp. in 1828)—unpublished
c) Rob. Schumann Toccata opus 7.
6. Songs.
7. Ludwig v. Beethoven Sonata (E major) op. 109.

Imagine playing such demanding works as the Beethoven, op.
109; Schumann, Fantasie and Toccata; his own Handel Variations;
as well as smaller works by Scarlatti, Bach, and Schubert and perhaps even accompanying the (unspecified) songs, all in a single recital! What superpianist would undertake such a marathon today,
and what audience would listen to it?

In piano playing it was not only the music that interested
Brahms. His *51 Studies*—published for the first time when Brahms
was 60 years old but certainly dating, for the most part, from
much earlier times—demonstrates his great fascination with special domains of technique and, most of all, with polyphonic *legato*
playing.[25] He practiced the often uncomfortable stretches involved
here and sometimes went to extremes.

These exercises help us recognize the same kind of stretches
when they occur in his piano pieces. Brahms meant for them to be
executed exactly as written, that is, by finger *legato* and not to be
replaced (as often happens) by approximate solutions through
pedaling. Never mind how much Brahms himself may have over-
used the pedal in his late years: here scores speak louder than personal memoirs. The following are a few examples at random:
Capriccio in C major, op. 76, no. 8 (Exx. 33a, b); Capriccio in D
minor, op. 116, no. 1 (Ex. 34, showing Brahms's fingerings); In-

Capriccio in C major, op. 76, no. 8.
Ex. 33a mm. 56–58. as written

Ex. 33b mm. 57–58, upper voices

termezzo in A minor, op. 118, no. 1 (Exx. 35a, b, in which the intricate polyphony is shown); and Intermezzo in C major, op. 119, no. 3 (Ex. 36). In all the right-hand examples it was as important to the composer *not* to hold notes too long as it was to hold them long enough.

Ex. 34 Capriccio in D minor, op. 116, no. 1, mm. 38–48, left hand.

Intermezzo in A minor, op. 118, no. 1, mm. 25–28.
Ex. 35a right hand

Ex. 35b showing polyphony

Ex. 36 Intermezzo in C major, op. 119, no. 3, mm. 56–58.

In many cases Brahms's fingerings are actually "handings" (a Schnabel term), in which several registers are bridged quickly by using the entire hand, from thumb to little finger, for arpeggios, on both white and black keys. A typical example occurs in the E-flat major Rhapsody, op. 119, no. 4 (Ex. 37). Brahms's extra stems for quarter notes make the use of the fifth finger for the beginning

Ex. 37 Rhapsody in E-flat major, op. 119, no. 4, mm. 39—40, left hand.

of each four-note group mandatory. The combination of finger *legato* in the leading parts with arpeggiated chords all over the piano accounts for the typical deep, full, mellow Brahms sound, especially in the slow movements of the two piano concertos. The hands are buried in the instrument, which seems one with the human body. To get the feel of these sonorities it is often helpful, as a game, to sit far away with stretched elbows, as Brahms does in the famous cartoons of his playing, where he leans back so far that his beard becomes almost horizontal. (Not that today's performer should sit this way while playing in public!)

It is often mentioned that Brahms liked to add thirds-plus-octaves or sixths-plus-octaves to his melodies, perhaps as an imitation of certain stops on the organ. Actually it is only one of his many devices to use all registers of the piano simultaneously. Occasionally these settings have a technical, etude-like goal. In a letter from early October 1892, to Clara Schumann, Brahms speaks about the E minor Intermezzo, op. 116, no. 5 (Ex. 38), which begins with such a tone constellation in both hands. He advises her to take an easier hand distribution in which the thumbs are not interlocked, adding: "True, this ruins the particular attraction inherent in technically difficult passages[!]; in this case, in the strong pliable flexions of the hands—*big hands!*"[26] (Clara Schumann's hands were quite small.)

Ex. 38 Intermezzo in E minor, op. 116, no. 5, mm. 1—2.

In addition to the 51 exercises and five transcription-etudes (among which the Bach Chaconne stands out), Brahms, like most composers before him, also used the variation form for an etude-like display of virtuosity. However he was not as universal in his technical ambitions as Chopin and Liszt had been, probably because, in Brahms's day, the piano did not change as much as it had in the first half of the century; essentially it just became bigger, stiffer in its action, and louder.

CONCLUSION

Brahms's immense popularity is by no means confined to the United States. Even in France, where he was practically unknown 50 years ago, his music has become a normal part of the standard repertoire. Brahms festivals abound everywhere.

Nobody would be as surprised by this development as Brahms himself. In his lifetime, when the attention of the population at large was preoccupied with technological progress and geopolitical expansion, Brahms—whom these things did not interest—was forced to look at himself as reactionary. In today's atomic age, we have begun to see the dangers that come with technology and expansion, and this has reflected on our appreciation of art. We cherish the subtlety and intimacy of earlier times probably more than our parents did. On the other hand, we are not ready to give up what was good about nineteenth-century progress toward peace, prosperity, and scholarship. Neither do we want to diminish the artistic importance of the experiments in abstraction that occurred in the beginning of the twentieth century. Here is where Brahms's music is now filling a need. His full textures make us feel that music has a solid substance, like nineteenth-century living quarters. At times, even the greatest Mozart lover may need a momentary change from the thin texture of Mozart's piano sonatas. On the other hand, Brahms's subtle, moderate, yet challenging experiments satisfy our hunger for abstract, intellectual probing in art. Dryden said of Shakespeare that he is "the very Janus of poets, he wears almost everywhere two faces,"[27] and so we may perhaps call Brahms the very Janus of composers: like Nietzsche's Germany, he represents the time Before Yesterday and that After Tomorrow.

Conclusion

Music is a most potent force through which we may reach up and out. For some of us, this happens in stages. At first we experience the thrill of great performances and are fascinated by the artists. Eventually we become preoccupied by individual composers, their styles and their personalities. Here is where this book wants to be helpful. Finally, we may be able to enter the realm of all music and go further from there. Each earlier stage remains active but also becomes absorbed in the next, in an ever more encompassing ecstatic comprehension.

Notes

For complete bibliographic data on the references
cited see Selected Bibliography.

Chapter 1. Bach

1. See Erwin Bodky, *The Interpretation of Bach's Keyboard Works,* p. v.
2. See Philip Barford, *The Keyboard Music of C.P.E. Bach,* p. 96.
3. See *The Bach Reader,* p. 238.
4. Leopold Mozart, *Gründliche Violinschule,* chap. 1, sec. 3, no. 11.
5. A. Dolmetsch, *The Interpretation of the Music of the 17th and 18th Centuries,* p. 65.
6. Thurston Dart, *The Interpretation of Music,* p. 81.
7. Bodky, p. 198.
8. See, most recently, Frederick Neumann, *Ornamentation in Baroque and Post-Baroque Music with Special Emphasis on J.S. Bach.*
9. F. W. Marpurg speaks with contempt of "fifth-catchers" and states that *"you can neither forbid nor permit anything without admitting exceptions* [italics Marpurg's]" (*Handbuch bey dem Generalbasse und der Composition,* pp. 51 ff.). This may have been written under Bach's influence.
10. Andreas Moser, Preface to an edition of Bach's solo violin music, dating from the turn of the century; reprint by International Music Company.
11. See Pierre Pidoux, Introduction to *G. Frescobaldi: Orgel- und Klavierwerke,* vol. 4; and Willi Apel, *The History of Keyboard Music to 1700,* translated and revised by Hans Tischler (Bloomington: Indiana University Press, 1972), p. 456.
12. Elmar Seidel, "Ueber eine besondere Art Bachs, die Tonart der IV. Stufe zu verwenden," *Music Theorie,* 1/2 (1986).
13. Friedrich Neumann, "Typische Stufengänge im Bachschen Suitensatz."
14. Christoph Wolff, "Bach's 'Handexemplar' of the Goldberg Variations: A New Source," p. 227.
15. "These forms [dances] are small models for the later compositions" (H.C. Koch, *Versuch einer Anleitung zur Composition,* 1782–93), quoted in Leonard G. Ratner, "18th Century Theories of Musical Period Structure," p. 447. See also Ratner, *Classic Music,* pp. 231 ff.
16. René Leibowitz and Konrad Wolff, *Erich Itor Kahn* (Paris: Corrêa Ed., 1958), p. 165.
17. See Jörgen Jersild, "Die Harmonik J.S. Bachs," pp. 68–69.
18. See Ernst Schwarzmaier, *Die Takt- und Tonordnung Josef Riepels,* pp. 33–34.
19. See Ernö Lendvai, *Béla Bartók* (London: Kahn and Averill, 1971), pp. 17–27.
20. Robert Marshall speaks of "thoroughgoing periodicity of phrase structure" ("Bach the Progressive," p. 313).
21. Walter Schenkman, in "The Establishment of Tempo in Bach's Goldberg Variations," *BACH,* vol. 6, no. 3, pp. 3–10, agrees that the two parts of the vari-

ation must be in "viable relation" to each other, and his metronomic indications set the speed of the second part at four times that of the first.

22. See Ratner, *Classic Music,* p. 38.

23. Ibid., pp. 9 ff.

24. Robert Schumann, *Musik und Musiker,* p. 214.

25. August Halm, *Von Zwei Kulturen der Musik,* 1920.

26. The polyphonic detail of this fugue has been analyzed by August Halm, ibid., pp. 205 ff.; and by Imogen Horsley, *Fugue,* p. 138.

27. About the somewhat uncertain chronology of this transcription, see Werner Breig, "J.S. Bach und die Entstehung des Klavier-Konzerts," *Archiv für Musik-wissenschaft,* 1979: 21–48; esp. pp. 31–34.

28. Konrad Wolff, "On Tonal Relations in Classical Music," p. 12.

29. Praeludium and Fughetta in C major, in Bach-Gesellschaft, *Johann Sebastian Bachs Clavierwerke,* vol. 4, p. 224; see also p. xciv, printed from autograph source. (*Collected Works,* vol. 36, edited by Ernst Naumann [Leipzig: Breitkopf & Härtel, 1890].)

30. See Albert Schweitzer, *J.S. Bach,* p. 343.

31. Ralph Kirkpatrick, Introduction to the *Goldberg Variations,* pp. 20–23. See also John Boe, "Fully Notated Articulation in Bach's Mature Keyboard Music," *BACH,* vol. 7, no. 1, pp. 12–19; no. 2, pp. 14–22.

32. Georg von Dadelsen, in "Die Crux der Nebensache," gives the "Presto" (Finale) of the solo Violin Sonata in G minor, with its detailed, constantly changing phrase marks, as an example of Bach's typical phrasing. The six continuous sixteenth notes in this piece are sometimes subdivided into 1 + 5, 3 + 3, 3 times 2, etc.

33. "Bach, the Teacher," in *The Bach Reader,* chap. 2.

34. Schweitzer, p. 352.

35. Vianna da Motta, in "Zur Pflege der Bachschen Klavierwerke," as quoted by Schweitzer (pp. 329, 378), actually used the metaphor of terraces in a narrow conception: "This music is at all times to a certain extent majestic. It constantly builds itself in broad terraces comparable to the ancient temples of the Assyrians." Thus he relates the terrace principle, it seems to me, to a certain "affect" or character he sees in Bach's piano music, and not to the composer's and performer's structural concerns.

36. F. W. Marpurg, "Kritische Briefe über die Tonkunst," quoted in *The Bach Reader,* p. 257.

37. See Charles Rosen, "Bach and Handel," in *Keyboard Music,* edited by Denis Matthews (New York: Praeger, 1972), p. 729 (as quoted by Malcolm Bilson, *Notes,* vol. 29 [1973]).

38. On the adding and subtracting of voices, see George Kochevitzky, "Dynamics, a Postscript," *BACH,* vol. 7, no. 1, pp. 3–11. He quotes Quantz on the subject on p. 4.

39. The titles used in these examples are those of the Wolfgang Graeser edition (Wiesbaden: Breitkopf & Härtel, n.d.).

40. On insertions in general, see Schwarzmaier, p. 37.

41. Reprinted in the Bach-Gesellschaft edition, vol. 36.

Chapter 2. Haydn

1. See William S. Newman, "The Pianism of Haydn, Mozart, Beethoven, and Schubert—Compared."

2. See Christa Landon's excellent Preface to the Vienna Urtext edition of Haydn's piano sonatas.

3. Hermann Abert, "Joseph Haydns Klaviersonaten," esp. Year 2, p. 556 and 567.

4. Karl Geiringer, *Haydn*, p. 85; see also H.C. Robbins Landon, *Haydn: Chronicle and Works*, vol. III: *Haydn in England*, pp. 140–41.

5. Maynard Solomon, *Beethoven*, pp. 68 ff.

6. Charles Rosen, *Sonata Forms*, p. 229.

7. "Haydn had always been deeply religious and free from doubt and skepticism and was really sincere when he wrote the words *Laus Deo* at the end of each of his compositions" (Geiringer, p. 144).

8. Zelter's article, "Franz Joseph Haydn," was originally published in *Die Musikpflege*. Most of it is reprinted in Pierre Barbaud, *Haydn*, pp. 145 ff. But Barbaud erroneously attributed it to Goethe because he reprinted it in his journal *Über Kunst und Alterthum*. Further tributes to Haydn are in H.C. Robbins Landon, vol. V: *Haydn: The Late Years 1801–1809*, pp. 407–30.

Chapter 3. Mozart

1. Alfred Einstein, *Mozart*, p. 94.

2. For the *Magic Flute* as an expression of unity, see Alexander Hyatt-King, *Mozart in Retrospect*, pp. 141 ff.

3. Pichler's memoirs were published in 1844; the scene she describes occurred more than 50 years earlier. This passage is reproduced in Otto Erich Deutsch, *Mozart: Die Dokumente seines Lebens*, p. 472.

4. Georges de Saint-Foix, *Mozart, Sa Vie Musicale*, vol. 5, p. 319.

5. Published in Hinrichsen Editions as op. V, no. 5.

6. Hans Georg Nägeli, *Vorlesungen über Musik mit Berücksichtigung der Dilettanten*, p. 47. See K.G. Fellerer, "Mozart in der Betrachtung Nägelis," for an extensive analysis of Nägeli on Mozart.

7. *Denkmäler der Tonkunst in Bayern*, vol. 4.

8. Eva and Paul Badura-Skoda, *Interpreting Mozart on the Keyboard*, chap. 1.

9. See "Janizary Music," *Harvard Dictionary of Music*, 2nd ed. (Cambridge: Harvard University Press, 1969), p. 431.

10. Shelley Davis, "Harmonic Rhythm in Mozart's Sonata Form," *Music Review*, 1966, pp. 25–43.

11. A. W. Byler, "First-Movement Form in Mozart's Piano Concertos."

12. See the interesting analysis by Charles Rosen in *The Classical Style*, p. 285.

13. Leopold Mozart, *Gründliche Violinschule*, chap. 9, no. 4 (end), p. 197.

14. C. M. Girdlestone, *Mozart's Piano Concertos*, p. 382.

15. See Malcolm Cole, "The Rondo Finale," p. 256.

16. Leopold Mozart, chap. 12, no. 20, and footnote (e).

17. Sandra Rosenblum, *Performance Practices in Classic Piano Music* (Bloomington: Indiana University Press, 1988), p. 75.

18. James Grassineau, *A Musical Dictionary*, p. 3. Sébastien Brossard's *Dictionnaire de Musique* of 1703 (Paris: Christophe Ballard), of which Grassineau's work was an enlarged translation, did not yet include this remark.

19. See D. G. Türk, *Klavierschule*, chap. 1, sec. 5, no. 72, in which Quantz's statements are discussed.

20. The importance of cyclic relationships is exhaustively discussed by William S. Newman in *The Sonata in the Classic Era*, pp. 138–39.

21. Anthony van Hoboken, *Joseph Haydn: Thematisch-bibliographisches Werkverzeichnis*, vol. 1 (Mainz: Schott, 1957), p. 761; and H. C. Robbins Landon, *Haydn: Chronicle and Works*, vol. 2 (1978), p. 430.

22. See Hans Neumann and Carl Schachter, "The Two Versions of Mozart's Rondo, K. 494." I agree with the authors that if the Rondo is played by itself, it should be performed without the cadenza. Wolfgang Hildesheimer, *Mozart* (Frankfurt: Suhrkamp, 1979), p. 200, is wrong.

23. Konrad Wolff, *Schnabel's Interpretation of Piano Music*, p. 92.

24. Otto Erich Deutsch, *Mozart: Die Dokumente seines Lebens*, p. 453.

25. Ibid., p. 397.

26. Konrad Wolff, "J.S. Schroeter," p. 349.

27. Hugo Riemann, *L. van Beethoven Sämtliche Klaviersonaten*, 3rd ed., vol. 1 (Berlin: Max Hesse, 1919), p. 231.

28. See Hermann Abert, *W.A. Mozart*, vol. 1, p. 866.

29. Sol Babitz's guide, "Modern Errors in Mozart Performance," is—despite debatable details—still an excellent reference.

30. *Thayer's Life of Beethoven*, p. 88.

31. Abert, pp. 201–41.

32. Ibid., pp. 225–26, including footnote 1.

33. J. N. Hummel, *A Complete Theoretical and Practical Course of Instructions on the Art of Playing the Piano-Forte.*

34. Wolfgang Amadeus Mozart, *Neue Ausgabe sämtlicher Werke*, Series IX, Werkgruppe 28, vol. 2, *Einzelstücke für Klavier*, edited by W. Plath (Kassel: Bärenreiter, 1982), pp. 171–72.

Chapter 4. Beethoven

1. Romain Rolland, *Beethoven* (1903).

2. W. J. Turner, *Beethoven: The Search for Reality.*

3. J. W. N. Sullivan, *Beethoven: His Spiritual Development.*

4. Rudolf Kolisch, "Tempo and Character in Beethoven's Music."

5. Alfred Einstein, *Mozart*, p. 193.

6. Wilhelm von Lenz, *Beethoven: Eine Kunststudie*, vols. 1 and 2.

7. Paul Bekker, *Beethoven.*

8. Carl Dahlhaus, "Cantabile und Thematischer Prozess," pp. 81–98.

9. See T. W. Adorno, "Der Spätstil Beethovens"; and Alfred Brendel, *Nachdenken über Musik*, pp. 73 ff.

10. Dagmar Beck and Grita Herre, in "Anton Schindlers fingierte Eintragungen in den Konversationsheften," list all Schindler's forgeries. See especially pp. 40 and 49.

11. William S. Newman, *The Sonata in the Classic Era*, p. 513 and n.63, gives a detailed list of secondary sources. See also Ludwig Misch, *Beethoven-Studien*, pp. 42–55.

12. August Halm, *Von Zwei Kulturen der Musik*, p. 79.

13. See T. W. Adorno, *Aesthetische Theorie*, p. 299.

14. Anton Schindler, *Beethoven*, English edition by Ignaz Moscheles, pp. 153 ff. Maynard Solomon was kind enough to make this information available to me. It appears in a reprint of the original English translation of Schindler's book.

15. Adolf Bernhard Marx, *Ludwig van Beethoven*, 3rd ed., pp. 163 ff.

16. William S. Newman, *The Sonata in the Classic Era*, pp. 513–14, including nn.65–66.

17. Peter Stadlen, "Zu Schindlers Fälschungen in Beethovens Konversationsheften," *Oesterreichische Musikzeitung* 32 (1977), p. 250.

18. Marx, *Ludwig van Beethoven.*

19. "The first movement is an idyll of spring. At first there are light floating rhythms. . . . Later we hear the twittering of birds . . . then a song blossoms forth. . . ." From Thomas K. Sherman and Louis Biancolli, *Beethoven Companion* (Garden City: Doubleday, 1972), p. 280.

20. Bekker, pp. 38 ff.

21. August Halm, *Beethoven* (Potsdam: published by the author, 1917), pp. 114 ff.

22. Albert Hensel, *Beethoven; der Versuch einer musik-philosophischen Darstellung* (Berlin: Jatho-Verlag, 1918).

23. See Jürgen Uhde, *Beethovens Klaviermusik,* vol. 3, p. 277.

24. See Dahlhaus, pp. 93–94; and Allen Forte, *The Compositional Matrix.* Heinrich Schenker, *Beethoven: Die Letzten Sonaten,* devotes 54 pages of analysis to the op. 109 Sonata, yet never mentions these connected bass motives.

25. Arnold Schönberg, *Harmonielehre,* 3rd ed., p. 459.

26. Bekker, p. 189.

27. Richard Goode, "The 32 Beethoven Piano Sonatas," program introduction, New York, 1986/7.

28. M. Hürlimann, ed., *Beethoven: Briefe und Gespräche,* pp. 216–17.

29. See Maynard Solomon, *Beethoven's Tagebuch of 1812–1818,* nos. 94, 105, etc. For Beethoven's reading of Oriental literature, see *Thayer's Life of Beethoven,* p. 480.

30. Halm, *Beethoven* (1927), pp. 153 ff.

31. Konrad Wolff, *Schnabel's Interpretation of Piano Music,* p. 177.

32. Beethoven's diary of 1820; see Hürlimann, p. 239. See also Solomon, *Beethoven's Tagebuch,* p. 261; and idem, *Beethoven,* p. 37.

33. *Thayer's Life of Beethoven,* p. 963.

34. Schenker, Sonata, op. 110, frontispiece.

35. Schenker overlooked this detail (ibid., p. 63).

36. Paul Badura-Skoda, Introduction to Carl Czerny, *On the Proper Performance of All Beethoven's Works for the Piano,* p. 3.

37. Anton Schindler, *Beethoven as I Knew Him,* pp. 416 ff.

38. Wolff, pp. 152 and 163.

39. See Deryck Cooke, "The Unity of Beethoven's Late Quartets," *Music Review,* 1963, pp. 31–49.

40. Details in Schindler, *Beethoven as I Knew Him,* p. 252. It is amazing that William Drabkin's article "Rosalia," in *The New Grove,* vol. 16, p. 192, never mentions this most famous instance! See the excellent article "Rosalie," in *Brockhaus Riemann Musiklexikon,* vol. 2, which provides information not available anywhere else.

41. See William Kinderman, "The Evolution and Structure of Beethoven's 'Diabelli' Variations," especially p. 322, for the relationship between the *Diabelli* and the *Goldberg* variations. In addition to the circumstantial evidence for Beethoven's familiarity with the *Goldberg Variations,* there is also his use, in Variation 24, of the relatively rare term *Fughetta,* which was employed by Bach in his Variation 10. Finally, the peculiar trill in m. 337 of the Finale of Beethoven's A major Sonata, op. 101, is perhaps an imitation of m. 14 of the last Goldberg variation, "Quodlibet."

42. See Gustave Reese, *Music in the Renaissance* (New York: W. W. Norton, 1954), example on p. 73, mm. 6 ff.

43. See Imogene Horsley, *Fugue,* pp. 290 and 292; and John V. Cockshoot, *The Fugue in Beethoven's Piano Music,* p. 198.

44. Solomon, *Beethoven,* p. 26.

45. "He and his friends combed the libraries of Lobkowitz and Archduke Rudolph in search of old music and treatises on liturgical procedures" (ibid., p. 307).

46. Anatole France, *L'Ile des Pingouins* (Paris: Calmann-Levy, 1908), p. ii.

47. See Badura-Skoda, Introduction to Czerny; and Kenneth Drake, *The Sonatas of Beethoven,* pp. 36 ff.

48. Schindler, *Beethoven as I Knew Him,* pp. 415 ff. and 433 ff.

49. Czerny, pp. 104–105.

50. Kolisch, "Tempo and Character in Beethoven's Music."

51. William S. Newman, "Tempo in Beethoven's Instrumental Music."

52. *The Art of Josef Szigeti* (New York: Columbia Masterworks, 1972), record 2.

53. Schindler, *Beethoven as I Knew Him,* p. 401.

54. Czerny, p. 107.

55. G. Nottebohm, *Beethoveniana,* vol. 2, pp. 356 ff. Translated in part in R. R. Gerig, *Famous Pianists and Their Technique,* pp. 92 ff.

56. Badura-Skoda, Introduction to Czerny.

57. Gerig, p. 91.

58. See Nottebohm. The authenticity of Beethoven's alleged comments on the Cramer Etudes is suspect, since they are only preserved in a copy made by Schindler. See G. Jarecki, "Beethovens Anmerkungen zu Etuden von Cramer"; and Isolde Ahlgrimm, "Barocke Tradition bei Beethoven."

59. *Thayer's Life of Beethoven,* p. 526.

60. Edward Rothstein, "Discovering the Beethoven inside the Monument," *New York Times,* January 23, 1983.

Chapter 5. Schubert

1. O. E. Deutsch, *Schubert—Thematic Catalogue of All His Works* (London: J. M. Dent & Sons, 1951), no. 328(c).

2. See Jörgen Jersild, "Die Harmonik J. S. Bachs," pp. 68–69.

3. Albert Schweitzer, *J. S. Bach,* pp. 419–20.

4. See Konrad Wolff, *Schnabel's Interpretation of Piano Music,* p. 136.

5. Robert Schumann, *On Music and Musicians,* p. 110.

6. Konrad Wolff, "Schubert's 'Istesso Tempo,'" pp. 38–39.

7. Ibid.

8. Paul Henry Lang, *Music in Western Civilization,* pp. 734 ff.

9. Details in William S. Newman, "Tempo in Beethoven's Instrumental Music," p. 27.

10. See Konrad Wolff, "Observations on the Scherzo of Schubert's B-flat Major Sonata, op. posth."

11. See Christa Landon and Walther Dürr, in *Neue Schubert Ausgabe,* series VII, 2, vol. 5 (Kassel: Bärenreiter, 1984), p. viii.

12. See Konrad Wolff, "Accent? Decrescendo?" *American Music Teacher,* 38/3 (January 1989), pp. 14–17, 63.

Chapter 6. Chopin

1. Eugène Delacroix, *Journal,* April 13, 1860, p. 779.
2. Moritz Karasowski, *Friedrich Chopin,* pp. 147 ff., see also p. 169.
3. Krystyna Kobylanska, *Chopin . . . Werkverzeichnis,* pp. xvii–xviii.
4. See Jeanne Holland, "Chopin the Teacher"; and Jean-Jacques Eigeldinger, *Chopin: Pianist and Teacher.*
5. André Gide, *Notes sur Chopin,* p. 94.
6. Ibid., pp. 79 ff.
7. Joseph Elsner, Chopin's teacher, considered the pianistic styles of Mozart and Beethoven outdated (letter to Chopin, November 27, 1831, in Karasowski, pp. 145–46).
8. According to Adolf Gutmann (see Jeanne Holland, "Chopin's Teaching and His Students," p. 221).
9. Eigeldinger, pp. 277–78.
10. Holland, "Chopin's Teaching," p. 247; and Eigeldinger, pp. 58–59.
11. Johann Nepomuk Hummel, *Méthode Complète et Pratique pour le Piano-Forte* (reprint, Geneva: Minkoff, 1981); and Eigeldinger, p. 131 n.126.
12. See Eigeldinger, pp. 166–67.
13. *The New Columbia Encyclopedia* (New York: Columbia University Press, 1975), "versification," p. 2882.
14. See Boris Schwarz, *Great Masters of the Violin* (New York: Simon & Schuster, 1983), pp. 207–26.
15. Maurice Hinson, "Pedaling the Piano Works of Chopin," in Banowetz, *The Pianist's Guide to Pedaling.*
16. Wilhelm Jerger, *Franz Liszts Klavierunterricht von 1884–1886: Dargestellt an d. Tagebuchaufzeichnungen von August Göllerich* (Regensburg: Gustav Bosse, 1975), pp. 53–54, no. 5.
17. Karasowski, p. 116; and Hedley, *Selected Correspondence of Fryderyk Chopin,* p. 72.
18. Karasowski, pp. 127–28.
19. Among other studies, see the dissertations by Anne Swartz and Frank W. Marks listed in the Bibliography.
20. Eigeldinger, p. 147 n.172, reaches a similar conclusion.
21. Ibid., p. 73.
22. Johann Mattheson, *Grosse General-Bass-Schule,* 1731 (reprint, Hildesheim, 1968).
23. Karasowski, p. 165.
24. As quoted by Robert Schumann, *On Music and Musicians,* p. 143.
25. See, for instance, the fascinating correspondence between Goethe and Schiller in April 1797, in *Briefwechsel zwischen Schiller und Goethe,* vol. 2 (Stuttgart: Cotta, n.d.), letters 300–304.
26. See William Kinderman, "Directional Tonality in Chopin," in Samson, ed., *Chopin Studies,* pp. 70 ff.
27. Eigeldinger, p. 70.
28. See Eugene Narmour, "Melodic Structuring of Harmonic Dissonances," in Samson, ed., *Chopin Studies,* pp. 77 ff.
29. Schumann, pp. 137–38.
30. See Humphrey Searle, "Miscellaneous Works," in Walker, *Chopin,* pp. 223–24.
31. Karasowski, pp. 191–92.

32. Alan Walker, "Chopin and Musical Structure," in *Chopin,* pp. 250 ff.
33. From an unpublished biography by Douglas Ashley.
34. Letter to Chopin's family, October 11, 1846 (Hedley, p. 268).
35. Letter to Chopin's family, May 14, 1831 (ibid., p. 81).
36. Letter to T. Woyciechowski, December 16, 1831 (Karasowski, pp. 152–53).

Chapter 7. Brahms

1. Friedrich Nietzsche, *Jenseits von Gut und Böse* (Leipzig: C. G. Naumann, 1899), no. 240, pp. 205–206.
2. See Karl Geiringer, *Brahms, His Life and Work,* pp. 303, 305, 338–39.
3. Lina Ramann, *Lisztiana,* text revisions by Friedrich Schnapp (Mainz: Schott, 1983), p. 276.
4. Arnold Schoenberg, "Brahms the Progressive."
5. Richard Heuberger, *Erinnerungen an Johannes Brahms,* p. 94.
6. Brahms, . . . *im Briefwechsel mit Joseph Joachim,* vol. 2, p. 149.
7. Ibid., p. 152.
8. Heuberger, p. 94.
9. Eigeldinger, *Chopin: Pianist and Teacher,* p. 63.
10. Edited by Mayer-Mahr, 1926.
11. Robert Haven Schauffler, *The Unknown Brahms,* pp. 63–64, calls them "little greetings to the past masters of music."
12. See Michael Struck, "Revisionsbedürftig: zur gedruckten Korrespondenz von Johannes Brahms und Clara Schumann," *Die Musikforschung,* 41 (1988), p. 239.
13. See, for instance, Geiringer, pp. 192–93; and Heinrich Reimann, *Johannes Brahms,* p. 25.
14. Schauffler, pp. 303–12, analyzes Brahms's melodic patterns.
15. Heinrich Heine, "Ueber die französische Büne," letter 9, in *Sämtliche Werke* (Leipzig: P. Reclam jr., n.d.), vol. 4, p. 502.
16. Richard Wagner, "Unendliche Melodie" (1860), in *Brockhaus Riemann Musiklexikon,* edited by C. Dahlhaus and H. H. Eggebrecht (Wiesbaden and Mainz: Brockhaus-Schott, 1979), p. 673.
17. See David Epstein, *Beyond Orpheus: Studies in Musical Structure* (Cambridge: MIT Press, 1978), pp. 175–76.
18. *Clara Schumann Johannes Brahms Briefe,* vol. 2, letter 651, p. 513 (my translation).
19. Ibid., letter 636, p. 496.
20. Ernst Toch, *The Shaping Force in Music* (New York: Criterion, 1948).
21. Arnold Schoenberg, *Structural Function of Harmony* (New York: W. W. Norton, 1954), at Ex. 87.
22. *Clara Schumann Johannes Brahms Briefe,* vol. 2, letters 658, 659, 664, pp. 519–20, 525.
23. Konrad Wolff, *Schnabel's Interpretation of Piano Music,* pp. 94–95.
24. Facsimile reproduced in Reimann, *Johannes Brahms.*
25. Brahms, . . . *im Briefwechsel mit Philipp Spitta,* letter of December 5, 1893, p. 95.
26. *Clara Schumann Johannes Brahms Briefe,* vol. 2, letter 622, p. 479 (key misprinted as C minor instead of E minor).
27. John Dryden, *Essay on the Dramatic Poetry of the Last Age* (1668).

Selected Bibliography

not including current reference books and music editions

Only books and articles actually consulted—whether quoted or not—are listed here.

General Sources

Adorno, T. W. *Aesthetische Theorie.* Frankfurt: Suhrkamp, 1970.

Brendel, Alfred. *Nachdenken über Musik.* Munich: R. Piper, 1976.

Dahlhaus, Carl. "Der rhetorische Formbegriff H. Chr. Kochs und die Theorie der Sonatenform." *Archiv für Musikwissenschaft,* 1978, pp.154–77.

Dart, Thurston. *The Interpretation of Music.* London: Hutchinson, 1954.

Dolmetsch, A. *The Interpretation of the Music of the 17th and 18th Centuries.* London: Novello & Co., 1915.

Gát, József. *The Techniques of Piano Playing,* 2nd ed. London: Collet, 1965.

Gerig, R. R. *Famous Pianists and Their Technique.* New York and Washington: Robert B. Luce, 1972.

Halm, August. *Von Zwei Kulturen der Musik.* Munich: Georg Müller, 1920.

Horsley, Imogene. *Fugue: History and Practice.* New York: Free Press, 1966.

Lang, Paul Henry. *Music in Western Civilization.* New York: W. W. Norton, 1941.

Newman, William S. *The Sonata in the Classic Era.* Chapel Hill: University of North Carolina Press, 1963.

———. "The Pianism of Haydn, Mozart, Beethoven, and Schubert—Compared." *Piano Quarterly,* 105 (Spring 1979).

Ratner, Leonard G. "18th Century Theories of Musical Period Structure." *Musical Quarterly,* 1960, pp.439–54.

———. "Joseph Riepel." *New Grove,* vol.16 (1980), p.7.

———. *Classic Music.* New York: Schirmer Books, 1980.

Riemann, Hugo. *Brockhaus Riemann Musiklexikon,* 2 vols. Mainz: B. Schotts Söhne and Wiesbaden: F. A. Brockhaus, 1978/79.

Rosen, Charles. *The Classical Style.* New York: Viking Press, 1971.

———. *Sonata Forms.* New York: W. W. Norton, 1980.

Schönberg, Arnold. *Harmonielehre,* 3rd ed. Vienna: Universal Edition, 1922.

———. *Style and Idea,* edited by Leonard Stein. London: Faber & Faber, 1975.

Schumann, Robert. *Musik und Musiker,* 5th ed. Leipzig: Breitkopf & Härtel, 1914.

———. *On Music and Musicians* [selected writings]. New York: Pantheon, 1946.

Schwarzmaier, Ernst. *Die Takt- und Tonordnung Josef Riepels.* Regensburg: Gustav Bosse, 1978.

Türk, D. G. *Klavierschule* (1780). Reprint, Kassel: Bärenreiter, 1962.

Wolff, Konrad. "On Tonal Relations in Classical Music." *Piano Quarterly,* 102 (Summer 1978), pp.36–40.

———. *Schnabel's Interpretation of Piano Music.* New York: W. W. Norton, 1979.

Bach

The Bach Reader, rev. ed., edited by H. T. David and A. Mendel. New York: W. W. Norton, 1966.

Barford, Philip. *The Keyboard Music of C.P.E. Bach.* London: Barrie & Rockliff, 1965.

Blankenburg, Walter. "Die Bachforschung seit etwa 1965, Teil III." *Acta Musicologica,* LV (1983), pp. 1–58.

Bodky, Erwin. *The Interpretation of Bach's Keyboard Works.* Cambridge: Harvard University Press, 1960.

Boe, John. "Fully Notated Articulation in Bach's Mature Keyboard Music." *BACH: The Quarterly Journal of the Riemenschneider Bach Institute.* Beria, OH: Riemenschneider Bach Institute, vol.7, in instalments.

Breig, Werner. "J.S. Bach und die Entstehung des Klavier-Konzerts." *Archiv für Musikwissenschaft,* 1979, pp.21–48.

von Dadelsen, Georg. "Die Crux der Nebensache." *Bach-Jahrbuch,* 1979, pp.95–112. Berlin: Evangelische Verlagsanstalt, 1979.

Da Motta, Vianna. "Zur Pflege der Bachschen Klavierwerke." *Neue Zeitschrift für Musik,* 1904, pp.678–79.

Jersild, Jörgen. "Die Harmonik J. S. Bachs." *Bach-Jahrbuch,* 1980, pp.53–82. Berlin: Evangelische Verlagsanstalt, 1980.

Kirkpatrick, Ralph. J. S. Bach, *Goldberg Variations,* Introduction. New York: G. Schirmer, 1938.

Kochevitzky, G. A. "Performing Bach's Keyboard Music." *BACH,* vols.4–8, in instalments.

Marpurg, F. W. *Handbuch bey dem Generalbasse und der Composition,* 1755. Reprint Hildesheim: Georg Olms, 1974.

Marshall, Robert L. "Bach the Progressive: Observations on His Later Works." *Musical Quarterly,* 1976, pp.313–57.

Mattheson, Johann. *Der Vollkommene Capellmeister,* 1739. Facsimile edition by Margarete Reimann. Kassel: Bärenreiter, 1954.

Neumann, Frederick. *Ornamentation in Baroque and Post-Baroque Music with Special Emphasis on J. S. Bach.* Princeton: Princeton University Press, 1978.

Neumann, Friedrich. "Typische Stufengänge im Bachschen Suitensatz." *Bach-Jahrbuch,* 1967, pp.28–56.

Pidoux, Pierre, ed. G. *Frescobaldi: Orgel- und Klavierwerke,* vol.IV. Kassel: Bärenreiter, 1948.

Rosen, Charles. "Bach and Handel." In *Keyboard Music,* edited by Denis Matthews. New York: Penguin Books (Praeger), 1972.

Schenkmann, Walter. "The Establishment of Tempo in Bach's Goldberg Variations." *BACH,* vol.6, in instalments.

Schweitzer, Albert. *J. S. Bach,* 3rd ed. Leipzig: Breitkopf & Härtel, 1907.

Siegele, Ulrich. *Kompositionsweise und Bearbeitungstechnik in der Instrumentalmusik Johann Sebastian Bachs.* Neuhausen-Stuttgart: Hänssler, 1975.

Spitta, Philipp. *J. S. Bach,* 3rd [unchanged] ed., 2 vols. Leipzig: Breitkopf & Härtel, 1921.

Wolff, Christoph. "Bach's 'Handexemplar' of the Goldberg Variations: A New Source." *Journal of the American Musicological Society,* vol.XXIX (1976), pp.224–41.

Wolff, Konrad. "Fugue Subjects without Leading Tone in the Well-Tempered Clavier." *Piano Quarterly,* 100 (Winter 1977/78), pp.13–14.

Haydn

Abert, Hermann. "Joseph Haydns Klaviersonaten." *Zeitschrift für Musikwissenschaft,* Year 2, pp.552–73; Year 3, pp.535–52 [1920/1].

Barbaud, Pierre. *Haydn.* Translated from the French by K. Sorley Walker. New York: Grove Press, 1959.

Geiringer, Karl. *Haydn.* London: George Allen & Unwin, 1947.

Landon, Christa. Preface, *Haydn: The Complete Piano Sonatas.* Vienna Urtext Edition, vol.1. Vienna: Universal Edition, 1966.

Landon, H. C. Robbins. *Haydn: Chronicle and Works.* Bloomington: Indiana University Press. Especially vol.3, 1976; vol.5, 1977.

Mann, Alfred. "Haydn's 'Elementarbuch': A Document of Classic Counterpoint Instruction." In *Music Forum,* edited by William J. Mitchell and Felix Salzer, vol.3, pp.179–238. New York: Columbia University Press, 1973.

Sisman, Elaine R. "Small and Expanded Forms: Koch's Model and Haydn's Music." *Musical Quarterly,* vol. LXVIII (1982), pp. 444–75.

Zelter, K. F. "Franz Joseph Haydn." *Die Musikpflege,* 3rd Year, pp.49–52. Leipzig: 1826.

Mozart

Abert, Hermann [Jahn-Abert]. *W. A. Mozart,* 2 vols. Leipzig: Breitkopf & Härtel, 1923/4.

Babitz, Sol. "Modern Errors in Mozart Performance." *Mozart-Jahrbuch,* 1967, pp.62–89. Salzburg: Mozarteum, 1967.

Badura-Skoda, Eva and Paul. *Interpreting Mozart on the Keyboard.* New York: St. Martin's Press, 1962.

Byler, A. W. "First-Movement Form in Mozart's Piano Concertos." Master's thesis, University of Chicago, 1947.

Cole, Malcolm. "The Rondo Finale." *Mozart-Jahrbuch,* 1968–70, pp.242–56. Salzburg: Mozarteum, 1970.

Deutsch, Otto Erich. *Mozart: Die Dokumente seines Lebens.* Kassel: Bärenreiter, 1961.

Einstein, Alfred. *Mozart.* Oxford: Oxford University Press, 1945.

Fellerer, K. G. "Mozart in der Betrachtung Nägelis." *Mozart-Jahrbuch,* 1957, pp.25–36. Salzburg: Mozarteum, 1958.

Girdlestone, C. M. *Mozart's Piano Concertos.* London: Cassell & Co., 1948.

Grassineau, James A. "Allegro." In *A Musical Dictionary.* London: J. Wilcox, 1740. [Enlarged English version of Sébastien de Brossard's *Dictionnaire de Musique* of 1703.]

Grave, Floyd K. " 'Rhythmic Harmony' in Mozart." *Music Review,* XLI (1980), pp.87–102.

Hummel, J. N. *A Complete Theoretical and Practical Course of Instructions on the Art of Playing the Piano-Forte.* London, 1829. Reprint, Leipzig: Breitkopf & Härtel, 1923.

Hyatt-King, Alexander. *Mozart in Retrospect.* Oxford: Oxford University Press, 1956.

La Rue, Jan. Symposium: *Der Gegenwärtige Stand der Mozartforschung. Kongressbericht der Internationalen Gesellschaft für Musikwissenschaft, Salzburg 1964,* vol.2, p.91. Kassel: Bärenreiter, 1966.

Mozart, Leopold. *Gründliche Violinschule,* 1756. Reprint, Leipzig: Breitkopf & Härtel, 1956.

Nägeli, Hans Georg. *Vorlesungen über Musik,* 1826. Reprinted as *Von Bach zu Beethoven,* edited by Willi Reich. Klosterberg (Basel): B. Schwabe, 1946.
Neumann, Hans. "The Two Versions of Mozart's Rondo, K. 494," revised and completed by Carl Schachter. In *Music Forum,* vol.1, edited by William J. Mitchell and Felix Salzer. New York: Columbia University Press, 1967.
Rendleman, R. *A Study of 18th Century Improvisation through the Cadenzas of Mozart.* Ann Arbor: University Microfilms, 1979.
Saint-Foix, Georges de. *Mozart: Sa Vie Musicale,* vol.5. Paris: Desclée de Brouwer, 1946.
Turner, W. J. *Mozart: The Man and His Works.* New York: Knopf, 1938.
Wolff, Konrad. "J. S. Schroeter." *Musical Quarterly,* 1958, pp.338–59.

Beethoven

Adorno, T. W. "Der Spätstil Beethovens." In *Moments Musicaux.* Frankfurt: Suhrkamp, 1964.
Ahlgrimm, Isolde. "Barocke Tradition bei Beethoven." *Beethoven Almanach,* 1970, pp.156–68. Vienna: Elisabeth Lefitre, 1970.
Beck, Dagmar, and Herres, Grita. "Anton Schindlers fingierte Eintragungen in den Konversationsheften." In *Zu Beethoven,* pp. 11–89. Beiträge zur Musikwissenschaft. [East] Berlin: Verlag für Neue Musik, 1979.
Bekker, Paul. *Beethoven.* Berlin: Schuster & Löffler, 1916.
Boucourechliev, A. *Beethoven.* Paris: Editions du Seuil, 1963.
Cockshoot, John V. *The Fugue in Beethoven's Piano Music.* London: Routledge & Kegan Paul, 1959.
Czerny, Carl. *On the Proper Performance of All Beethoven's Works for the Piano.* Reprint, edited by Paul Badura-Skoda. Vienna: Universal Edition, 1970.
Dahlhaus, Carl. "Cantabile und Thematischer Prozess." *Archiv für Musikwissenschaft,* 1980, pp.81–98.
Drake, Kenneth. *The Sonatas of Beethoven: As He Played and Taught Them* [1972]. Reprint, Bloomington: Indiana University Press, 1981.
Forte, Allen. *The Compositional Matrix.* New York: Da Capo, 1974.
Halm, August. *Beethoven.* Berlin: Max Hesse, 1927.
Hürlimann, M., ed. *Beethoven: Briefe und Gespräche.* Zurich: Atlantis, 1944.
Jarecki, G. "Beethovens Anmerkungen zu Etuden von Cramer." *Beethoven Almanach,* 1970, pp.169–76. Vienna: Elisabeth Lefitre, 1970.
Kaiser, Joachim. *Beethovens 32 Klaviersonaten und ihre Interpreten.* Frankfurt/Main: S. Fischer, 1976.
Kinderman, William. "The Evolution and Structure of Beethoven's 'Diabelli' Variations." *Journal of the American Musicological Society,* 35 (1982), pp.306–28.
Kolisch, Rudolf. "Tempo and Character in Beethoven's Music." *Musical Quarterly,* 1943, pp.169–87, 291–312.
Kullak, Franz. *Beethoven's Piano Playing* [1901]. New York: Da Capo, 1973.
Lenz, Wilhelm. *Beethoven: Eine Kunststudie,* 2 vols. Hamburg: Hoffman & Campe, 1855/60.
Marx, Adolf Bernhard. *Ludwig van Beethoven,* 3rd ed., 2 vols. Berlin: Otto Janke, 1863.
Misch, Ludwig. *Beethoven-Studien.* Berlin: W. de Gruyter, 1950.
Newman, William S. *Performance Practice in Beethoven's Piano Sonatas.* New York: W. W. Norton, 1971.

————. "Tempo in Beethoven's Instrumental Music." *Piano Quarterly,* 116 (Winter 1981/2), pp.22–29; 117 (Spring 1982), pp. 22–31.

Nottebohm, G. *Beethoveniana* [1872]. New York: Johnson Reprint Corp., 1970.

————. *Zweite Beethoveniana* [1887]. New York: Johnson Reprint Corp., 1970.

Rolland, Romain. *Beethoven: Les Grandes Epoques Créatrices,* 7 vols. Paris: Sablier, 1930–1949.

————. *Beethoven.* Paris: *Cahiers de la Quinzaine,* 1903. German edition, Zurich: Rascher & Co., 1925.

Schenker, Heinrich. *Beethoven: Die Letzten Sonaten,* 4 vols. Edited by Oswald Jonas. Vienna: Universal Edition, 1971.

Schindler, Anton. *Beethoven as I knew Him.* Edited by D. W. McArdle. Chapel Hill: University of North Carolina Press, 1966.

————. *Beethoven.* English edition 1841. Boston: Oliver Ditson [1841?].

Schneider, Norbert J. "Mediantische Harmonik bei Ludwig van Beethoven." *Archiv für Musikwissenschaft,* 1978, pp.210–30.

Solomon, Maynard. *Beethoven.* New York: Schirmer Books, 1977.

————. *Beethoven's Tagebuch of 1812–1818.* Beethoven Studies 3, Alan Tyson, ed., pp.193–285. Cambridge: Cambridge University Press, 1982.

Subotnik, R.R. "Adorno's Diagnosis of Beethoven's Late Style." *Journal of the American Musicological Society,* XXIX (Summer 1976), pp.242–75.

Sullivan, J. W. N. *Beethoven: His Spiritual Development.* London: Jonathan Cape, 1927.

Thayer, A. W. *Thayer's Life of Beethoven,* 2 vols. Revised and edited by Elliot Forbes. Princeton: Princeton University Press, 1964.

Tovey, Sir Donald Francis. *Beethoven.* Edited by H. J. Foss. London: Oxford University Press, 1944.

Turner, W. J. *Beethoven: The Search for Reality,* 2nd ed. London: Ernest Benn, 1933.

Uhde, Jürgen, *Beethovens Klaviermusik,* 2nd ed., 3 vols. Stuttgart: Philipp Reclam jr., 1980.

Zenck, Martin. "Rezeption von Geschichte in Beethovens 'Diabelli-Variationen.' " *Archiv für Musikwissenschaft,* 1980, pp.61–75.

Schubert

Brown, Maurice J. E. *Schubert: A Critical Biography.* London: Macmillan & Co., 1958.

————. *Essays on Schubert.* London: Macmillan, 1966.

Deutsch, Otto Erich. *Schubert: A Documentary Biography.* London: J. M. Dent & Sons, 1946.

Einstein, Alfred. *Schubert.* London: Cassell & Co., 1951.

Reed, John. *Schubert: The Final Years.* London: Faber & Faber, 1972.

Wolff, Konrad. "Observations on the Scherzo of Schubert's B-flat Major Sonata, op. posth." *Piano Quarterly,* 92 (Winter 1975/6), pp. 28–39.

————. "Schubert's 'Istesso Tempo.' " *Piano Quarterly,* 106 (Summer 1979), pp. 38–39.

Chopin

Atwood, William G. *Fryderyk Chopin, Pianist from Warsaw.* New York: Columbia University Press, 1987.

Chopin, Frédéric. *Correspondance de Frédéric Chopin,* vol. I: *L'Aube, 1816–1831.* Edited by B.E. Sydow. Paris: Richard-Masse, 1953.

Delacroix, Eugène. *Journal, 1822–1863.* Paris: Plon, 1980.

Dunn, John Petrie. *Ornamentation in the Works of Frederick Chopin.* New York: Da Capo Press, 1971.

Eigeldinger, Jean-Jacques. *Chopin: Pianist and Teacher as Seen by his Students.* Cambridge: Cambridge University Press, 1986.

Gide, André. *Notes sur Chopin.* Paris: L'Arche, 1948.

Grenier, Jean-Marie. *Frédéric Chopin.* N.p.: Les Editions Seghers, 1964.

Hedley, Arthur, ed. *Selected Correspondence of Fryderyk Chopin.* New York: McGraw-Hill, 1963. Reprint, New York: Da Capo Press, 1980.

Hinson, Maurice. "Pedaling the Piano Works of Chopin." In Joseph Banowetz, *The Pianist's Guide to Pedaling.* Bloomington: Indiana University Press, 1985. An exhaustive study, necessary for grasping the problems.

Holland, Jeanne. "Chopin's Teaching and His Students." Diss., University of North Carolina, 1972.

————. "Chopin the Teacher." *Journal of the American Musicological Society,* 38 (Summer 1985), pp. 39 ff.

Karasowski, Moritz. *Friedrich Chopin.* New ed. Berlin: Ries & Erler, [1877].

Kleczynski, Jean. *The Works of Frederic Chopin,* 6th ed. Translated by A. Whittingham. London: William Reeves, n.d.

Kobylanska, Krystyna. *Frederic Chopin, Thematisch-Bibliographisches Werkverzeichnis.* Munich: Henle, 1979.

Marks, Frank William. "Form and the Mazurkas of Chopin." Diss., University of Washington, 1970.

Samson, Jim, ed. *Chopin Studies.* Cambridge: Cambridge University Press, 1988.

Swartz, Anne. "The Mazurkas of Chopin." Diss., University of Pittsburgh, 1973.

Walker, Alan, ed. *Frederik Chopin.* London: Barrie & Rockliff, 1966. Anthology.

Weinstock, Herbert. *Chopin.* New York: Alfred A. Knopf, 1969.

Weissmann, Adolf. *Chopin.* Berlin and Leipzig: Schuster & Loeffler, 1912.

Brahms

Brahms, Johannes. *Clara Schumann Johannes Brahms Briefe,* edited by Berthold Litzmann. 2 vols. Leipzig: Breitkopf & Härtel, 1927.

————. *Johannes Brahms im Briefwechsel mit Heinrich und Elisabeth von Herzogenberg,* edited by Max Kalbeck. Berlin: Deutsche Brahms-Gesellschaft, vol. 1, 1908; vol. 2, 1912.

————. *Johannes Brahms im Briefwechsel mit Joseph Joachim,* vol. 2, edited by Andreas Moser. Berlin: Deutsche Brahms-Gesellschaft, 1908.

————. *Johannes Brahms im Briefwechsel mit Philipp Spitta.* Tutzing: H. Schneider, 1974.

Fellinger, Imogen. *Ueber die Dynamik in der Musik von Johannes Brahms.* Berlin: Max Hesse, 1961.

Geiringer, Karl. *Brahms, His Life and Work,* 2nd ed. New York: Anchor Books, 1961.

Henschel, George. *Personal Recollections of Johannes Brahms.* Boston: Richard G. Badger, 1907.

Heuberger, Richard. *Erinnerungen an Johannes Brahms,* edited by Kurt Hofmann. Tutzing: Hans Schneider, 1971.

Kraus, Detlef. "Das Andante aus der Sonate Op. 5 von Brahms." In *Brahms Studien,* vol. 3. Hamburg: Karl Dieter Wagner, 1979.

———. *Johannes Brahms, Composer for the Piano,* translated by Lillian Lim. Wilhelmshaven: Florian Noetzel, 1988; distributed by C.F. Peters, New York. The definitive book on Brahms performance practice.

Niemann, Walter. *Brahms.* New York: Knopf, 1929; reprint, Totowa, NJ: Cooper Square Publishers, 1969.

Reimann, Heinrich. *Johannes Brhams.* 5th ed. Edited by Bruno Schräder. Berlin: Schlesische Verlagsanstalt, 1919.

Schauffler, Robert Haven. *The Unknown Brahms.* New York: Dodd, Mead & Co., 1933.

Schoenberg, Arnold. "Brahms the Progressive." In *Style and Idea,* edited by Leonard Stein. New York: St. Martin's Press, 1975. Pp. 398–441.

Index

Page numbers containing examples are printed in italics. Movements are listed in roman numerals: "op. 31/2 II" = opus 31, number 2, second movement. Compositions are identified according to needs, including the Hoboken catalog for Haydn, the Deutsch catalog for Schubert, and of course the Köchel for Mozart. "p. 61n" = page 61, footnote. Capital letters denote major keys; lower-case letters, minor keys.

KONRAD WOLFF is author of *Schnabel's Interpretation of Piano Music* and of numerous articles appearing in *Clavier, Piano Quarterly,* and *Journal of the American Liszt Society.*